Pensions f
You and Your
Business

Pensions for You and Your Business

Robin Ellison

crimson

Every effort has been made to maintain accuracy in this book. However, legal require-ments are constantly changing so it is important for readers to check for updates carefully, and to seek professional advice as appropriate. The author and publisher cannot be held responsible for any inaccuracies in information supplied to them by third parties or contained in resources and websites listed in the book.

Pensions for You and Your Business

This first edition published in 2012 by Crimson Publishing Ltd, Westminster House, Kew Road, Richmond, Surrey TW9 2ND

© Robin Ellison 2013

British Library Cataloguing in Publication Data
A catalogue record for this book is available from the British Library

ISBN 978 1 85458 678 0

Typeset by IDUSK (DataConnection) Ltd
Printed and bound in Great Britain by Ashford Colour Press, Gosport, Hants

CONTENTS

PREFACE

From the end of 2011, all businesses have had to think about pensions for their workforce, even if they only employ one person. The Pensions Acts 2007, 2008 and 2011 require you to establish a pension scheme of your own to certain minimum standards, or to ensure that you pay at least 3% of salary (and that your employees pay 4%) into a scheme set up by the government as a last-resort pension scheme, known as NEST (National Employers Savings Trust). If you do not comply with the extensive and complex duties you face substantial fines.

Consequently, you have probably been tackling inquiries from employees about whether they really need to pay this money; from your finance director, who is looking to save as much as possible; and from pensions salesmen (also known as independent financial advisers or pensions providers) seeking to provide alternatives to the NEST system.

What should you do? Should you simply make sure your payroll systems can cope? Should you set up a scheme of your own which may offer you and your staff better advantages and value for money? How will you cope with the potential criminal and civil penalties if you try to advise your employees on whether to join or not? What are the pros and cons of doing it yourself – or joining the government system?

This radical change to the UK pension system offers a host of challenges and opportunities. The changes come at a time when confidence in the private pension system is not high – and confidence in the state pension system is even lower.

This book is intended to enable you and your colleagues to review the situation as a whole, to put the changes in context and to help you come to a considered conclusion as to what you should do.

It is written at a time when many issues are still not yet known, and many alternatives are still developing. It might be sensible to try to defer decision-making as long as possible. On the other hand, provision for old age is much cheaper the sooner it is started.

So it might be best to view this book as a work in progress, intended as a guide to help you think about company policy. Suggestions for improvements for any future edition, or gentle notes pointing out any errors, are always welcome. In the meantime, I thank my colleagues at Pinsent Masons for their help and support, and in particular Simon Tyler, the fount of technical wisdom, Tom Barton, who knows everything about auto-enrolment, and Holly Ivins, as the strictest editor ever.

Finally, a caveat. This book is not for purists or techies; it tries to explain what is going on, sometimes at the expense of compliance with the strict technicalities. For example, the Pensions Act 2008 does not actually require employees to make pension provision through NEST; what it requires is compulsory auto-enrolment of all employees in a company pension scheme, with a government-sponsored scheme (NEST) being available for companies who cannot or do not want to establish a scheme of their own, but it is simpler to talk about the NEST requirements as a shorthand for that mouthful. Similarly, the NEST system itself is determined to be known as a privately managed occupational pension scheme managed under an independent trustm, but it is simpler (and closer to the truth) to talk about it as a form of fourth state pension. The desire for accuracy has occasionally been sacrificed for clarity, and no apology is made for that.

Robin Ellison
robin@pensionslaw.net

INTRODUCTION

BACKGROUND

None of us are getting any younger. In fact, with luck, we are all getting a lot older. The statistics show that with every hour that passes, our life expectancy increases by 15 minutes – or, to put it another way, for with every year that passes we can expect to live another three months. Some people believe that the first person has been born who will live to be 1,000 years old.[1]

In many respects this increasing life expectancy is a boon; some of us will live to see our children, grandchildren and great-grandchildren. We will probably be around to see things that our forefathers could never have dreamed of. But this demographical achievement also brings with it a problem. If we continue to work for the same number of years as before (say, 40), can we save enough to keep us alive for maybe 30 years in retirement?

Another way of looking at it is to observe a modern life cycle: we might study or earn very little until we are 30; we might work for another 30 years, and then live in retirement for another 30 years. We will only have worked for around 30 or 40 years, out of the 90 years we might live. Therefore, saving enough while we work to keep us going for those final 30 years will be a challenge. The other challenge is not knowing when we will actually die (or, if we are in a relationship, who will be the last to die), which means we do not know exactly (or even roughly) how much we need to have set aside financially to ensure our money lasts long enough.

In order to meet these challenges, humans invented pensions,[2] which provide a form of financial security against the risk of living too long (ie longer than our money lasts). For the last hundred years in the UK, both state pensions and private pensions have flourished and have dealt with the problem that has arisen since the Industrial Revolution: we can no longer expect our families to look after us in our old age. Firstly, families now spread themselves around the country and overseas, and, secondly, the Industrial Revolution meant that agricultural subsistence in small communities no longer applied – and we all have much smaller families, so there are fewer children around to take care of their parents, financially or otherwise. Countries that are beginning to move into similar economic positions, such as China, are now faced with similar problems and are racing to establish pension plans as fast as they can.

However, as we know, pension arrangements in the last few years in the UK have hit a few problems. First of all, the state decided it wanted to play a smaller role in pensions and limited the amount it wanted to spend on them. Secondly, private pensions faced a barrage of disincentives. Pensions became more expensive because people started living longer, accounting rules made them harder to provide, investments performed erratically, and adviser costs shot up because the government imposed astonishing quantities of legislation, regulation and levies – and withdrew essential tax neutrality (ie imposed double taxation on pensions). A perfect storm assailed company pension provision, and the destruction of good and sensible schemes by well-meaning but counterproductive government policy will haunt us for many years to come.

Table 1: Penalties for breach

Kind of penalty	Amount		Example of breach
Fixed penalties (Civil fines)	£400		Failing to comply with a previously issued compliance notice by the Pensions Regulator or the requirements under any of the automatic enrolment regulations
Escalating penalties (Civil fines)	Size of workforce	Amount per day	Failing to comply with a previously issued compliance notice or unpaid contribution notice or provision of information notice issued by the Pensions Regulator; inducing employees not to join
	1 – 4	£50	
	5 – 49	£500	
	50 – 249	£2,500	
	250 – 499	£5,000	
	500+	£10,000	
On conviction on indictment (Crown Court/High Court/ criminal court)	Imprisonment for up to two years or an unlimited fine		Wilful failure to comply with auto-enrolment or re-enrolment or employee right to opt-in requirements
On summary conviction (Magistrates Court/ Sheriff Court)(Criminal)	Fine up to £5,000 (Level 5, statutory scale)		Wilful failure to comply with auto-enrolment or re-enrolment or employee right to opt-in requirements
The Pensions Regulator	Up to £5,000 for individuals or £50,000 for corporate bodies		Failure to maintain records (any person, not just employer)

Nonetheless, despite the government's attempts to make retirement provision difficult and expensive, all of us (unless we are rich or have a large and loving family) need to make some kind of financial provision for our old age – indeed, the need is increasing every day. History has shown that provision through a company is sensible and highly efficient. The costs of collective provision are much lower than individual or personal provision, and companies have the expertise (or access to expertise) to manage schemes which individuals lack.

This book explores what your company might want to do to meet these challenges, which can no longer be ignored. The reason is that the government is now enforcing some form of company pension provision for almost everyone, which will be phased in by 2018. The penalties for ignoring the law can be considerable, as the table above shows.

STAGING DATE TIMELINE
Your staging date is determined by the total number of persons in your largest PAYE scheme, based on information held by HMRC as at 1 April 2012. Any changes to your PAYE scheme before this date, may not be reflected in the information used to determine your staging date.

Table 2 shows the full list of staging dates in table format.

To look up your staging date, you need to know

■ the size of your PAYE scheme and
■ PAYE scheme reference.

If you have more than one PAYE scheme, your staging date will be determined by the largest. You may also choose to bring your staging date forward.

Small employers

If you had fewer than 50 workers on 1 April 2012 but you had or were part of a PAYE scheme that has more than 50 people in it, you are a 'small employer'. This could apply to you if you're part of a corporate group and share your PAYE scheme with other employers, or if there are people in your PAYE scheme who aren't workers (eg if you're paying pension benefits to retired members of staff). Because your staging date is determined by the total number of persons in your PAYE scheme on 1 April 2012, it will be earlier than it would have been, if it were based on the number of workers you have. For this reason, you can, if you wish, move your staging date to a later prescribed date. To do this, look up your original staging date in Table 2, then look up the corresponding later staging date in Table 3.

Table 2: List of staging dates by PAYE scheme size or reference

PAYE scheme size or reference	Staging date
120,000 or more	1 October 2012
50,000–119,999	1 November 2012
30,000–49,999	1 January 2013
20,000–29,999	1 February 2013
10,000–19,999	1 March 2013
6,000–9,999	1 April 2013
4,100–5,999	1 May 2013
4,000–4,099	1 June 2013
3,000–3,999	1 July 2013
2,000–2,999	1 August 2013
1,250–1,999	1 September 2013
800–1,249	1 October 2013
500–799	1 November 2013
350–499	1 January 2014
250–349	1 February 2014
160–249	1 April 2014
90–159	1 May 2014
62–89	1 July 2014

61	1 August 2014
60	1 October 2014
59	1 November 2014
58	1 January 2015
54–57	1 March 2015
50–53	1 April 2015
Fewer than 30 with the last 2 characters in their PAYE reference numbers 92, A1–A9, B1–B9, AA–AZ, BA–BW, M1–M9, MA–MZ, Z1–Z9, ZA–ZZ , 0A–0Z, 1A–1Z or 2A–2Z	1 June 2015
Fewer than 30 with the last 2 characters in their PAYE reference number BX	1 July 2015
40–49	1 August 2015
Fewer than 30 with the last 2 characters in their PAYE reference number BY	1 September 2015
30–39	1 October 2015
Fewer than 30 with the last 2 characters in their PAYE reference number BZ	1 November 2015
Fewer than 30 with the last 2 characters in their PAYE reference numbers 02–04, C1–C9, D1–D9, CA–CZ or DA–DZ	1 January 2016
Fewer than 30 with the last 2 characters in their PAYE reference numbers 00 05–07, E1–E9 or EA–EZ	1 February 2016
Fewer than 30 with the last 2 characters in their PAYE reference numbers 01, 08–11, F1–F9, G1–G9, FA–FZ or GA–GZ	1 March 2016
Fewer than 30 with the last 2 characters in their PAYE reference numbers 12–16, 3A–3Z, H1–H9 or HA–HZ	1 April 2016
Fewer than 30 with the last 2 characters in their PAYE reference numbers I1–I9 or IA–IZ	1 May 2016
Fewer than 30 with the last 2 characters in their PAYE reference numbers 17–22, 4A–4Z, J1–J9 or JA–JZ	1 June 2016
Fewer than 30 with the last 2 characters in their PAYE reference numbers 23–29, 5A–5Z, K1–K9 or KA–KZ	1 July 2016
Fewer than 30 with the last 2 characters in their PAYE reference numbers 30–37, 6A–6Z, L1–L9 or LA–LZ	1 August 2016
Fewer than 30 with the last 2 characters in their PAYE reference numbers N1–N9 or NA–NZ	1 September 2016

Fewer than 30 with the last 2 characters in their PAYE reference numbers 38–46, 7A–7Z, 01–09 or 0A–0Z	1 October 2016
Fewer than 30 with the last 2 characters in their PAYE reference numbers 47–57, 8A–8Z, Q1–Q9, R1–R9, S1–S9, T1–T9, QA–QZ, RA–RZ, SA–SZ or TA–TZ	1 November 2016
Fewer than 30 with the last 2 characters in their PAYE reference numbers 58–69, 9A–9Z, U1–U9, V1–V9, W1–W9, UA–UZ, VA–VZ or WA–WZ	1 January 2017
Fewer than 30 with the last 2 characters in their PAYE reference numbers 70–83, X1–X9, Y1–Y9, XA–XZ or YA–YZ	1 February 2017
Fewer than 30 with the last 2 characters in their PAYE reference numbers P1–P9 or PA–PZ	1 March 2017
Fewer than 30 with the last 2 characters in their PAYE reference numbers 84–91, 93–99	1 April 2017
Fewer than 30 unless otherwise described	1 April 2017
Employer who does not have a PAYE scheme	1 April 2017
New employer (PAYE income first payable between 1 April 2012 and 31 March 2013)	1 May 2017
New employer (PAYE income first payable between 1 April 2013 and 31 March 2014)	1 July 2017
New employer (PAYE income first payable between 1 April 2014 and 31 March 2015)	1 August 2017
New employer (PAYE income first payable between 1 April 2015 and 31 December 2015)	1 October 2017
New employer (PAYE income first payable between 1 January 2016 and 30 September 2016)	1 November 2017
New employer (PAYE income first payable between 1 October 2016 and 30 June 2017)	1 January 2018
New employer (PAYE income first payable between 1 July 2017 and 30 September 2017)	1 February 2018

There is no requirement for you to tell the Regulator if you choose to move your staging date to one of the prescribed dates in the table below. The Regulator will however write to all employers 12 and 3 months before their staging date, so it is sensible to tell the Regulator that you have chosen to move your staging date, who may ask for confirmation that you were able to move your staging date, so you should keep a record of the number of people in your PAYE scheme and the number of workers you had on 1 April 2012.

Table 3: Modified staging dates for small employers

Original staging date	Prescribed date to which you can choose to move
1 May 2013 and 1 June 2013	1 February 2016
1 July 2013 and 1 August 2013	1 March 2016
1 September 2013 and 1 October 2013	1 April 2016
1 November 2013 and 1 January 2014	1 May 2016
1 February 2014 and 1 April 2014	1 July 2016
1 May 2014 and 1 July 2014	1 September 2016
1 August 2014 and 1 October 2014	1 November 2016
1 November 2014 and 1 January 2015	1 February 2017
1 March 2015 and 1 April 2015	1 April 2017

Bringing your staging date forward

To allow some flexibility, you can bring your staging date forward. A list of early staging dates and the information you will need to provide to the regulator is set out below.

To bring your staging date forward, you must:

■ have an existing staging date
■ have contacted a pension scheme that can be used to comply with the employer duties and secured the agreement of the trustees or managers, provider, or administrator of the scheme you have chosen, that the scheme will be used to comply with those duties from the new (earlier) staging date
■ notify The Pensions Regulator in writing (letter, fax or email) at least one calendar month before the new (earlier) staging date you choose, providing all the information set out below.

The information includes:

1. employer name
2. employer paye reference number(s) eg 123/4ab (you can find this on your p35 employer annual return), including all paye scheme reference numbers that you operate
3. your name
4. your job title within your organisation
5. your contact telephone number, email address and business address
6. the new (earlier) staging date chosen and your original staging date
7. employer's address (including postcode) and email address

Table 4: Bringing your staging date forward

Available dates		
1 January 2013	1 October 2014	1 June 2016
1 February 2013	1 November 2014	1 July 2016
1 March 2013	1 January 2015	1 August 2016
1 April 2013	1 March 2015	1 September 2016
1 May 2013	1 April 2015	1 October 2016
1 June 2013	1 June 2015	1 November 2016
1 July 2013	1 July 2015	1 January 2017
1 August 2013	1 August 2015	1 February 2017
1 September 2013	1 September 2015	1 March 2017
1 October 2013	1 October 2015	1 April 2017
1 November 2013	1 November 2015	1 May 2017
1 January 2014	1 January 2016	1 July 2017
1 February 2014	1 February 2016	1 August 2017
1 April 2014	1 March 2016	1 October 2017
1 May 2014	1 April 2016	1 November 2017
1 July 2014	1 May 2016	1 January 2018
1 August 2014		

8. Companies House registration number or equivalent, eg registered charity number, VAT registration number or industrial provident society number
9. a declaration from the employer that they have contacted a pension scheme and have obtained the agreement of the trustees or managers, provider, or administrator, that the scheme can be used to comply with the employer duties from the new (earlier) staging date
10. your own declaration that you are authorised to apply for a change of staging date.

Employers with multiple PAYE schemes
If you operate more than one PAYE scheme, you will need to include all PAYE reference numbers when notifying the Regulator of bringing your staging date forward. Staging dates are based on an employer's largest PAYE scheme. If you share a PAYE scheme with another employer, or operate your PAYE through an umbrella company, your staging date will be based on the total number of persons within that PAYE scheme. You can submit your notification either by email (customersupport@autoenrol.tpr.gov.uk) or in writing to The Pensions Regulator, PO Box 16314, Birmingham B23 3JP.

WHAT DO COMPANIES WANT?
Why on earth would your company want to get involved with pensions? Your company probably does not provide clothes, food, education or, nowadays, even cars for employees. The usual method of payment is the oldest one: an employee is paid for his or her

labour and they then have the freedom to spend their money as they wish. Some people (spouses or the independently wealthy, perhaps) do not want or need a pension. Why should your company go to all the bother and expense of administration and compliance, not to mention additional payroll, legal, accounting and other costs – as well as the cost of contributions – when perhaps the employees might manage their own retirement like they manage their own groceries or choice of television set?

Some companies, of course, do just that, ie leave pensions issues to be dealt with by employees themselves. In many cases that is a sensible solution. Others, however, for equally valid reasons, wish to provide some form of retirement income for employees, especially longer-serving ones, perhaps out of a sense of duty or paternalism or even as a recruitment and retention (and redundancy) tool.

In addition, providing pensions for a workforce may make it easier to provide pensions to the managers and directors; indeed, at one time in the United States there was no tax relief for companies who discriminated by providing pensions for senior management but not for ordinary employees.

Pensions provided by your company can be, if properly marketed and managed, not only a critical tool in human resource management but also much better value for money than alternative methods of providing retirement income.

Finally, a hundred years ago, even when capitalism was at its most raw, many companies provided pensions for their workforces, because it was an efficient way of managing workers and it engendered goodwill with the staff. It also left employees free to get on with their jobs, rather than worry about how they were going to manage in later life. Even today, with all the competition for employment in the Far East and the drive to reduce costs, many companies think a decent pensions policy provides a calm and reliable cadre of employees, who appreciate what the company is doing for them and respond accordingly.

However, even when your company has decided it is good policy to provide a pension arrangement, increasingly you need such a scheme to be:

- simple to understand
- simple to administer
- with low compliance and management costs
- appreciated by the beneficiaries
- offering security of income in old age, which is:

  - tax efficient
  - good value
  - safe.

Achieving all those objectives concurrently may be a challenge, but this book will try to suggest a few ways of getting to the end of the yellow brick road.

You should not feel embarrassed for being confused about whether you really want to introduce a scheme. Your company might very sensibly both **want** and **not want** a pension scheme for your workforce. Here are some of the reasons why you might want one.

- It can act as **a tool for recruitment and retention**. In times when good staff are hard to find (and those times do come around), the provision of a decent pension scheme can give you an extra advantage when staff decide to choose which company to work for. The same benefit can be used also to retain staff – although, since it is now illegal to forfeit a pension if someone moves, it is less useful than it used to be.

- They are **a tax efficient (tax neutral) way of providing additional income**. They are not quite as tax efficient as salesman say they are (see Chapter 4) but they are handy, although the benefits for the higher paid are not quite as useful as they used to be.
- They provide **a way of allowing people to leave your company after many years' service** without being a reproach to you; the paternalistic element of employment is still fortunately alive and well in many companies.
- They offer **a way for employees to provide for their old age in a very efficient manner**. Pension provision through the workplace is the most trusted form of pension provision, not least because it is very good value (the expenses are low because there's no marketing and distribution costs are modest).
- They increase **a sense of bonding between your company and the employee**; the pension is a form of salary paid until death, especially where the payment can be branded.
- The payment of pensions to retired employees gives **a sense of comfort to existing employees**; they can see that your company cares about the retired workforce, which improves morale.
- Your company might prefer **employees simply to think about work** and not be distracted about their future finances, spending time and effort working on something they may be ill-equipped for.
- **Personal pension provision is inefficient**, complicated and usually poor value for money – and it takes time and expertise to manage; collective provision through the workplace offers advantages of scale and simplicity.
- **The Pensions Act 2008 requires you** to provide a company scheme – or at least pay minimum contributions into the government-run scheme (NEST).

However, at the same time, your company might struggle with the notion of providing pensions to your team for the following reasons.

- **Pensions can prove expensive**, especially where margins are tight. Offering a decent pension might cost your company (together with employee contributions) around 30% of salary if the intention is to provide around two-thirds of pre-retirement income, whatever the nature of the pension scheme.
- **Pensions can prove a disincentive to moving**; this is especially the case for some pension schemes where the rules can make it expensive for employees to move. They can therefore be a barrier to efficient manpower planning.
- Pension provision, especially if it is a final salary-related scheme, can have **an adverse impact on your company balance sheet**, making it difficult to finance the company or making the balance sheet unreasonably volatile.
- Your company might feel inhibited from restructuring where a scheme is in place, because of **inappropriate regulation** (you might need to get consents or clearances from regulators).
- **Compliance costs**, trustee costs, the Pension Protection Fund levy and other matters may make you conclude that the pension scheme takes up too much management time and distracts from running the business. Your company does not want to be in the business of pension provision; you just want to ensure your employees are well looked after.
- The provision of a benefit can in itself give rise to **complaints and litigation**, which would not arise if employees were simply given money to spend on the retirement of their choice.

■ **One size fits all may not be helpful**, especially for the very highly paid (who need something different, or even in some cases nothing at all) and, equally importantly but in a different way, for the very lower paid, for whom state provision is normally more efficient.

WHAT DO EMPLOYEES WANT?

Employees, coming from very different personal positions, may want rather different things. It is not always possible for employers to find out what the workforce wants and needs, and much will also depend on the nature of the workforce. Your employees may be rapidly turning over, staying for only a short time, and thus pensions won't exactly be at the top of their wish list. On the other hand, some members of your workforce could end up staying for half of their working life – and may even introduce their children to your company in due course. Ultimately, it is not unreasonable to conclude that, generally, most employees would like to make – or have made for them – some provision for an income when they stop working.

In practice, only a few employees will have either the financial or intellectual resources or desire to make their own provision. Some will hope the problem will go away, or that they will work until they drop, or that their spouse will provide for them, or that they might inherit their parents' house. Most, however, will want to do something – or rather, have something done for them. Their problem is that they do not know what to do, and they have many other pressing priorities. Moreover, many independent financial advisers or other salesmen find such individuals hard to advise, since the cost of advice has been pushed up by regulation, so that cheap and dirty advice is no longer possible – and, in any event, many people often do not trust financial advisers. Nor do they trust insurance companies, given their rather mixed track record over the years. Finally, pensions in general have also had a rather unattractive press in recent times: scheme failures, high charges, low annuity rates. There is no doubt, however, that most employees are worried about how they will cope financially after retirement.

In a perfect world, of course, they (and you, and me) may therefore dream of a defined benefit, preferably final-salary, scheme paid for without any personal contributions, with a retirement on full pension at age 60. This aspiration is hard to achieve for anyone outside the public sector, or the oil industry, at a cost which is affordable, so ambitions may have to be toned down. Whatever the level of benefits, most employees would welcome provision of some sort being organised by their employer. The reasons are obvious. First of all, they trust you (usually). Secondly, they understand that you have the resources to make proper investigation as to the best (or at least not the worst) arrangements. Thirdly, it is easier to have a default scheme where the deductions, if any, are less noticeable, as they are abstracted along with other deductions before the net salary hits the bank account.

Finally, many people want to live in a comfortable retirement. The idea of retirement is barely 100 years old. Other than the wealthy, not that long ago most people worked until they dropped, and pensions were there to help them in sickness rather than as a form of long-term financial holiday in their old age. Now retirement is a widespread aspiration, although, as the population ages, it is becoming increasingly difficult to achieve.

In theory, employees simply want to have enough to live on when they retire. They mostly do not want to think about it at all – or they tend to focus on the following aspects.

- To **trust you as their employer** to make provision; it avoids all the hassle with insurance salesmen, providing passports and gas bills to banks, making decisions on investments and the like.
- To **let others (ie you) make the decisions** on matters with which they feel ill-equipped to deal.
- To allow their employer (ie you) to inter-relate the pensions system with the **redundancy and retirement policies**.
- To be allowed to take their pension arrangements to their **next employer**.
- To have the level of pension provision (and provision for dependents) at an amount **adequate to maintain the standard of living** they enjoyed before retirement.
- To have the pension proofed against **inflation**.
- To have the pension proofed against **falls in fund values**.
- To have to pay **no contributions**.

In real life these ambitions are either unachievable, or achievable only at an expense which is unacceptable to both parties. You may find that this shopping list will be a list too far; however, some of the items on the list may be available at a cost which is manageable, and even a modest pension is usually better than no scheme at all (except for the very poor or the very rich).

WHAT DOES THE GOVERNMENT WANT?

The message sent by the government on pension provision over the last few years has been mixed; on the one hand, there have been frequent ministerial statements indicating that policy should be to encourage the growth of company-backed pension schemes, and especially defined benefit schemes. The Labour Government of 1997, for example, developed a policy aimed to encourage around 40% of pension expectations to be provided by the state and 60% by employers.

On the other hand, regulatory, tax and accounting changes have imposed considerable barriers of cost and complexity, sending a very different message. As the impact of well-meaning but counter-productive pension legislation began to bite, it became increasingly clear that the state's original objective was more and more unachievable. By the turn of the century, the plan had changed. In principle the desire was still to encourage private provision for retirement but, in practice, it became obvious that this was just too hard for most people – and while private provision was diminishing, the strain on the state system was also proving difficult to manage because of the following factors.

- The population was ageing (ie there were more people to whom to pay pensions).
- There were fewer workers who paid the National Insurance contributions to pay for the pension benefits.[3]
- Other priorities emerged in the national budget.

Pensions are politically important but, in practice, other issues, such as defence or health, often have to be dealt with urgently, whereas in most cases politicians can put off difficult pensions decisions for another year or two.

By 2004, the pendulum had swung again. A government report[4] on the provision of private pensions ignored the question it had been asked to answer and concluded that the real problem was that of inadequate state pensions. It recommended that private or company pensions be encouraged and, since such encouragement was difficult, should be semi-compulsory. It shied away from making it fully compulsory – doing so would have made it appear like a tax – and it recognised that there had been consumer complaints in the past about the occasional failings of company schemes. Therefore, it introduced added legislative controls on company pensions (making such schemes paradoxically harder to provide), and the Treasury became paranoid about the perceived (though not actual) tax loss involved by the need for tax neutrality for pension provision. The Treasury's agenda was in direct conflict with the objective of the Department for Work and Pensions (ie that increased private pension provision is a good thing). It proved (and still proves) hard, if not impossible, for governments of any political persuasion to provide a joined-up workplace pensions policy; in other words, the UK pensions policy is a mess, and the government is hoping that you and your company can clean up some of it.

SOME OTHER ISSUES

Even if you have now decided what to do about your company's pension policy, there are a few other things to consider. Some of the main ones include:

- what to do about trustees
- what to do about coping with the explosion in regulation
- what to do about tax
- what to do about the costs of administration.

The conflict between companies and trustees

If you have set up a pension scheme without any law saying you have to do so, you might be forgiven for thinking that changing, improving or reducing it was a matter for you and your employees. And you might also be forgiven for thinking that the trustees of the pension scheme – there to manage the money and the benefits separate from the company – would nonetheless appreciate that it was the company which provided the pension and that it would therefore be sensible to keep it sweet. In other words, it should be fairly obvious that it is in the interests of everyone to work together in harmony, not least because the senior management of the company is also in the pension scheme. Basically, there is a community of interest between you, as the company, and the trustees of the scheme.

It is in no one's interest for your company to struggle commercially and financially because the trustees' demands are excessive. However, regulators today like to see some tension between companies and trustees, and for the trustees to take sides on behalf of the members against the company. This unwelcome development worsened when schemes started to develop deficits rather than surpluses, and regulators today require:

- trustees to treat **any deficit as a bank debt** due from the company (though not any surplus as a credit for the company)
- **trustees to be consulted** before the company takes any action which may affect its ability to pay pensions contributions or make-up deficits
- the **regulator to be consulted** before any major restructuring of the company takes place – and, if not, possibly make the directors of the company personally liable for the costs of the scheme.

In addition, in 2003 the law converted a company's best intentions (ie to fulfil members' expectations) into guaranteed legal rights, which was the job of trustees to enforce as best they could.

The curse of regulation

It is not possible even for an expert to be aware of all the laws that govern pension schemes in the UK – and you are not supposed to be an expert. Every government calls for the reduction and simplification of regulation, and every government fails to do so; the claims by pressure groups are simply too great to resist. So pensions' regulation has increased from around 100 pages 30 years ago to around 50,000 pages today and some of it is very complicated indeed. It shows no sign at present of diminishing, and the NEST scheme itself has spawned several hundred new pages of rules. You might at some stage consider registering your pensions scheme outside the UK to avoid all (or at least most) of this.

The cost of administration

There is nothing inherently complicated about providing pensions. You save money now and draw it later – similarly to Aesop's fable of the ant and the grasshopper. However, due to the impact of regulation, administering a pension scheme is now immensely complicated and sometimes all but impossible. Indeed, the forthcoming NEST system (modelled on overseas systems, one of which is the Japanese system) may prove hard to manage. The Japanese system failed after 15 years, with the loss of the records of 50 million contributors in 2008. Fortunately, this could never happen in the UK;[5] since our systems are much more robust than those of the Japanese.

The issue of trust

Despite the Maxwell episode (see Appendix III), most employees still trust employers in relation to pension provision more than any other intermediary – or even themselves. Research by the National Association of Pension Funds suggests that employers are rated higher than insurance companies, independent financial advisers or even the government. The newspapers seem to delight in blowing up every pensions failure (and there have been a few: ASW, Equitable Life, pensions mis-selling and many others) but are less good at putting pensions in context. Whilst there are (still) failures in pension schemes and sometimes some of us are led to expect more than was ever promised by an employer or a scheme, the risk of failure is actually very low. More importantly, the risks of not having enough to live on during retirement, which are posed by *not* making provisions, are much higher. The issue of trust in the pensions system is one which concerns industry and the government very much, although the latter in particular seem to struggle to do much about it.

HOW DO PENSIONS WORK IN THE UK?

If you really want to understand the UK state pension system, Chapter 1 looks at it in detail. However, it might be useful here just to spend a few minutes getting the hang of the outline of the system as a whole, ie both **state** and **private** pensions. Understanding a simple outline is rather handy if implementation of your company pension policy is not to prove expensive or wasteful.

Company pension funds in the UK are now a major economic force: UK pension fund assets are estimated at a shade under £1 trillion, with liabilities, including unfunded public sector liabilities, of around £3 trillion. This compares with a GDP of around £1 trillion, and mortgage assets in building societies (£300 billion) and mortgage banks (£600 billion).

Therefore, it is not surprising that the government has a significant interest in the affairs of pension funds – and has introduced extensive legislation to control them. There is a tension in the legislation: on the one hand, much is tax-driven, initially largely by HMRC, to limit the benefits of (and hence the perceived tax relief on) pensions. At the same time, though, the Department of Work and Pensions is deeply concerned about demographic profiles (ie more older people and fewer children) which will mean significantly increased state pension costs by the turn of the half century, with fewer contributors available to pay for them. In contrast with HMRC, it wishes to encourage the development of private pension arrangements.

Background: the system in outline

Most techies explain pension systems around the world using 'tiers' or 'pillars' of provision. There are usually said to be three pillars:[6]

1. the state
2. private pensions
3. private savings.

Splitting retirement income provision in this way means that there is diversification of income; this should protect workers a little in case one of the pillars does not deliver as it should. In practice, the UK system follows this pattern, although there is considerable overlapping between the pillars.

In addition, certain pensions offered by the state to its own employees do not fit easily into this structure. Many public sector arrangements are unfunded or, even more impenetrably, 'notionally funded' – and some are funded, but not in the usual fashion.

The first pillar: the state scheme

The first pillar is the state scheme, which is often described in three (and now four) pillars:

- the **basic state pension**, and other broadly universal benefits
- the **additional state pension** – including the former graduated retirement scheme (1961 to 1975) and the former state earnings related scheme (1978 to 2002) – whose current version came into operation in 2002 (known as the state second pension: S2P)
- a **third state pension** – the pension credit – with two elements: a means-tested guarantee element and a savings credit
- a **fourth state pension**, which is a funded system started in 2012 (NEST: National Employment Savings Trust).

The second pillar: private pensions

The second pillar is a complex amalgam of private pensions. It is usually convenient to describe it in terms of:

- **occupational** (workplace) **pension schemes**, provided through the employer
- **personal pensions**, provided by an individual for himself or herself.

As ever, there are hybrid arrangements (mixtures of the two), and of course there are special arrangements for civil servants, although their generous pension arrangements are being cut back slowly.

The third pillar: private savings

The third pillar consists of private savings. Due to public disaffection with pension arrangements in recent years, increasing numbers of people have been simply saving through tax-efficient ISAs and by buying property. These savings, even if used to support income in retirement, are only dealt with incidentally in this book.

State pensions
In simple terms, there are four state pensions, and they are described more in-depth below.

The basic state pension
If you work for at least 30 years, you will get a basic state pension of around £100 per week. That's the easy bit; in fact, the details of the basic state pension are rather complicated, and it is available in around five different forms,[7] with:

- a pension being paid for those who work
- a pension for those married (or are civil partners) of those who work
- a completely pointless extra special pension of 25p a week for those over 80.

This is one of the lowest state pensions in the European Union, and if that's all you get, you will also get additional state benefits, since it is not enough to keep body and soul together. Both the **employed** and the **self-employed** get a basic state pension.

The additional state pension
The additional state pension (once known as SERPS: the state earnings-related pension scheme) now known as the state second pension (S2P) gives you a very complicated additional pension to the basic state pension – if you are employed (it gives nothing to the self-employed).

In theory it tops up your basic pension to around £140 per week. The only practical way to work out how much it will actually get is to fill in a form on the Pension Service website to get a quotation (see www.gov.uk/state-pension-statement). Since the government almost certainly has imperfect information about your earnings record, the quotation will probably be wrong, but it is virtually impossible to query the calculations. You just have to hope that the National Insurance numbers on which it is based are accurate (many are not).

The state pension credit/guarantee
A third state pension is available, but you have to pass a means test.

- If the first two pensions are not enough to add up to £140 a week, the **state pension guarantee** will top it up to that amount.
- Also, there is a reward for you (the **state pensions credit**) if you have in fact managed to save a modest amount during your working life (though not too much), amounting roughly up to £50 per week (if you fill the form in).

The form is almost purpose-built to put you off applying and in fact around £5.5 billion a year goes unclaimed because it is so hard to complete it.

NEST and auto-enrolment
Pretty soon your company – and all employers – are going to have to consider what to do about a semi-compulsory fourth state pension system. If you already have (or are going to have) a basic company pension scheme for all your staff then you will be exempt, but you have to have a system that all staff, must join (unless they sign a

difficult-to-find form saying they don't want to join); this is called '**auto-enrolment**'. Otherwise, your company will have to deduct 4% of your employees' salary, add 3% of your own money and send it to **NEST**: a government-backed fourth state pension system.

This means that in theory all employees in the country will have 8% (the government gives 1% tax relief) – up to an income of around £35,000 – put into a funded pension scheme.

NEST stands for National Employee Savings Trust, which is totally not what it says on the tin.

- It is not national (most people will not join).
- It is not for employees (it has to be organised by the employer).
- It is not savings (it is to provide pensions, which are not savings).
- It is only nominally a trust (it is really a statutory body).

It was invented to try to get the lower paid on the workplace pension ladder, but no one yet knows:

- whether the administrative system will cope (nothing like this has ever been done before)
- whether the policy objective will be achieved (ie to help the lower paid, many of whom would be better advised to opt out since they would get better value from state benefits – and in any event the benefits on offer will be very modest).

Private pensions
Since most of us know that the state pensions will not give us enough to live on when we've stopped working, generally those who can afford it try to organise private pensions as well. There are two main systems for private pensions.

1. **Defined benefit (DB) systems**, which provide benefits linked to income; these systems are dying rapidly due to a destructive regulatory environment, though they still exist predominantly in large companies (eg Tesco) and in the public sector. There is now an alternative to the dying DB schemes, called a **career average system** (which the civil service is adopting), which lowers the benefits that you get, as it is based on the average of the salary you have earned over the years, rather than your final salary. Pure defined benefit schemes are disappearing because they have become prohibitively expensive and complicated; in 2006 there were 3 million people contributing to such schemes, but by 2009 there were only 2.4 million.[8] There had at one time been around 12 million in such schemes – around half the workforce.
2. **Defined contribution systems**, which simply take money from the employer and/ or employee every year; once you see how much there is in the kitty at retirement, you then go and buy an annuity from an insurance company. It's a bit risky because you are never sure how much there will be – the investment values, the expenses and the tax change all the time – and the amount the pot will buy varies depending on mortality and interest rates at the time you retire.

In recent years, there have been attempts to encourage the use of 'third-way' systems, which share some of the risks between employer and employee, or between different generations (as happens for example in the Netherlands, with some success, where they are called 'collective defined contribution' schemes or CDCs).[9]

If you are earning a little more than the norm, there are varieties of these schemes which either provide higher benefits or benefits outside the tax limits, or where the individual has the right to manage their own investments. The essential details of these higher-earner arrangements – and the options available – are explored later in the book.

WHY IS IT ALL SO COMPLICATED, AND WILL IT CHANGE?

The UK pension system is one of the most (if not *the* most) complicated pension systems in the world. The state system offers four varieties of benefits, some of which are contracted out and some contracted in; some are flat rate and some of them earnings-related, and some are automatic and some means-tested. Thousands of pages of regulations cover the state scheme; around 30,000 pages cover the private pensions sector and there are around 4,000 pages of tax rules (most countries manage with a page and a half). There are also innumerable agencies charged with looking after the system: the Department of Work and Pensions, the Treasury, Her Majesty's Customs and Excise, the Pension Protection Fund, the Pensions Regulator, the Financial Services Authority (soon to be the Prudential Regulatory Authority), the Pensions Registry, the Pensions Ombudsman, The Pensions Advisory Service and several tribunals. It is all rather a mess. The record shows that companies over the last 10 years have understandably tried to reduce their involvement in pension provision.[10]

However, there is no need for you to despair. It is true that there are periodic attempts to try to simplify the system, though every effort seems to produce even more regulation.

- No government has yet managed to produce a consistent pension policy.
- The Treasury is obsessed with trying to cut back on tax relief (although for the most part pension systems are fiscally neutral).
- The Department of Work and Pensions is worried about:

  □ the ageing of the population (the state pension system will not be able to pay)
  □ continual complaints about the failures of the private pension system.

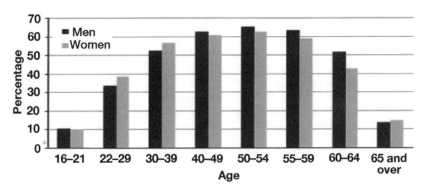

Graph 1: Employee membership of an employer-sponsored pension scheme:[1,2] by sex and age range, 2009.

Source: Annual Survey of Hours and Earnings, Office for National Statistics.

1. Pension is arranged through an employer, main pension only.
2. Between 2008 and 2009 Lloyds Banking Group, the Royal Bank of Scotland Group and HBOS plc were reclassified from the private sector to the public sector.

■ All the experts argue all the time about what is the role of the state, what is the role of the private sector and how the tax system should work (although I know what the answer should be).

Until we have a holistic pensions policy for the UK, all you can do in your company is:

■ take note of the inconsistencies
■ try to work around them
■ focus on what you want to do for your company and your staff.

WHAT THIS BOOK COVERS, AND WHAT IT DOES NOT . . .

This book does not attempt to be a complete encyclopaedia of pensions for everyone. It does not look at:

■ the problems of the government in setting down a pensions policy
■ the problems of the public sector
■ the self-employed
■ detailed issues of investment, law and administration, or actuarial issues.

It is simply designed to help you and your company to come to terms with determining your own pension policy, which is not easy with the current complexities and frequent policy, tax and accounting changes.

Just to be clear: there are more changes likely to come. For example, the government is gently panicking because company pension schemes are changing and people are not saving enough for their old age. Therefore, it is looking at bringing in ad hoc changes, such as allowing people early access to their pension cash to ensure they remain within those schemes.[11] Whatever you do, you will need to look at it again from time to time.

CHAPTER 1
THE STATE SYSTEM AND NEST

If all you are going to live on when you retire is your state pension, you are going to live a very simple life. The state pension system, complex and contradictory as it is, will deliver, even after recent reforms, one of the lowest state pensions in Europe.

Nevertheless, although the money that the state will deliver is modest (and likely to get more modest), it would be foolish for your company to ignore it when designing the private pension arrangements.

The reasons that it might be better for the lower paid employees you may have (say under £25,000 pa) *not* to join a pension scheme at all – and for you *not* to put money into it for them – are because:

- improving their private pension simply gets them out of means-tested state pensions
- forcing them to make contributions to a pension scheme might deprive them of money they could use better in other ways, eg paying off credit card debt.

It may be better, therefore, for all concerned to take into account the state pension position of your workforce when designing your company scheme, rather than wasting your money and theirs on a pointless exercise.

You will also need to think about how things will change in the future. Means testing may or may not go, and certainly no one knows now how things will turn out tomorrow in pensions – never mind the next 30 years. The government cannot decide what it wants private pensions and state pensions to do and makes continual changes in policy, rather like a butterfly hopping from stamen to stamen.

Governments of all persuasions have been unable to settle on a stable pensions policy in the last 50 years, and changes in direction on state pensions and public sector pensions, as well as private sector pensions, tax and regulation, have resulted in confusion for both employers and employees.

So what should you do? The first thing is to try to understand what concerns the government about pensions.

THE POLITICAL BACKGROUND

The government is obsessed with pensions. It's why politicians keep changing their mind about what to do and changing their pensions ministers about every nine months. So far, state pensions have been low in the UK because private pensions did most of the job. The success of the growth of private pensions over the last century (driven by market forces rather than government policy) produced fantastic pools of capital which partly led to the pre-eminence of London in world capital markets. Today even in bad times, total UK pension fund assets are estimated at a shade under £1 trillion. The promises (or expectations) made by pension funds, including unfunded public sector liabilities, seem to be around £3 trillion – and on top of that is the cost of state pensions. To put this into perspective: the UK's gross domestic product is around £1 trillion a year, and mortgage assets in building societies and mortgage banks are about the same.

You can only build a decent company pension on the foundation of a decent and stable state system. The changing state pensions makes it hard for you and your company to plan, but there are some basic principles you can be pretty sure of.

- The state system is likely to change forever.
- The state system is likely to become worse rather than better, because the population is ageing and there will be fewer working taxpayers in relation to older people.
- Rather like no one expects the Spanish Inquisition, no one understands the state pension system – except for the fact that most of us will not be able to afford to live on state benefits.
- More than 10 million people in the UK today can expect to live to see their 100th birthday – 17% of the population:

  - ☐ 3 million are currently aged under 16
  - ☐ 5.5 million are aged between 16 and 50
  - ☐ 1.3 million are aged between 51 and 65
  - ☐ around 875,000 are already aged over 65.

By 2066, there will be at least half a million people aged 100 or over, which will include nearly 7,700 supercentenarians, ie those aged 110 or over.[1]

So company pensions are going to be critical for your own survival and that of your workforce. In order to design a decent and cost-effective company plan, you need to know what the state thinks it will do for pensions (even though it will probably change the deal in the next few years).

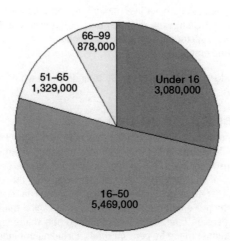

Graph 2: Number of people currently alive who can expect to see their 100th birthday, by age in 2010.

Source: 2008 based People Projections (UK), Office for National Statistics

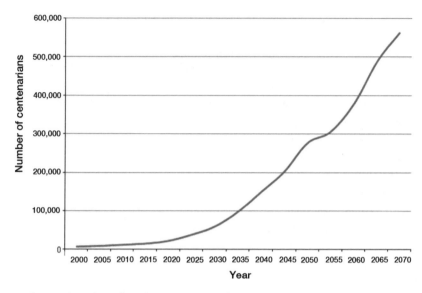

Graph 3: Projected number of centenarians in the UK.

Source: 2008 based People Projections (UK), Office for National Statistics

Background: the system in outline

Providing pensions for all of us ageing people is a bit of a challenge for the state. The pension system is being cut back so that state pension ages are rising for women from 60 to 65 (between 2010 and 2020) and for everyone to age 66 (from 2016) and to 68 (from 2046). It's probable that if you are presently under 45, you will not get your state pension until age 70 – or even 75.

The following tables show the revised state pension ages for women under the Pensions Act 1995 and as revised for both men and women under the recent proposals. These dates not only affect the start date for receipt of the state Retirement Pension (if not deferred), but also delay the time at which the requirement to pay personal National Insurance contributions ceases.

Even when you get your pension it might not be worth all that much. The basic state pension was approximately 40% of national average earnings after the war, 22% of national average earnings by 1975, and it is expected to fall to about 6% by 2020, although it was later increased slightly.[2] These days you will usually get something in addition from the state second pension and maybe means-tested benefits, but it is not generous.

So what will you and your workforce get from the government? There are four main state benefits:

1. the basic pension
2. the additional pension
3. means-tested pensions
4. NEST.

Table 5: Increased pension ages for women (date of birth (DOB) up to 5 April 1953, under Pensions Act 1995)

Date of birth	Pension age (years.months)	Pension date
For women (DOB up to 5 April 1953, under Pensions Act 1995)		
6 April 1950 to 5 May 1950	60.0 – 60.1	6 May 2010
6 May 1950 to 5 June 1950	60.1 – 60.2	6 July 2010
6 June 1950 to 5 July 1950	60.2 – 60.3	6 Sept 2010
6 July 1950 to 5 Aug 1950	60.3 – 60.4	6 Nov 2010
6 Aug 1950 to 5 Sept 1950	60.4 – 60.5	6 Jan 2011
6 Sept 1950 to 5 Oct 1950	60.5 – 60.6	6 Mar 2011
6 Oct 1950 to 5 Nov 1950	60.6 – 60.7	6 May 2011
6 Nov 1950 to 5 Dec 1950	60.7 – 60.8	6 July 2011
6 Dec 1950 to 5 Jan 1951	60.8 – 60.9	6 Sept 2011
6 Jan 1951 to 5 Feb 1951	60.9 – 60.10	6 Nov 2011
6 Feb 1951 to 5 Mar 1951	60.10 – 60.11	6 Jan 2012
6 Mar 1951 to 5 April 1951	60.11 – 61.0	6 Mar 2012
6 April 1951 to 5 May 1951	61.0 – 61.1	6 May 2012
6 May 1951 to 5 June 1951	61.1 – 61.2	6 July 2012
6 June 1951 to 5 July 1951	61.2 – 61.3	6 Sept 2012
6 July 1951 to 5 Aug 1951	61.3 – 61.4	6 Nov 2012
6 Aug 1951 to 5 Sept 1951	61.4 – 61.5	6 Jan 2013
6 Sept 1951 to 5 Oct 1951	61.5 – 61.6	6 Mar 2013
6 Oct 1951 to 5 Nov 1951	61.6 – 61.7	6 May 2013
6 Nov 1951 to 5 Dec 1951	61.7 – 61.8	6 July 2013
6 Dec 1951 to 5 Jan 1952	61.8 – 61.9	6 Sept 2013
6 Jan 1952 to 5 Feb 1952	61.9 – 61.10	6 Nov 2013
6 Feb 1952 to 5 Mar 1952	61.10 – 61.11	6 Jan 2014
6 Mar 1952 to 5 April 1952	61.11 – 62.0	6 Mar 2014
6 April 1952 to 5 May 1952	62.0 – 62.1	6 May 2014
6 May 1952 to 5 June 1952	62.1 – 62.2	6 July 2014
6 June 1952 to 5 July 1952	62.2 – 62.3	6 Sept 2014
6 July 1952 to 5 Aug 1952	62.3 – 62.4	6 Nov 2014
6 Aug 1952 to 5 Sept 1952	62.4 – 62.5	6 Jan 2015
6 Sept 1952 to 5 Oct 1952	62.5 – 62.6	6 Mar 2015
6 Oct 1952 to 5 Nov 1952	62.6 – 62.7	6 May 2015
6 Nov 1952 to 5 Dec 1952	62.7 – 62.8	6 July 2015
6 Dec 1952 to 5 Jan 1953	62.8 – 62.9	6 Sept 2015
6 Jan 1953 to 5 Feb 1953	62.9 – 62.10	6 Nov 2015
6 Feb 1953 to 5 Mar 1953	62.10 – 62.11	6 Jan 2016
6 Mar 1953 to 5 April 1953	62.11 – 63.0	6 Mar 2016

Table 6: Increased pension ages for women (born after 5 December 1953) under Pensions Act 2011

Date of birth	Pension age (years.months)	Pension date
For women (DOB up to 5 Dec 1953, under Pensions Act 2011)		
6 April 1953 to 5 May 1953	63.2 – 63.3	6 July 2016
6 May 1953 to 5 June 1953	63.5 – 63.6	6 Nov 2016
6 June 1953 to 5 July 1953	63.8 – 63.9	6 Mar 2017
6 July 1953 to 5 Aug 1953	63.11 – 64.0	6 July 2017
6 Aug 1953 to 5 Sept 1953	64.2 – 64.3	6 Nov 2017
6 Sept 1953 to 5 Oct 1953	64.5 – 64.6	6 Mar 2018
6 Oct 1953 to 5 Nov 1953	64.8 – 64.9	6 July 2018
6 Nov 1953 to 5 Dec 1953	64.11 – 65.0	6 Nov 2018
For men and women (DOB to 5 April 1954, under Pensions Act 2011)		
6 Dec 1953 to 5 Jan 1954	65.2 – 65.3	6 Mar 2019
6 Jan 1954 to 5 Feb 1954	65.5 – 65.6	6 July 2019
6 Feb 1954 to 5 Mar 1954	65.8 – 65.9	6 Nov 2019
6 Mar 1954 to 5 April 1954	65.11 – 66.0	6 Mar 2020
6 April 1954	66.0	6 April 2020

Table 7: When to stop paying Class 4 National Insurance contributions

Date of birth	Pension age (years.months)	Final Class 4 liability
For women		
6 April 1950 to 5 Oct 1950	60.0 – 60.6	2010/11
6 Oct 1950 to 5 April 1951	60.6 – 61.0	2011/12
6 April 1951 to 5 Oct 1951	61.1 – 61.6	2012/13
6 Oct 1951 to 5 April 1952	61.6 – 62.0	2013/14
6 April 1952 to 5 Oct 1952	62.1 – 62.6	2014/15
6 Oct 1952 to 5 April 1953	62.6 – 63.0	2015/16
6 April 1953 to 5 July 1953	63.2 – 63.9	2016/17
6 July 1953 to 5 Oct 1953	63.11 – 64.6	2017/18
6 Oct 1953 to 5 Jan 1954	64.8 – 65.3	2018/19
6 Jan 1954 to 5 April 1954	65.5 – 66.0	2019/20
For men		
6 Dec 1953 to 5 Jan 1954	65.2 – 65.3	2018/19
6 Jan 1954 to 5 April 1954	65.5 – 66.0	2019/20

Each of those is now explained below. It's not an easy read (it's not an easy system), and you will still be able to plan your company pension and understand the rest of this book even if you skip the rest of this chapter, or at least merely skim-read it.

THE BASIC STATE PENSION

There is, of course, no money backing the basic state pension; when you pay your National Insurance contributions, the money goes into a black hole (the consolidated fund at the Treasury). The basic state pension operates as a 'pay-as-you-go' system, ie the National Insurance contributions and tax paid by the workers in each year pays the pensions for the oldies.

- Nothing has been set aside to save for these pensions.
- The basic pension is not universal; you won't get it all (or even any) if you have not paid enough NI contributions.
- You only get it from state pension age (at present, 60-ish for women and 65 for men), changing to 65/66 by 2020. The state pension age for men is edging up to 66 and for women it is increasing in monthly steps between April 2010 and April 2020.[3]
- It is possible to increase the amount of the pension by deferring receipt of it beyond retirement age.
- It is a 'redistributive' pension: provided an adequate number of contributions have been paid, individuals receive the same level of benefit, regardless of the size of contributions.

An individual with a complete contribution record receives a full basic state pension of just over £107 per week (2012/13). The state pension is increased every year from April, broadly in line with inflation.

Sadly, there is not just one state pension; in fact, there are five – and the five categories apply also to the state second pension.[4] They are:

1. Category A
2. Category B
3. Category C (now obsolete)
4. Category D
5. Category E.

Category A

The Category A pension is **contributory**, ie you only get it if you have paid sufficient contributions. It consists of two parts, either or both of which may be payable.

1. **Basic state pension**: dependent upon the number of qualifying years a person has worked in their life.
2. **Additional state pension** (either SERPS or the state second pension): dependent upon earnings, or deemed earnings, in a person's working life since April 1978.

If you have an incomplete contribution record, you can use the qualifying years of a 'former spouse' (separated either through bereavement or divorce) to provide a higher basic state pension.

Category B

The Category B pension is also **contributory, but it is a derived pension**, ie based on someone else's contribution record. Like a Category A pension, it can consist of a basic state pension, an additional state pension, or both. You get it on the basis of a spouse's or civil partner's qualifying years and earnings. It is payable to married women, widows and widowers, and nowadays whatever sex you are you can get a basic state pension based on your spouse's NI record, if this is better than yours.

If both you and your spouse/civil partner have a satisfactory NI contribution record, then you each get the full basic state pension when you reach state pension age. If your wife (but not your husband) is entitled to less than 60%, she may be able to claim a dependent adult's addition based on her husband's contribution record, which would increase her pension to 60% of the full rate.

Category C
Category C is now obsolete.

Category D
The Category D pension (the '**over 80 pension**') is non-contributory, ie you get it even if you've paid no National Insurance – or not enough. You will get it when you:

■ reach age 80 or above
■ have been resident in the UK for at least 10 years in the previous 20 and either:

☐ are not entitled to another category of state pension
☐ are entitled to one at a lower rate than the Category D rate.

Category E
Rather like your appendix, the final category is completely pointless and is based on an historical accident. Category E pension is in fact called the '**Age Addition**' and is payable to all recipients of state pensions aged 80 or above. It is 25 pence a week – worth around 4.2% extra to the basic pension in 1971 and now worth an additional 0.3% of the basic pension – subject, of course, to any tax payable. It probably costs more to administer it than the £13 a year it pays to pensioners.

THE ADDITIONAL STATE PENSION
Since the basic state pension is not enough to live on, the additional state pension – an umbrella term covering the state second pension (S2P) and the state earnings-related pension scheme (SERPS) – was invented at a time when Britain could not afford to increase the basic pension. It is complicated and an anomaly, and it will eventually die.

In the meantime, we have to cope with it. Since 1961, there have been three versions, little bits of which still remain.

1. The graduated retirement scheme, which operated from 6 April 1961 until 5 April 1975, offers a maximum weekly benefit (provided there is a full contribution record). Based on graduated NI contributions paid between April 1961 and April 1975, it pays less than £12 per week.
2. The **state earnings-related pension scheme (SERPS)**, which operated from 1978 until 2002, offered a maximum in 2009/10 of £154.71 to a single person. It was intended originally to provide a pension of 25% of 'band earnings' but was subsequently much reduced, and has now been replaced by the state second pension, although existing rights are protected.

3. Little is currently being paid out under the state second pension (S2P). It is even more complicated than SERPS, which itself was a byword for complexity. It is based on three earnings bands and three accrual rates (rather than one of each). For low earners, a flat rate of S2P pension is guaranteed. Higher earners accrue (for the moment) an earnings-related benefit. Disabled people and some carers are given credits into the flat-rate part of S2P. If you think you understand it, you haven't studied it enough and life is too short to do so.

STATE SECOND PENSION (S2P)

As well as the basic state pension, you will get, as an employee, the state second pension. If you earn (or are treated as earning) between two arbitrary numbers (the *lower earnings limit* and the *upper earnings limit*) you will build up a state second pension on a cumulative basis – depending on the level of your earnings. Earnings above the upper earnings limit do not count.[5]

The aim of the state second pension was to provide greater resources to the lower paid than the old SERPS did, and to provide pension benefits for some carers and individuals with a long-term disability. However, it works rather like SERPS did.

- It is funded through National Insurance contributions on a pay-as-you-go basis.
- The pension is payable from state pension age and is taxable.
- All employees, as opposed to the self-employed, are members of S2P, and you earn S2P for any periods of employment, unless you:

  - ☐ earn below the lower earnings limit; or
  - ☐ are aged over state pension age; or
  - ☐ are a married woman or widow paying reduced rate NI contributions.

You do not get any state second pension for those times when you were self-employed or unemployed. The way in which you calculate how much pension you should get is designed to be impossible to understand and can be summarised as follows.

- If you earn below the lower earnings threshold of £14,700 per year (April 2012), you are treated as if you earn £14,700 and the accrual rate is twice the rate under SERPS.
- If you earn between £14,700 per year and £40,040 per year, you build up benefit at a faster rate than under SERPS, with the additional benefit reducing as earnings increase.
- If you earn above the upper accrual point of £40,040 per year, (20012/13), you build up benefits at the same rate as under SERPS.
- Some carers (caring for either children under six years old or disabled relatives) and people with a long-term illness or disability are treated as if they are employees earning £14,700.

Simple, eh?

How much pension will the state second pension scheme give you?

The old system (SERPS) was designed to try to give you (if you had a full work record) a pension of around a fifth of your earnings between the bands. The current S2P is designed to give lower earners slightly higher benefits than before. It does this using a phenomenally complex structure.

Under the old SERPS, the benefit accrual was based on all earnings between the lower earnings limit (LEL) and the upper earnings limit (UEL) ('the earnings band'). With S2P there were at one time *three* (now only two) separate bands (all rates as at April 2012):

■ the first band, between the LEL and the lower earnings threshold (LET) (£5,564 and £14,700)
■ the second band, between the LET and the upper accrual point (UAP) (£14,700 and £40,040).

The UEL now matches the threshold for higher-rate income tax and is used to calculate National Insurance contributions, but not to calculate S2P or contracted-out rebates. These are both based on earnings between the LEL and yet another acronym: the UAP. This is £40,040 and does not increase with time so that the S2P slowly, over time, (depending on inflation rates) converts into a flat-rate pension.

Under SERPS, an individual with potentially 49 years of membership (ie working from age 16 to 65) each year accrued a pension of 20% of band earnings divided by 49. However, under S2P, the accrual rate varies with the bands; for an individual with a potential total membership of SERPS and S2P of 49 years, the accrual rates for S2P are (since April 2010):[6]

■ 40% of band earnings divided by 49 for earnings in the first band
■ 10% of band earnings divided by 49 for earnings in the second band.

If you do not understand any of this, do not despair – simply pray that the government computers in Newcastle have the right information about you, and are correctly programmed, to be able to calculate your eventual pension.

Table 8: How much will the state second pension give me (2012/13)?

Earnings from employment	Band earnings	S2P accrual pa
Carer – £0	-	£74
£3,000	-	£0
At LEL (£5,304)	-	£74
£5,504	£200	£74
£10,000	£4,696	£74
At LET (£14,400)	£9,096	£74
£19,000	£13,696	£84
£25,000	£19,696	£96
£32,600	£27,296	£111
£35,000	£29,696	£116
At UAP (£40,040	£34,736	£127
£50,000	£34,736	£127

Contracting out

Your company can, if it wants, make a deal with the government about the state second pension. You can agree that, in exchange for paying lower NI contributions, you will take over responsibility for paying the state second pension.

Don't do it. At one time the deal to contract out the state scheme was mildly attractive; now it is suicidal.

There is a small legacy of older pension schemes which continue to offer such benefits, and for whom it is too much trouble to change, but no one today would agree to engage in contracting out. In any event, it is now no longer available for defined contribution plans and is due to be phased out for DB schemes as well.[7]

THE THIRD STATE PENSION

If you didn't understand the previous couple of pages about the state second pension, you will probably struggle with the third state pension. The idea of it, though, is simple. If state pension no. 1 and state pension no. 2 are not enough to meet a target (say around £140 a week at the moment) then the government will top you up to just that amount.

It is, of course, means-tested (you have to fill in a 28-page form) and at present it covers about half the retired population. Paradoxically, because it is means-tested, there is an incentive if you are lower paid not to save for your retirement, so there is at the same time a means-tested bonus for having saved for retirement. There are, therefore, two forms of state pension credit:

1. guarantee credit
2. savings credit.

The guarantee credit

The pension guarantee credit is a means-tested income support for people over state retirement age (which is rising every month) and is taxable, although the full amount of guarantee credit is invariably below the tax threshold for someone aged 65 or older. In 2011/12, it guaranteed single pensioners around £140 a week and around £200 a week for couples.

You are eligible for guarantee credit if you:

■ are aged 60 or over (either person, in the case of a couple)
■ are on a low income
■ work less than 16 hours a week (and any partner working less than 24 hours a week).

Guarantee credit is higher where:

■ you are disabled and living on your own or living with another disabled person
■ you are a carer receiving invalid care allowance
■ you are in receipt of child benefit
■ there are housing costs not fully covered by Housing Benefit.

Lower levels are paid where pensioners have savings of more than £10,000. The credit is reduced by £1 a week for each £500 (or part thereof) in excess of £10,000.

The savings credit

The other part of the third state pension gives you a reward for having tried to save for your retirement. The savings credit pays you a (tax-free) allowance of 60 pence per £1 for any income between basic state pension and the guarantee credit threshold. This includes income from employment, SERPS, graduated retirement scheme, occupational pensions, personal pensions and income from savings. The amount of savings credit then reduces by 40 pence for every £1 of income above the threshold. The maximum that can be received is around £20 for single pensioners and £27 for couples. You stop getting savings credit when your weekly income exceeds £189.

FINDING OUT ABOUT THE BASIC STATE PENSION AND THE ADDITIONAL STATE PENSION

Due to the complexity of the system, it is all but impossible for individuals to calculate their own pension expectations, and companies usually are not permitted to do so on their employees' behalf – and in any event should not attempt to give advice to their employees. Anyone who wants to know what they might expect to get from their state plans can do so by filling in a form, available on the internet.[8] In practice, it is not possible to challenge the quotation – certainly not cheaply.

THE FOURTH STATE PENSION, NEST AND AUTO-ENROLMENT

Some years ago a government report concluded that state pensions were inadequate. However, instead of improving the state pension for everyone (and taxing the rich on it), the report recommended what everybody agreed should not be done: invent a fourth state pension.

The introduction of this fourth state pension is really the reason for this book. It is intended to help those on modest incomes to have an additional pension, but as ever in these matters it does so in a complicated way.[9]

Very simply, the new rules require **you:**

- to establish a new pension scheme, **or**
- to amend your existing pension scheme if necessary, in order to ensure a minimum contribution is paid in on behalf of your employees, **or**
- to pay the equivalent amount to a government sponsored occupational-style scheme called NEST.

They also require **all employees** to join and pay minimum contributions **unless** they make a formal decision not to join **or** their existing scheme is good enough.

If any of your employees decide not to join:

- they must take active steps to do this
- you as their employer cannot encourage them (or even provide the paperwork)
- they will be put back in the scheme every three years unless they repeat the form filling.

This is called 'auto-enrolment': a fancy name for membership by default. In theory, every employee in Britain will have to be a member of a fourth state pension arrangement.

Problems with the fourth state pension

There are some major design issues with the new system.

- It is not cost-effective for very low earners to join the system, since it simply takes them out of the means-tested system, which provides a free pension for them.
- The amounts involved at present are too low in most cases to provide a meaningful benefit.
- It is not certain that the administration system will work.
- There is a risk that the investments will not perform as expected.
- The costs are not as low as some private pension arrangements, and costs are a major problem when low contributions are involved.

This fourth new state system (although it is marketed as a private pension system) came into operation as a rolling programme in 2012; employees must normally pay 4% of their salary up to £42,475 and, if they do:

- you must pay 3%
- the government must add a further 1%.

The total 8% is invested through a national system (called NEST) or through a company plan into a funded arrangement, and the amount at retirement is used to purchase an annuity.

Some of the details

The basic framework includes the following.[10]

- Everyone over 22 and earning more than £8,105 a year must join a scheme but has the opportunity to 'opt out', ie not to join.
- There is a minimum contribution of 4% from the individual on band earnings between £5,564 and £42,475 a year. This is matched by a minimum 1% contribution of band earnings from the government and a compulsory 3% contribution of band earnings from the individual's employer.
- In theory, at least, the overheads should be low.

All these numbers are subject to change, but the ranges are about right.

Semi-automatic membership was outlawed in the 1980s but has now come back into favour. Its re-introduction follows an understanding of behavioural economics that indicates the following.[11]

- Automatic enrolment can combat people's tendency not to act when faced with difficult financial decisions.
- Automatic enrolment is associated with increased participation rates. On average, only 56% of those who are eligible to join a pension scheme in the workplace do so. This compares to 90% where auto-enrolment exists.
- There is evidence that employers and individuals are in favour of automatic enrolment.

There are, however, two major concerns related to the risks involved when introducing a near-universal new auto-enrolment system with severe penalties on employers who advise employees on the pros and cons of joining.

1. There remains the risk (as yet untested) of employers 'levelling down' their contributions to existing pension provision in response to the increased costs that they may face from the increased participation rates.
2. There is a severe risk of employees being auto-enrolled into a product which may not be suitable for them.

Your own pension scheme or NEST?

You are now required to establish a company pension scheme and put all your staff in it. However, you do not have to have your own scheme – and if you do not, or do not want to put certain sections of the workforce into your scheme, you can (or must) use the government's own 'private scheme', known as NEST.

In theory, NEST is a useful back-up or alternative to private pension arrangements, but there are still some outstanding issues to be addressed before you decide to commit to NEST (as opposed to setting up your own scheme). Some of these are listed below:

■ whether the NEST systems will be robust enough to cope with all sizes of employers, from the one-man band to the very largest; such a computerised system has not yet been operated anywhere else in the world
■ whether it will be able to cope with the particular issues of employees who are only short-term employees; staff who are only with you for a short time may be hard to manage
■ what happens if the wrong payments are paid (in hindsight) – and whether you later have to pay more or less (ie depending on whether the value of payments has to be increased or decreased if markets fluctuate)
■ what happens if you go bust and have not paid over contributions which have been deducted
■ what happens if one of your employees wants to opt out and does not complete the forms in time.

Policing the fourth state pension

The government is so concerned that you will not do as you are required that it has hired an additional 300 'policemen' run by the Pensions Regulator to check up on you. You must pay the right amounts, sometimes quite small, into (and arrange for your staff to pay into) your own scheme (or NEST instead) on time.

There are bound to be mistakes from time to time, and the cost of remedying those mistakes might be quite high. However, the Regulator has been told to try to help employers to get things right, rather than behave like a traffic warden determined to chalk up a record number of parking tickets.

A mini history

The government has made a bit of a mess about introducing the fourth state pension. The rules are spread over (at least) three Acts of Parliament and several more statutory instruments.

■ The **Pensions Act 2007 s20** set up the predecessor to NEST: the Personal Accounts Delivery Authority (PADA). It was wound up on 5 July 2010 and its functions are now run by the NEST Corporation.
■ The **Pensions Act 2008** established the constitution and structure of NEST, the process of auto-enrolment and the level of compulsory employer contributions.
■ The **Pensions Act 2011** amends some of the terms following the 2010 general election and the then-new coalition government, examining and revising some of the terms. This was the case especially:

    ☐ in relation to re-enrollment after a period away from the scheme
    ☐ in relation to the 'earnings trigger', ie 'Earns more than £8,105'. But if the employee does join, he has to pay contributions on income over a lower figure . . .

☐ in allowing the employer to impose a waiting period for up to three months (to avoid unnecessary administration in relation to staff who may not stay long)

☐ in ensuring that re-enrolment is not to happen more than every two years and nine months and

☐ in allowing employers to self-certify that their scheme meets the necessary minimum requirements.

Most of the detailed provisions of the NEST system are contained in secondary legislation (statutory instruments) made under the Pensions Act 2008; there are now at least 12 such sets of regulations – and more to come.[12]

WHAT DO I HAVE TO DO?

The most important job you have is to make sure that:

- **all** your employees are members of your pension plan (or NEST)
- the plan is good enough to meet the legal requirements
- you do this in time to meet the deadlines.

Employers' duties

This is what you **must do**.

- Ensure all employees are enrolled in a company pension plan or in NEST.
- Pay the contributions on time.
- Re-enrol the employees every three years.
- Ensure the scheme stays compliant.

What you **must not do** is advise employees on how not to join.

Which employees do I have to do all this for?

Any employees who meet the following conditions have to be in a suitable scheme.

- **They work (or ordinarily work) in Great Britain** under a contract (including temporary workers and in some cases agency workers). 'Employees' includes directors who are employed under a service contract but not non-executive directors.
- **They are at least 22** and not over state pension age (although employees aged over 16 and under 75 can join if they wish).
- **They earn more than the income tax personal allowance (£8,105 in 2012/13)** including bonuses, overtime and statutory maternity, paternity and adoption pay. The qualifying earnings band is reviewed annually and revalued to allow for inflation. Although the regime is directed at low earners, employees earning more than the qualifying earnings band are subject to auto-enrolment, too. However, their contributions are paid on a different basis, ie on earnings over the National Insurance Primary Threshold (£7,605 in 2012/13).

In order to decide whether an employee's earnings are sufficient to qualify him or her for auto-enrolment, you can use your normal pay cycle (for example, weekly or monthly) as the pay reference period. If you wish to reduce the number of employees who accidentally have to join when they wouldn't otherwise have to (for example, if their earnings briefly rise above the threshold), a pay reference period of 12 months from their employer's staging date applies to employees whose contractual pay is less than the threshold (if you do not expect their pay to exceed the threshold).

What is a 'good enough' scheme?

You have to put your staff into a pension scheme; this can be either your own scheme (or one you have organised) or NEST.

It has to be a scheme which does not oblige the employee to make a choice or provide information, so in practice there will be 'default options', ie you or your advisers will take investment and other decisions on your employees' behalf.

Your duty to ensure your staff stay in the scheme

You have a duty not to do anything (or not to do something) to stop your employee being a member or to disqualify your scheme as being a qualifying one. The only excuse for this occurs when the employee is an active member of another qualifying scheme. However, if you reduce your contributions or remove employees from membership, you are in breach. You are given a one-month breathing space to allow staff to move from one scheme to another.

Employees who do not want to join

You have to put your staff into a scheme – whether yours or NEST's – but they have an equal right not to join anything they don't want to, and to get their contributions back if they have been put into a scheme they did not want to join. They can also leave or join at any time, but, in order to save administration costs, they can only do this once in any 12-month period.

Employees who are not able to join

Some of your staff cannot be forced to be auto-enrolled into your scheme or NEST. This is usually because they:

- are under 22 or over state pension age
- earn less than £8,105 a year (in 2012/13).

However, even if they are outside the normal age limits, they can ask to join the scheme; again, they can only do this once in a 12-month period.

Low earners can also ask to join the scheme, although it does not have to be an automatic enrolment scheme (ie meet the quality requirements, including the requirement for minimum employer contributions), so you could have a cheaper or easier scheme for them.

Anyone who does not have to join must be told of their right to join if they want.

When do I have to do all this?

Since it is so expensive – and so complicated – and because so many things can go wrong along the way, the auto-enrolment/NEST system is being phased in over four years, with the first phase having started on 1 October 2012. The government thinks that between 5 million and 9 million people will start pension saving for the first time or increase their existing savings.

Nothing in pensions is simple, though. You will be in one of 43 bands, according to size, and each band is given a monthly 'staging date' (only a civil servant would see this as a simplified system). Larger employers are subjected to the enrolment duties before smaller employers (the thinking being that they are probably going to have their own schemes anyway and will not need to do much to comply – or need to join the NEST system).

If you have a smaller business, or a new business, you are required to begin towards the end of the phasing in. For example, a new employer that first pays employees between 1 April 2012 and 31 March 2013 has a staging date of 1 March 2016. These dates are subject to change and you will need to check periodically on the Pensions Regulator's website (www.thepensionsregulator.gov.uk).

You can, if you wish, start before you have to, but you have to sign a form saying that you understand the implications and have a scheme in place.

Repetition

If you thought that, once you'd done the things you have to do, you could rest easy, you need to think again. You are required to re-enrol your staff automatically every three years after they first become subject to the statutory employer duties. This is designed to force those employees who have opted out to reconsider their pension provision at regular intervals. You can choose a date within one month of the three-year anniversary of its staging date (and for the future, within one month of the three-year anniversary of its first re-enrolment date).

You have to re-enrol the staff for as long as they stay with you, although employees who have opted out in the 12 months just before the re-enrolment date do not have to be re-enrolled.

DOES MY SCHEME COUNT AS 'GOOD ENOUGH'?

If you have one, your scheme is already probably good enough; it is almost certainly:

- either an occupational or personal pension scheme
- registered with HMRC
- satisfying certain quality requirements.

Encouragingly, you can self-certify that your existing scheme meets the requirements.

Defined contribution (DC) schemes

If you have a defined contribution (DC) scheme, it is good enough if:

- you make minimum contributions of at least 3% of the jobholder's (fancy word for employee) 'qualifying earnings' (ie, earnings between £5,564 and £42,475) over a 12-month pay reference period (ie during the year)
- the total amount of contributions paid by the jobholder and you must be at least 8% of the jobholder's qualifying earnings over a 12-month period
- these provisions may be varied for schemes that are contracted out of S2P.

If you run a group personal pension scheme (GPPP) instead, you must:

- make minimum contributions of at least 3% of the jobholder's qualifying earnings (as for occupational DC schemes) over a 12-month period
- have an agreement with the pension provider (insurance company) under which you must make up the shortfall if the total contributions are less than 8%; this is called a 'section 26 agreement' (PA 2008 s26).

You also have to make sure that you deduct contributions from the jobholder's earnings and pay these direct to the scheme (this is almost certainly technically illegal under EU law, but the European Commission has said it's OK, even though it's against the normal consumer protection law).

If you have an existing scheme, your trustees have the power under law to change the contribution levels made to the scheme to make sure they comply with the conditions for an auto-enrolment scheme, but only with your consent (PA 2008 s32).

Self-certifying compliance in advance
You can self-certify that your scheme is good enough, even though the details of what is good enough are still not settled. Your certificate lasts 12 months, so even if things change a bit during the year (and your scheme is in breach from time to time), there is no penalty. You have three months from the date you decide to designate as the certification date to fill in the forms.

Defined benefit (DB) schemes
If you are one of the fortunate few who still run a defined benefit scheme, your scheme must offer benefits which match or exceed a 'test scheme'. A test scheme is an occupational pension which provides that:

- members receive a pension for life
- beginning at the age of 65
- at an annual rate that is 1/120th of average qualifying earnings in the last three tax years preceding the end of pensionable service multiplied by the number of years of pensionable service, up to a maximum of 40.

It is likely that the test scheme must provide for pensions to be:

- revalued in line with inflation
- increased annually in line with inflation.

Additionally, if a scheme is contracted out of S2P (unlikely for new schemes, since contracting out is too complicated and expensive), it may be that the benefits must be increased to at least 1/80th.

Certifying a DB scheme
The government does not trust you on your own to certify a DB scheme. Only you and the actuary can certify that a scheme meets the test scheme standard, and you cannot give a certificate in relation to any matter requiring calculation or which otherwise falls within the province of the actuary. Meanwhile, the actuary cannot:

- take into account contingent or ancillary benefits, such as dependants' pensions, death benefits, pension credit benefits or money purchase benefits
- certify that the scheme meets the required standard if the pensions to be provided for more than 10% of relevant members are not 'broadly equivalent' to the pensions that would be provided under the test scheme.

If your scheme is a **career average scheme** it does not count as a qualifying scheme unless:

- it gives discretionary revaluation increases at a rate of 2.5% LPI
- this is provided for in the scheme's statement of funding principles.

Other stuff
There is quite a lot of other stuff you have to do, including what is listed below.

- Register your scheme with the Pensions Regulator; you now have four months after your staging date (ie the date you have to start your scheme) to tell the Regulator that you have done it.
- Tell your staff of your duty to provide a qualifying scheme if their membership is lost because your company (or a subsidiary) closes down or you change your scheme (although not because of what your employee does or does not do).
- Tell employees they have the right to join the scheme even during any waiting period.
- Self-certify that your scheme meets at least one of these:

  ☐ a minimum of 9% contribution of the employee's pensionable earnings, including a 4% employer's contribution (pensionable earnings is the higher of your company's definition of either pensionable earnings or basic pay)

  ☐ a minimum of 8% contributions of the employee's pensionable earnings (including a 3% employer's contribution) provided that the total pensionable earnings of all the employees to whom the criteria applies constitutes at least 85% of their total earnings

  ☐ a minimum of 7% contribution of the employee's total earnings (including a 3% employer's contribution).

Not quite DB and not quite DC: hybrid schemes

Your scheme might be one of the very few that tread a very sensible path between defined contribution and defined benefit; such schemes are called hybrids. If you have one of these, you have caused the regulators some anguish because they are not quite sure how to decide if your scheme is good enough. Detailed (although rather different) quality tests also apply for hybrid schemes. In general, the provisions of a scheme that relate to DB benefits and the part that relates to DC benefits should be treated as though they provided those benefits under separate schemes. Once this is done, you apply the relevant DB or DC test and, in most cases, your scheme needs only to satisfy one of the tests. For example, if the DB test is met then it is irrelevant whether the DC test is met or not.

Schemes across the water

The UK is a very unattractive place to have a pension scheme, and EU laws now make it possible to have your scheme registered in another country within the EU. In this case, you can use your non-UK scheme for auto-enrolment if it:

- meets the necessary quality requirements applying to UK schemes (either DB, DC or hybrid)
- is regulated by a regulatory body
- uses at least 70% of the benefits to provide an income for life for its members.

The DWP rules do not require your scheme to be tax-recognised in its country of origin, although HMRC probably do. The self-certification provisions for DC schemes do not apply for non-UK DC schemes.

If you already have a good scheme

You can postpone auto-enrolment if your employees are to be enrolled in a high-quality scheme (other than NEST). Provided your scheme meets certain quality criteria, you can operate a three-month waiting period before the auto-enrolment requirements are effectively triggered. This might save money and administrative costs if employees are only with you for a short time.

TRANSITIONAL ARRANGEMENTS

In order to avoid giving your cash flow a shock by requiring you to pay the full contributions at once, if you wish you can phase them in over several years.

DC schemes: minimum contributions to be phased in over five years

If you have a DC scheme, you can phase the contributions in over five years as shown in the table below.

Year	Employer contribution	Employee contribution including tax relief
1–4 (first transitional period)	1%	1%
5 (second transitional period)	2%	3%
6 onwards	3%	5%

DB schemes: four-year period of grace

If you have a defined benefit scheme (or a hybrid) you could enjoy a four-year transitional period; this corresponds to the staging period during which you can delay the auto-enrolment requirements as a whole. Even so, an employee is able to opt into your employer's qualifying DB scheme during this period if they want to do that. If you close your DB scheme, you must provide an alternative qualifying scheme.

EMPLOYEE PROTECTION

There are rules to stop you encouraging employees not to join. The general principle is that you cannot contract out of, limit or exclude any of the new duties imposed on you, except under a compromise in relation to proceedings in an employment tribunal (PA 2008 s58).

Prohibited recruitment conduct

In particular, you are not allowed to ask job applicants at interview whether they plan to opt out of auto-enrolment. The Pensions Regulator could issue a compliance notice on you if you do so and a penalty notice if you ignore the compliance notice. No one seems to know whether job applicants could seek compensation or other redress at an employment tribunal, although it seems unlikely.

Inducements

You must not offer a financial inducement to your staff for opting out of membership. The Regulator will get annoyed if you do this and issue a compliance notice if you offer money for the 'sole or main purpose' of inducing your employees to opt out of NEST or your own scheme (PA 2008 s54). You should be particularly careful not to offer a higher salary or one-off bonus in exchange for opting out of scheme membership. However:

- providing factual information about the implications of membership for those who claimed enhanced protection (a tax arrangement) does not count as an inducement
- providing factual information about the implications of the restriction of tax relief for high-earners does not count as an inducement.

You might find yourself offering a flexible benefits package where an employee can select benefits from a range of options that have equivalent value and decide that he or she prefers something else to a pension. This is a rather grey area, but if the pension fund membership is a core benefit, clearly there will be no breach.

Right not to suffer detriment

You are also going to have to face the fact that, despite the government's intentions to contain employee rights generally, employees have rights under the Pensions Act 2008 not to suffer any detriment in their employment because of your breach. This protection does not cover detriment arising from an unfair dismissal. However, any dismissal arising from your breach of the auto-enrolment requirements or the prohibited recruitment conduct is automatically unfair (Employment Rights Act 1996).

THE PENSION POLICE

The Pensions Regulator has the job of ensuring that you comply with your duties and is also responsible for providing you with information about your staging date and auto-enrolment responsibilities. Once the system is up and running, the Regulator is responsible for policing compliance with your new duties. The Regulator has been given another 300 staff to ensure compliance, which sounds like a lot ... but not to cover 25,000,000 people.

THE UNKNOWNS (AT THE TIME OF WRITING)

For a simple pension scheme, there are still many unknowns.

- **Salary sacrifice** means taking a reduced salary (which is taxed) to enjoy instead additional pension contributions from the employer (which are not taxed). It looks as though salary sacrifice is not necessarily incompatible with auto-enrolment, although this might be the case where an employee has to consent to salary sacrifice, and those employees who do not want to use salary sacrifice must be offered alternative arrangements.
- **Flexible benefits** means having an option to enjoy benefits over and above salary, so you might choose to have a car instead of a pension, for example. The rules seem to suggest that you cannot offer a flexible benefits package that helps to induce people not to take a qualifying pension (but no one is quite sure).
- Employees who have '**enhanced protection**' (a special form of tax protection for pension rights of higher paid people) could lose it if they automatically join a new pension scheme; accidentally losing many tens of thousands pounds of tax relief will irritate highly-paid people so there needs to be a system to stop that happening.
- **Agency workers** have to be put into a qualifying scheme, and it is not certain whether it is the agency or the employer that has the duty to organise this (at the moment the legislation applying to such workers is not in force).
- **Overseas workers** are subject to the regulatory requirements of their home country (if they are in the EEA), which may be hard, if not impossible, for UK schemes to manage to do; this could be a bit of a problem for Republic of Ireland workers who work in a factory in Northern Ireland, for example.
- Schemes which are established as **group personal pensions** (ie a collection of personal pensions rather than a company pension scheme) require (if there is a shortfall in contributions) your employee to pay, and your employee has to sign up to that.

WHAT TO DO IN PRACTICE

In theory, you do not have to do anything about auto-enrolment until 1 October 2012 at the earliest (and probably in most cases for a few years after that). On the other hand, you might prepare for the changes sometime in advance (perhaps 18 months); items for the board agenda could include the following.

- How will you meet your basic auto-enrolment duty? If you operate an existing scheme, can (or should) this scheme be used for auto-enrolment?
- If your existing scheme (or one of them) is to be used (whether occupational or personal), is it good enough? If you have a DB scheme you need to get a certificate from your scheme actuary. If you have a DC scheme you need to ensure it meets the minimum contribution requirements.
- If you use an existing scheme, does it meet the provisions enabling employers with high-quality schemes to postpone auto-enrolment for three months?
- If you use your existing scheme, are any rule changes required (for example, relating to eligibility or waiting periods)?
- If you sponsor an occupational scheme with a waiting period, should it consider using two separate schemes in future (for example, NEST could be used as a 'nursery' scheme for new joiners)?
- If you use an existing DC scheme or group personal scheme, will it take advantage of the advance self-certification regime (assuming this is implemented)? If so, how will this be done? If sampling is to be used, procedures will need to be set up.
- If you use a DC or group personal pension arrangement, employees need to be enrolled in a default fund, as they must not be required to make any investment choices.
- What is the opting-out process for existing employees and new joiners?
- How will employees be informed of any changes? Is there a communications strategy?
- How will decisions by employees who are not automatic joiners or those who have opted out be processed? And how will they be advised?
- How will re-enrolment processes and communications be dealt with by HR systems?
- How will high earners who may be caught by tax limits be dealt with?
- How will low earners who may find that membership is inappropriate be dealt with?

Remember the limits

Starting from 2012, your staff will have the right to be enrolled into your pension scheme if they are:

- aged at least 16 but not yet 22 and have earnings of more than £5,564 a year. If these individuals ask to be enrolled you will have to make a minimum contribution
- aged at least state pension age but under 75 and have earnings of more than £5,564 a year. If these individuals ask to be enrolled you will have to make a minimum contribution
- aged at least 22 but not yet state pension age and have earnings between £5,564 and £8,105. If these individuals ask to be enrolled you will have to make a minimum contribution
- aged at least 16 but under 75 and have earnings that are less than £5,564. If these individuals ask to be enrolled you **will not** have to make a minimum contribution but can choose to do so if you wish
- in the NEST scheme and paying less than £4,400 pa (2012/13).

Make sure that you also bear in mind these two definitions.

1. **Qualifying earnings** are more than £5,564 but not more than £42,475 a year; these figures are being continually revised.
2. **Total earnings** include an individual's salary, wages, overtime, bonuses and commission, as well as statutory sick pay and statutory pay received during maternity, paternity or adoption leave.

HOW MUCH WILL ALL THIS COST?

Set-up costs depend on the complexity of your scheme (the NEST set-up costs are around £600 million, recovered through charges on the contributions).

The other costs are, of course, contributions to the scheme. If you are working on tight margins, the costs could come as quite a shock, amounting to around 3% of payroll plus administration charges.

You can always pay more (if you wish) than the minimum into a scheme for your staff.

In most cases, amongst low-to-moderate earners there is room within NEST's £4,400 annual contribution limit for employers and/or members to contribute more than the legal minimum contribution. Here some examples.

■ An 8% contribution on qualifying earnings for an employee with average earnings of around £25,000 a year is around £1,500 pa.
■ Within the contribution cap, there is flexibility around how contributions are structured. For example, you could make contributions on an employee's total earnings instead of their earnings above £5,564.
■ An 8% contribution on a wider band of earnings for someone earning £25,000 is around £2,000. This gives room for additional contributions by both you and the member of up to around £1,600.

SHOULD I USE NEST INSTEAD?

You do not, if you do not want to, have to set up a pension scheme of your own – you can use the one set up by the government for just this purpose: NEST. The latter looks on the outside just like any company pension scheme, with trustees and rules, and is registered with HMRC.

If you use NEST you have to make sure that it receives the minimum contributions (giving you a total of 8%):

■ employer contribution of 3%
■ member contribution of 4%
■ tax relief of 1%.

These are phased in over five years and only on qualifying earnings (between £5,564 and £42,475) as follows:

■ October 2012 to September 2016: total minimum of 2% of qualifying earnings, with at least 1% from the employer
■ October 2016 to September 2017: total minimum of 5% of qualifying earnings, with at least 2% from the employer
■ From October 2017, total minimum of 8% of qualifying earnings, with at least 3% from the employer.

NEST is seen as a threat to privately organised company pension plans, so it has had limits imposed on it.

■ It cannot accept contributions from any one member of more than £4,400 a year, which means that it may not be appropriate for salaries over £45,000 if the minimum is put in.
■ No transfers can be made into or out of NEST.

These limits may in future be removed.

NEST charges your staff:

■ an annual management charge of 0.3% of a member's fund value
■ an initial charge of 2% (currently cut to 1.8%, after some criticism) of the value of new contributions.

This doesn't sound a lot, but it may actually be more expensive than a private scheme.

NEST managers have set out how they hope NEST will operate:

■ simple and easy to administer, with straightforward and convenient online services and tools
■ flexibility over contribution levels and the way these are calculated
■ portable – your employees' membership of NEST can travel with them throughout their working life. There will be no continuing administration for employers when a NEST member leaves your company. For new joiners who are already members of NEST, all contributions made on their behalf can be added to their existing retirement savings pot. More than one employer can contribute to a member's NEST retirement savings pot at the same time
■ NEST Corporation is legally bound to run NEST in the interests of scheme beneficiaries (although in practice they will have to have conform to government objectives)
■ NEST Corporation has a public service obligation to run NEST so it's open to any employer that wants to use it to meet the new duties. This means that employers of all sizes and sectors can use NEST
■ NEST Corporation will set an investment approach for NEST that's specifically designed for the needs of low-to-moderate earners
■ up to £4,400 per year can be paid into each member's retirement savings pot
■ NEST Corporation is not allowed to accept transfers in or pay transfers out, except in very limited circumstances.

Uses for NEST

You can use NEST in a variety of ways. It could be the only scheme you offer your workers or sit alongside another scheme you already have. For example, you could use NEST as a foundation scheme on top of which you offer other schemes.

Alternatively, you could use NEST for a certain category, grade or group of workers. This might be seasonal workers, new joiners or staff who take career breaks.

Myths about NEST

NEST has issued a number of statements on what they see as myths about the service. Some of these are listed below.

Myth. All workers will be automatically enrolled into NEST.

Reality. Under the Pensions Act 2008, employers will be required to enrol automatically all eligible jobholders – and, when asked by them, any jobholder – into any workplace pension scheme that meets or exceeds certain legal standards and make a minimum contribution to that scheme. Other workers are also eligible to be enrolled into a workplace pension scheme but they must ask their employer to enrol them. These other workers are not entitled to have their employers make minimum contributions on their behalf, as they don't have qualifying earnings. However, an employer may make contributions if they choose to do so. It will be up to employers to choose a suitable pension scheme, which may mean using existing schemes, setting up a new one, using NEST or choosing a combination of options.

Myth. Automatic enrolment means that employers no longer have the freedom to choose the best pension scheme for their workers.

Reality. Employers can choose the pension scheme they believe is most appropriate. However, the new laws include certain legal standards that schemes must meet in order to comply with the legislation. NEST will be one of the schemes that meet these standards.

Myth. NEST is a pension scheme that's run by the government.

Reality. NEST Corporation is the trustee body that has overall responsibility for running NEST. It is a non-departmental public body that operates at arm's length from the government and is accountable to Parliament through the Department for Work and Pensions (DWP). NEST Corporation has a Chair and up to 14 Trustee Members. Together they form the scheme's Board of Trustees. As a trustee, they have an overriding legal duty to act in the best interests of scheme beneficiaries. NEST and NEST Corporation will be regulated by the Pensions Regulator.

Myth. NEST is only suitable for small companies.

Reality. NEST Corporation has a public service obligation to run NEST so that it's open to any employer who wants to use it to meet the new duties. This means that employers of all sizes and sectors can use it. NEST could be the only scheme an employer offers their workers or sit alongside an already existing scheme. Employers could use NEST as a foundation scheme on top of which they offer other schemes or, alternatively, they could use it for a certain category, grade or group of workers. This might be seasonal workers, new joiners or staff who take career breaks.

Myth. NEST will be a poor relation to other workplace pension schemes.

Reality. NEST will be high quality, low charge, easy to access and simple to use for both members and employers. It will also have high standards of governance and an investment approach specifically designed for its members.

Myth. NEST will compete with existing pension schemes.

Reality. NEST is being designed to complement existing workplace pension provision. It is being specifically conceived to meet the needs of low-to-moderate earners who are not currently served by existing pension providers. Currently, 750,000 employers in the private sector offer no workplace pension. NEST, together with the reform programme, will increase access to workplace pensions for millions of people.

Myth. The annual contribution limit of £4,400 for NEST will deter potential members.

Reality. In most cases, amongst low-to-moderate earners there will be headroom under the limit for employers and/or members to pay more than the legal minimum.

Myth. NEST will be difficult to administer.

Reality. NEST is being designed so employers can provide access to a pension scheme to their workers simply and easily. The scheme will need little administration and will be set up so that employers can appoint someone else to manage their participation for them if they wish. A worker's membership of NEST is portable – it can travel with them throughout their working life. This means there will be no continuing administration for an employer when a NEST member leaves their company. For new joiners who are already members of NEST, all contributions made on their behalf can be added to their existing retirement savings pot. Also, more than one employer can contribute to a member's NEST retirement savings pot at the same time.

Myth. NEST can only be used to meet the legal minimums required.

Reality. Employers can decide to offer more than the minimum requirements if they choose NEST or any other occupational scheme. NEST allows employers the freedom to choose the level of contributions they and their employees pay, and the way these contributions are calculated. Employers who choose NEST will have the option of either using the scheme simply to meet their minimum legal duties or using a more custom-ised approach that meets their specific business needs.

CHAPTER 2
WORKING OUT WHAT
YOU WANT

In theory, a generous pension for all would be ideal; in practice, such generosity is unachievable for most of us. Over-generous pension plans are said to be one of the reasons why the pensions movement has problems at the moment and why the government is trying to cut back on pensions for its own employees. There are, therefore, two basic preliminary questions.

1. Do we want to get involved in the pensions business at all (and it looks as though with auto-enrolment we have little choice)?
2. If so, what kind of pension system or systems do we want?

Sometimes even a basic pension may not be appropriate, either for your workforce as a whole or just part of it. If your company is a start-up, for example, you almost certainly have other priorities than pensions, as survival is normally your predominant aim. If you employ mostly part-time workers, although you must not, of course, discriminate against them, you might find that your workforce does not value pensions and will be relying on their spouses for pension provision. You might have a transient workforce (perhaps in the agricultural sector or perhaps from abroad) who mostly would prefer the cash and decide to make their own pension provision – or, more likely, no pension provision at all. If you employ a very highly paid workforce they may often prefer to make their own provision.

However, most of us would prefer our employer to help us make financial provision for old age. The question you must ask youself is: what kind of pension scheme is appropriate? There are lots of different kinds, and different people will want or need different types of pension protection. When planning to introduce or change a scheme, it is probably best if you examine first the kind of workforce you have.[1]

That probably means looking at the nature of your company, at your (and its) aspirations and those of the employees, and to reflect on a series of questions.

- What kind of workforce do you have?
- What kind of pension would they like?
- Is a pension important to them?
- Why should you and the company become involved in pensions?
- Do you want to do simply the absolute minimum (and maybe just join NEST), or do you want to do a bit more – or a lot more?
- Is the plan you are looking at a sensible use of company money?
- Are you prepared to take the risks of introducing and running a pension scheme – and enjoying the advantages?
- Should you manage the pension plan or should you outsource it?
- What advice do you need? Does it involve pension advisers, lawyers, accountants, tax advisers, communications consultants, insurers, actuaries, administrators or payroll managers?
- How much should you spend (or what is the budget)?

WHAT IS THE POINT OF THE PENSION SCHEME?

A useful starting point is to draft a position paper to the board or yourself which sets out not only the pros but also the cons of establishing a pension scheme in the first place. Obviously, if you have been encouraged to set one up, the representative will have explained the pros – he may have been less forthcoming about the cons. Each company will take a different view, so the list below may not be exhaustive or conclusive; however, a typical board paper might follow the points below.

■ The board have invited me to submit a paper on whether – and, if so, what – pension scheme we should introduce.
■ This is prompted by the forthcoming requirements to auto-enrol virtually all our staff into a scheme, so in due course we shall have to make a minimum 3% contribution to virtually all pensions. This is being phased in from [January 2013] to [January 2015].
■ The issue now is whether we do the absolute minimum, review our existing pension arrangements and/or install new ones.
■ The advantages of doing the absolute minimum are savings on costs and management time.
■ The advantages of a better-than-minimum plan generally include:

  ☐ an ability to compete in the market for staff
  ☐ savings on pension costs by making collective rather than individual arrangements
  ☐ facilitating retirement for older workers, now that compulsory retirement ages are illegal
  ☐ benefitting from increased employee satisfaction and employee retention.

■ The advantages of providing a plan through the company include:

  ☐ cost savings through central administration and absence of marketing costs
  ☐ comfort that the employees are protected
  ☐ ability to employ professional advisers rather than rely on salesmen.

■ There are, of course, downsides to providing a scheme. These include:

  ☐ additional contribution and management costs
  ☐ diversion of management time and distraction of attention.

■ When deciding to explore the option of putting in a decent pension scheme, the following will need to be considered:

  ☐ compliance, accounting administrative, investment and cost risks
  ☐ benefit levels appropriate for the workforce, with perhaps different arrangements for different groups
  ☐ whether to build on top of NEST or replace it.

DO YOU REALLY NEED A SCHEME?

It is perfectly possible to run a decent company without providing a pension scheme. Many small (and large) companies do so and prosper mightily, and their employees do not think they are cheapskates or spend much of their time looking elsewhere.

However, employees are increasingly worried about their pensions. There are legal obligations (NEST) to provide some form of private pension, and happy employees sometimes give better service. Long-term employees can be a detriment to employers if they find it difficult to retire – and there is no doubt that providing a pension scheme through a company is more efficient and easier than doing it as an individual.

WHAT KIND OF WORKFORCE DO YOU HAVE?

Not all kinds of workforce are suitable to have pensions provided for them. Construction companies, for example, are notorious for employing a workforce that really doesn't want pension provision. Putting in a decent pension plan might be a waste of your resources if your workforce:

- is transient
- is very lowly paid (where a pension would simply replace state benefits)
- depends on others for pensions
- has no pensions culture and would not appreciate the benefit.

It might be useful to bear in mind that employees will not appreciate having to give up money to their pension plan, but will be thankful they did so when they retire. Younger employees do not usually realise the benefits of pensions, as they are at an age when they find it almost impossible to believe that they may live to 60 – never mind 90. The risk of living too long will not hit them for maybe half a century.

WHAT ABOUT MERGERS AND ACQUISITIONS?

The introduction of the wrong kind of pension scheme can later prove an impediment if at some future time you want to restructure or sell your company. Private equity companies, in particular, find the existence of a defined benefit scheme very off-putting because it is hard to calculate the liabilities – and the regulatory overload can be very considerable.

Therefore, you will want to take your corporate objectives into account when designing the scheme; few companies these days wish to adopt a final-salary structure unless they have to (sometimes they might be obliged to do so when taking on public sector liabilities, for example), because the impact it can have on accounting and on the balance sheet of the company can prove too expensive and volatile, even though the actual cost of such schemes can be roughly that of a defined contribution scheme.

WHAT KIND OF BENEFIT STRUCTURE DO YOU WANT?

When designing the pension scheme, you need to take your workforce into account. In some cases, with a low-paid workforce, a simple pension system may be appropriate, sitting on top of the state system. Decisions to be made in the design of a pensions system include the following.

The anticipated or targeted level of pensions

Obviously, the point of a pension scheme is to provide a pension, predominantly for you and your employees. In a defined benefit (DB) scheme, the level of benefits you want to provide affects the costs and contributions. In a defined contribution (DC) scheme, the targeted level of benefits affects the level of contributions that probably need to be made. What kind of money are you talking about? You might be thinking of your company making a contribution of anywhere between 5% and 15%, with perhaps the employee putting in something similar, thus making a total contribution rate of somewhere between 10% and 25%. If the plan puts in much less than this, it will deliver pretty poor benefits. One solution is to match an employee's contribution – perhaps pound for pound (or maybe £2 for every £1) – up to a maximum of, say, 10%.

Contribution levels

You could of course pay all the contributions yourself; many DC plans did so for many years. On the other hand, it might make employees realise just how valuable a pension is if they also made a contribution. Depending on the level of targeted benefits, contributions can be made by the employee, and some must be made by the employer.

Survivor's benefits

Not all schemes have to provide survivor's benefits (ie benefits for widows and widowers, civil partners and infant children). Providing widows' and widowers' benefits can add to the cost – and if instead you have a personal pension (rather than a company pension), you can opt to use your money in due course to provide just a (higher) pension for yourself rather than a (lower) pension for you and your partner, and your partner would not find out until it was all too late. Thrillers have been written – and sold – on the way people have had revenge on an unsuspecting partner in this way. It can sometimes come as a shock to find that a spouse has not provided for you and so, in practice, most employers make survivor's pensions compulsory. Normally, the maximum that can be provided is a pension of two-thirds of the main pension.

Life benefits

Life benefits are usually death benefits, actually; if you die before retirement age it is common to provide a benefit of up to four times your salary, usually supported by a separate contract with a life insurance company. The cost is usually not excessive, depending on the level of salary covered.

Disability benefits

The pension scheme can also be used (commonly, in association with a permanent ill-health policy provided separately) to protect members against becoming ill whilst working. These can be useful but need to be carefully worded in order to avoid extreme costs arising, especially where there is protection against stress-related diseases, for example.

Discrimination

You must not discriminate in benefit provision on the grounds of race, sex, age, disability or sexual orientation. In fact, it is possible to provide different benefits where 'objectively justified', especially in relation to older people (the point of a pension is to discriminate on the grounds of age).

RETENTION AND RECRUITMENT

As well as the paternalistic objective of pension provision, one of the original reasons for the establishment of pension schemes in the last century was to respond to the shortage of labour at the time. Offering a decent pension was one way of attracting staff – and another objective of retaining staff was to make the pension forfeit (or at least much reduced) if they left the company's employment.

Today, it is a little harder to cancel the pension rights if an employee leaves, because of the law – 'preservation' (vesting) and transfer laws allow individuals to preserve most of their pension rights – but the provision of pension rights can still prove attractive if the benefits are properly communicated. As pension issues become ever more important for the workforce, since both the state and other private pensions are diminishing in real terms, pension provision becomes increasingly attractive.

COLLECTIVE OR PERSONAL PROVISION

In theory, there is nothing to prevent any of us from providing for our own old age individually. In former times, that is what most of us had to do – or work until we dropped. Today the self-employed still have no choice; they can save through personal pensions or through other savings vehicles, or in bank accounts or in other media, such as property or shares. However, providing for old age individually is very inefficient.

1. Distribution costs make individual arrangements **disproportionately expensive**; insurance companies and other costs are high when selling a pension to one human being, especially following the new regulations imposed by the Financial Services Authority.
2. An individual does not **know when they are going to die**. Pensions are a risk-management system for living too long (rather like life insurance is a risk-management system for not living long enough). A pension is a system that allows a person's mortality risk (ie the risk of not knowing when we are going to die) to be passed elsewhere at a reasonable cost. Otherwise, we would all individually need to save in case we lived to 120 years old; since on average we will all die at around 85, we can avoid the need to save extra money for a further 35 years, just in case. Pensions are for middle earners, as richer people can afford to live in retirement for a long time.
3. Due to regulations, **technicalities** of pension provision are now very complicated. Few of us will ever develop the skills needed to understand how pensions operate or be able to afford to retain experts to help us (charging around £150 per hour); therefore, using a company to spread the cost (ie amortise the cost amongst several people), find experts and organise the pensions through the payroll is very efficient and sensible.

CORPORATE OR PERSONAL PROVISION

For similar reasons, provision through an employer is sensible and efficient. As an employer, you can afford to investigate and manage pension schemes better than an individual can; you can hire actuaries, investment consultants and advisers, and lawyers and scheme designers – and give them proper instructions. They can arrange to share risks between all of us more than we can do individually, and in some cases they can carry risks that we cannot, such as investment risks or mortality risks. Sometimes they fail but, even when that happens, they will have done better than we could ever have done individually.

CONTRACTING IN OR OUT?

At one time, it was a matter of great concern whether a scheme should be contracted in or out. The term refers to the provision of the state second pension either through the company pension system (when it was contracted out) or through the government through the payment of a higher National Insurance contribution (when it was said to be contracted in). Nowadays, new schemes which are contracted out are hardly ever established, because the reduction in National Insurance contributions is so slight that it is not worth doing, and the administration costs and complications are high. Those schemes which are already contracted out wish daily that they weren't.

SCHEME DESIGN

You have the final say in choosing the kind of scheme that is offered to members; apart from auto-enrolment or NEST, you are not obliged to offer any kind of scheme at all. In practice, few employers nowadays offer the full-blown defined benefit scheme that everyone wants (and needs), and which the civil service for the moment enjoys. These decent schemes normally offer a percentage of salary, in real money, from retirement until death and are guaranteed by the company. This is the kind of scheme which the original state pensions offered, and which began to be developed in the middle of the 20th century for industries to protect members against some (though not all) of the issues of inflation. You almost certainly cannot afford it unless you are Google or own an oil well – not so much because of the cost, but due to the regulation.

DC OR DB?

In practice, mostly because of over-regulation, all companies today now offer some form of 'defined contribution scheme', ie a scheme which:

- sets out who pays what contributions
- leaves it to fate as to what level of pension that will in fact buy when retirement actually takes place.

There has been great pressure on the government to allow a kind of half DB/half DC, known as a hybrid scheme, which would enable the employer and employee to share risks rather than placing them all on one or the other. The government itself is introducing a different kind of hybrid scheme for its own workforce, known as a 'career average salary scheme', which is just like a DB scheme but uses a different definition of salary on which to base the benefits. This definition takes the salary for each year, revalues it to take account of inflation and then averages it. This means that it includes both low salaries, when the employee was starting out, and the later higher salaries as the member rises through the hierarchy. It is cheaper to provide for employers – and gives slower benefits than final salary schemes – but it is usually better appreciated than a pure defined contribution scheme.

At first some observers suggested that such schemes were simpler to operate than DB (ie final salary or salary-related schemes) but DC schemes, while limiting the financial risk for the employer, impose financial and retirement risks for the employee – and intangible risks for the employer as well, since if employees find it difficult to retire, manpower planning for the company can be made more difficult, especially once formal retirement ages are made unlawful.

Whatever scheme you introduce, the current trend is to try to build in as few options as possible to avoid the member having to agonise about decisions. Ideally such schemes simply require:

- a member's signature
- permission for them to change, for example, investment choices or retirement dates as they thinks fit
- the ability to do all this online.

Modern pension systems are remarkably efficient at this, but the legislation means that a member can be faced nonetheless with a battery of decisions phrased in impenetrable language, which are driven by compliance requirements.

However, there are some basic decisions to be made in designing a scheme – whether DB or DC – which will be examined now.

Contributions
How much should you and the employees put into the scheme?

■ On the one hand, you need to preserve the firm's resources and make as little a contribution as possible.
■ On the other hand, putting in a nominal amount is pointless and expensive if the only result is added administration and negligible retirement income.

As ever, the solution normally emerges as something in the middle. Not having a scheme sits at one extreme. At the other end, we find the option of putting in what is probably needed to provide a retirement income of around 60% of final salary – namely, around 30% of income. This percentage was the rule of thumb that was estimated to be needed to provide that kind of benefit in DB schemes. There is a very crude pension pot calculator on the web at www.thisismoney.co.uk/pension-pot-calculator, but this is really designed for personal pensions, and it does not factor in inflation, expenses, breaks in employment and other factors. Nor does it strip out pensions from all the other benefits that a good workplace pension scheme should cater for.

In addition to pensions, the benefits package might include:

■ permanent ill-health protection (either through the pension fund or separately)
■ a death-in-service benefit
■ (perhaps) some early retirement protection as part of a pre-planned redundancy system.

In practice, there are a variety of contribution options; some schemes might match £1 for £1 up to, say, £10 (at the higher end). Others might suggest £2 for every £1 of the employee contribution up to a maximum of 10% of salary. Anything much less than that is probably not worth bothering with, except as a signal of intent. Others suggest up to a maximum of, say, £500 a month (matching again).

Whatever the deal, it needs to be agreed at the outset that the pension is intended to be for the long term, although not guaranteed. You will not want to guarantee the payments indefinitely if times turn rough, although changing the deal if it is incorporated in the contract of employment may be a challenge.

Contributions in defined benefit schemes are usually on a different basis; you have to put in whatever the actuary certifies but may be given time to pay.

Investments
In DB schemes, investments are chosen by the trustees after discussion with the employer. The trustees need to keep a balance between choosing high performing assets (perhaps with higher risk) and less volatile investments. The former could keep the contributions from the employer down but may result in volatile valuations, which have to be reflected in the company balance sheet. On the other hand, the latter normally result in lower returns and higher employer contributions.

In DC schemes, the risks are different and there are several of them, as shown below.

- The amount put in might not be enough to provide a decent income on retirement.
- The investments might not perform.
- The investments could fall in value just at the time they need to be cashed in to buy an annuity.
- The tax rates could change.
- The annuity rates might change at retirement.

All these risks are borne by the employee – not by you as the employer. However, your employees will feel the need to keep on working if they cannot afford to retire and will also think that (unless it is clearly explained to them) the scheme was rather pointless – and will say so to other employees.

Defaults

Since employers are better equipped – and employees are poorly equipped – to manage their own pension arrangements, it is common for most plans to have 'default options', ie the investments will automatically be invested in a certain way unless the individual directs otherwise.

- The good news is that individuals do not have to think about it.
- The bad news is that the defaults are not always suitable for each individual and are based on common truths (eg that as individuals reach closer to retirement, they should have their assets moved more into bonds), which may actually not be as accurate as everyone thinks.

There are two main defaults.

1. An individual should be a member of the scheme unless he formally elects not to be; that is the NEST strategy.
2. An individual should have an investment strategy that is automatically set out, unless he formally elects to change it.

Default membership

One of the choices that employers face when designing schemes is whether to make membership of the scheme automatic (ie everyone is a member, unless they categorically ask to be removed) or whether employees have to make a positive decision to join.

Default membership normally results in around a 70%–90% take-up rate; it is easier to administer and ensures that employees have pension protection in due course. In con-trast, positive membership results in much lower rates of joining – and usually lower costs for employers. The NEST arrangement introduced by the government from October 2012 is a default scheme – everyone must join it (or an equivalent or superior scheme) and it has been made very hard not to join. Employers are not allowed to make forms available to individuals who feel that such a scheme is not for them (it is a criminal offence to offer such a form); the latter must find a copy themselves, probably on the web, and they are also not given any advice about how not to join. It is all rather unpleasant, but private pension schemes can indeed make opting out rather easier and simpler if they wish.

SMALLER COMPANIES

There is no doubt that smaller companies have always thought twice before installing a pension plan. They may not have the financial or administrative resources to pay into it or to manage it, and the trouble that regulators can make for them is well known. Smaller companies are frequently targeted by regulators who criticise them without taking into account the much smaller resources available, and without giving credit for the fact that it is better to have a Ford scheme that works than a Rolls-Royce scheme that no one can manage to afford. The figures reflect that reality: fewer small companies have pension arrangements.

Few smaller companies in particular can afford to run a defined benefit system. Accordingly, most of these schemes are group personal pension schemes, stakeholder or trust-based defined contribution schemes.[2] In such schemes the participation rate is around 60% of employees (with stakeholder only around 38%). The reasons why staff do not join are mostly cost (84%), a preference to spend (72%) and disillusionment with pensions (69%). Firms that do not provide pensions explain that the cost is too great (96%), economic conditions in their sector make it difficult (82%) and there is insufficient competitive pressure (53%).

Few firms target their pension costs but provide, on average, combined contributions of between 7.6% and 9.3% of earnings. This compares with average combined contributions into DB schemes of around 24% of earnings. These numbers show that DC schemes are in the end going to disappoint many members, unless the rates start to climb, because the benefits that will emerge will rarely provide the financial independence that so many seek.

In relation to NEST, the survey suggests that around a third of your employees will opt not to join (probably more if they are lower paid).

CONCLUSIONS
The design of pension plans in current conditions is probably easier than it has been for some time. You will normally want to provide something better than NEST default rates; it has to be simple to administer, provide something that will be a useful benefit and easy for employees to understand. The position of the higher paid is rather more complicated and is explored in more depth in Chapter 5.

CHAPTER 3
SOME TECHIE POINTS

Pensions have become notorious for their complexity but, in essence, they are pretty simple: we save now to spend later. It's rather like savings – except that we can only spend our pensions savings so that the money will last us to the end of our days.

This simplicity has been somewhat lost in the last few years. We now have:

- very complicated tax rules
- very complicated trust law rules
- unbelievably complicated regulation and compliance.

All this is despite several attempts at cutting the nearly 50,000 pages of rules, regulations, guidance notes and legal judgments.[1] The chart below demonstrates the growth in regulation since modern-style pension systems were introduced by the Finance Act 1921.

In many instances, the fact that something is complicated should not, of course, put us off. We manage to drive cars that few of us can fix; we watch televisions that some of us struggle to switch on; and computers always break down – but we use them all the time.

In practice, most of the day-to-day complexity of modern life is hidden from the user and, in some ways, the management of pensions is rather the same. It is important that you do not become embroiled in the complexities; you should use advisers and technicians to manage the technicalities of preservation, equal treatment, contracting out, solvency, reporting and many other matters. Even with cars, though, whilst we may not be able to fix the fuel injector, we are supposed to know the Highway Code. Pensions are the same: there are some things that you really need to know.

This chapter does not attempt to provide a guide to the technical intricacies of pensions, but it tries to explain why things are so unnecessarily complicated and where the

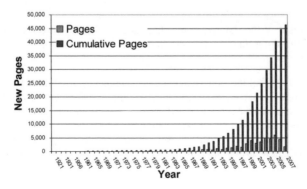

Graph 4: Pensions-related text: 1921–2005.
Source: Perspective.

complexities may be heading. It does not cover the detailed requirements; those will be dealt with by advisers – the actuaries, lawyers, technical consultants and others – who ensure there is proper management of the pensions system. But there are areas in which it might be helpful to have a general understanding. The next sections look at four separate issues:

1. tax
2. law
3. regulation
4. pension scheme governance.

TAX

Sensible tax treatment is an essential element of pension provision. In countries where there are significant rates of tax, pensions provision is not possible (or at least sensible) without proper tax treatment.

The main objective (as explained by the World Bank, the OECD and the EU) is that pension arrangements should not be subject to double taxation. In most countries there is an Exempt, Exempt, Taxed (EET) tax system.

■ The contributions (whether by employer or employee) are tax exempt.
■ The income on the savings backing the pension promise are tax exempt.
■ The benefits are taxable.

This is known as a 'fiscally neutral' pension tax system. It is the system nominally adopted in the UK, but it is not perfectly applied. For example, pension schemes pay corporation tax on the dividends they receive from their investments in shares; they also pay stamp duty on any property they purchase for their portfolios, and they pay VAT on the fees they pay. Nonetheless, by and large the pension system in this country was, until recently, broadly fiscally neutral. Today, the position is rather blurred.

■ You only get tax relief on contributions into the scheme under a certain limit.
■ The amount you can build up in the scheme is limited.
■ Any benefits taken in excess of a limit are taxed twice – sometimes with a penalty.

These limits, mostly pretty recent, are hard to manage in practice – and the tax rules keep changing as well. For you, without a long-term stable fiscal regime, long-term planning (which is what pension planning involves) is difficult. Long term arrangements are hard to achieve in many spheres, and few things stay the same for long; you only have to look at the changes in mobile phones in the last 10 years to realise that. Nonetheless, even if technology changes, the principles of taxation for old age provision really do not need to.

It was only in 1921 that the Finance Act allowed companies to set aside funds to protect members' pension expectations in case they become insolvent. Before that time, HMRC argued that there would be loss to the Treasury – despite the fact that the Treasury and other civil servants had pension arrangements which were identical but did not need funds to be set aside, since they were guaranteed by the government. The 1921 changes, which have lasted until this day, were simply made to allow parity for the private sector.

The current tax system has been significantly amended a number of times, since 1921, but it is only in the last few years that the EET system has been challenged. The present system allows pre-funded pension provision only within limits. The argument is that this protects the interests of the lower paid (otherwise the higher paid would get higher tax relief) and this is not fair. Pensions alone seem to have been singled out for this treatment; oddly, we do not argue that companies should not get tax relief on salaries paid over a certain limit.

The limits are arbitrary and sound quite generous. We get tax relief on annual contributions to a pension scheme, provided they do not exceed either our income or a maximum of £50,000 if more in any one year, and in our lifetime, we cannot have more than around £1.5m worth of private pension rights (say a pension of around £70,000 pa). Actually, we can have more than that; we just pay an excessive tax charge if we exceed that amount, which no longer makes it worthwhile.

These limits are imposed by a notoriously complex set of HMRC rules and regulations. The tax legislation was radically revised in 2006 (under the Finance Act 2004) to try to get rid of 1,300 pages of tax rules and around 13 different tax systems applying to pensions. We now have about three different systems and about 4,400 pages of tax rules. (Most other countries manage with roughly a page or two of tax rules.)

So far as your company is concerned, all you need to know is the following.

- You get tax relief on contributions to a pension scheme provided that the scheme is registered with HMRC. The scheme will be registrable if it meets the terms of registration and other conditions, and provides a limited list of benefits.
- Your scheme members are not taxed on company contributions to the scheme if the scheme is registered.

Finally, 'scheme administrators' (probably you) have reporting duties to HMRC and must inform it if you have made mistakes on investments or paid too much in benefits. Those mistakes can involve very high tax penalties (probably illegal, but who has the heart to challenge HMRC) so it is important to get the administration right.

However, there is no reason at this stage to have a deep understanding of HMRC rules in order to introduce a pension scheme (unless your staff are highly paid).

LAW
For many years there was very little law applying to pension funds; now there is an avalanche of it. Tax has already been mentioned, but there are also laws:

- dealing with equal treatment
- involving the protection of members who leave the scheme
- arranging for the interface with social security pensions
- applying employment law as it affects pensions
- trying to ensure that there are adequate funds in the scheme
- appointing regulators to apply governance
- ensuring there are proper dispute resolution procedures
- appointing member-nominated trustees where the scheme is a trust one.

Most company schemes were (and remain) established under trust, although a few were contractual, and while until recently there was a move towards having a contractual scheme (ie simply a deal with an insurance company), that trend seems to be reversing to having trustees to look after the interests of members, because not everyone trusts insurance companies or investment managers.

Contractual scheme

You could choose to have a contractual scheme, which involves signing a contract with a pension 'provider' (invariably an insurance company). The contract provides that you will pay money, and the insurer will receive it and look after it. It never includes a promise as to the amount of the pension, but it suggests how much that pension might be if the payments continued. There is always a risk that the investments will not perform well, the stock market will fall as retirement approaches or interest rates (and hence annuity rates) will fall.

The risk, of course, is usually that of the member and scheme expenses are hard if not impossible to manage, so that it is difficult to see if they are good value for money.

Trust-based schemes

From the 1960s onwards, most pension schemes were trust-based: a trust was established, money paid into it and a group of trustees appointed to look after the pot.

Even though there are more defined contribution than defined benefit schemes, this is still the preferred route today. Although in theory a contract is simpler – a provider manages everything, there are no trust laws and rules to follow, and no regulatory compliance to deal with – in fact contract-based schemes have emerged as much less flexible, more expensive and more difficult to change (and change is a recurring theme of pensions provision). Trusts, of course, need trustees, and trust law to the uninitiated looks formidable. The rules seem uncertain, trustees seem exposed to personal liability, and there seems to be more paperwork. However, trust law has developed as a user-friendly – and, until recent years, very cost-effective – and sensible way to run things.

Trust-based schemes are governed by the general principles of trust law – designed around 500 years ago to protect the interests of widows and orphans – and by more recent Pensions Acts, which set down some ways in which trustees have to behave in relation to pension schemes. As far as you are concerned, there is no need to be an expert, but it might be helpful to note the following.

■ There have to be member-nominated trustees on the trustee board (which can be a big advantage in communications).
■ There are certain limits on the kinds of investments which can be made.

Controlling personal liability

If you are prepared to be a trustee (and you should), the one point you need to consider is how to control your own personal liability. The good news about being a trustee is that you are looking after other people's money and helping them to enjoy a more satisfactory retirement (David Cameron might say that is part of his Big Society). On the other hand, a trustee could be sued by aggrieved members if things go wrong, so it is important to make sure that you are protected against personal liability. You do not want to lose your house because you are prepared to be a good citizen.

In practice, you do not need to know too much about trust law – apart from the fact that it exists – since you will be guided by your lawyers and other advisers, but the management of personal liability is important and you have to limit your liability.

■ Make sure the trust documents exempt you from liability. There is no rule against such a provision, and indeed few sensible trustees would take on the role, especially if they are unpaid, without it. The protection cannot protect you from liability for criminal acts (eg stealing the pension fund money) or from certain rules in Acts of Parliament (eg failure to take investment advice), but other than that, such a rule is very effective to protect you.

■ Make sure the documents provide for an indemnity from the pension fund and (if the company is still solvent) from the company as well. This gives protection against certain fines that the Pensions Regulator may at some time impose (although such fines have not been imposed in the decade since the Regulator was established).

■ Make sure you have proper insurance in place. Certain director's and officer's insurance policies also include pension trusteeship as part of the cover – but it may not be appropriate. The difference for pension funds is that any litigation may not emerge until several years after the alleged breach of trust or other complaint – by which time you may have already left. You need a specialist policy that covers you not only when you are a trustee but also after you have retired as trustee.

■ Make sure that you operate through a company rather than as an individual. If you are a director of a trustee company, even a purpose-built one, there is no absolute guarantee against a complaint being able to pierce the corporate veil – but it works in most cases.

Using these techniques, you can feel pretty safe. The courts (though not the Pensions Ombudsman or the Pensions Regulator) have repeatedly stated they appreciate the fact that if they make it hard for you to be a trustee then there will be a shortage of pension fund trustees. Contrary to popular belief, judges are not out to get trustees; in fact, it is absolutely the opposite.

REGULATION

At one time, largely before the Maxwell scandal in 1991, there was relatively little regulation of pension schemes, other than that imposed by the tax authorities, which was (in modern terms) relatively straightforward.

Today, there is a substantial regulatory and compliance requirement for company pension plans; some of which has resulted as a consequence of the Maxwell episode, but much of it is due to political initiatives in the belief that regulation would compel employers to improve their pension schemes – although there has never been a requirement that employers should have a scheme in the first place.

Regulations cover an immense range of activity. In practice, most employers delegate compliance to their advisers – the insurer, the investment consultant, the actuary or the lawyer – but it is handy to have a brief understanding of when regulation intervenes.

For DB schemes (and these include many schemes which are regarded by the sponsor as defined contribution) regulations can cover:

■ the right of individuals to move their pension rights elsewhere (transfer rights)
■ the right of members to have their benefits (in DB schemes) protected against inflation
■ the right of spouses and civil partners to take a share of their partner's pension rights on divorce
■ the outlawing of investing in the sponsor's own shares
■ what happens when the plan sponsor restructures the company, or buys or sells part of the company. The reason for this is because such transactions might affect the

ability of the employer to pay contributions (or make up any deficit) to the pension fund (and if it goes bust fall into the Pension Protection Fund, with the costs bearing on remaining pension funds)

■ the preparation of schedules of payments over the next year and the following three years so that the fund has enough to pay the benefits – and a schedule of how any deficit is to be dealt with

■ annual and triennial actuarial reports of the assets and liabilities under the scheme

■ annual calculations to determine the deficit and surplus of the pension fund for application to the company accounts

■ reporting, sometimes annually, to the Pensions Regulator and HMRC of certain aspects of the fund, sometimes at some length and sometimes including information as to the investments of the fund

■ responding to any complaints made by the members and any inquiries from the Pensions Ombudsman, the Pensions Regulator and the Pension Protection Fund

■ complying with the preservation, transfer and revaluation requirements imposed on pension schemes – and the equal treatment obligations in relation to disability, sex, age, race and sexual orientation.

In relation to DC schemes, while the compliance obligations are rather less, you are still required to make sure that:

■ there is proper governance of the pension scheme
■ contributions are paid on time and at the right amount
■ the administration is in good shape
■ the investments are properly managed.

There is also a small army of regulators to make sure that you behave yourself; they include:

■ the Pension Protection Fund (PPF)
■ the Pensions Regulator
■ HMRC
■ the Treasury
■ the Pensions Ombudsman
■ Financial Services Authority and its successors
■ the Pensions Register.

Levies have to be paid to the Pensions Regulator (and the PPF in relation to defined benefit schemes) for their services.

A levy for the Pension Protection Fund (PPF)

Payments to the PPF can be a significant amount if your company has a DB scheme; the amounts vary according to the size of the liabilities of the scheme and the strength of your company. The way this is measured is idiosyncratic, depending on a rating score from a company called Dun & Bradstreet. The risk profile of your company can, in practice, be quite easily manipulated (and the level of the levy payable reduced), sometimes quite simply, by clearing county court judgments.

Some of the rules apply to you, and some to trustees, but in the end the cost of responding to them falls on you. There is no doubt that the extent of the regulation has become excessive and is a deterrent to the introduction of schemes. Even contract-based schemes have a heavy cost of regulation; this is rather different, usually hidden, and includes obligations to meet requirements of the Financial Services Authority and its successors in terms of the provision of information to members, know-your-client letters and other documents which are often prepared by the pensions provider and advisers, and which are usually incomprehensible for most of us and rarely actually read by plan members.

OTHER TECHNICAL ISSUES
In addition to the tax, trust and compliance requirements, there are other general requirements which include the following.

- Pension arrangements must be set out in the contract of employment.
- Where there are unfair and other kinds of dismissal claims, the pension may need to be taken into account – and added to the pay-out costs where an award is made.

Contracting out
Contracting out – ie the provision of state benefits provided by the additional state second pension – was never a very attractive proposition for smaller schemes and companies. The reduction in National Insurance contributions does not reflect the cost to the company, the administration is hideously complicated and members never understood how it worked. However, for reasons now lost to sight, many companies did in fact arrange to contract out. In any event, contracting out is dying.

- Defined benefit arrangements contracting out is dying, as defined benefit schemes die.
- Defined contribution contracting out has been abolished (since 6 April 2012). Defined contribution contracting out certificates are being cancelled automatically, and there is no requirement to treat money purchase protected rights differently from other funds in the scheme, because the protected rights provisions (ie rules that prescribe that the private benefits under the scheme must reflect the state benefits) will have ceased to exist.

For your existing schemes the abolition of contracting out should come as a relief, as it should simplify your scheme administration. There are, however, some twists. Since contracting-out rebates are not always paid by the government on time, and not always at the correct amount, rebates for the tax year ending 5 April 2012 have to be calculated (and corrected in some instances!) and paid. You then have three years to resolve any rebate payment issues. During that period you have to notify HMRC of any transfers of protected rights (pension rights given by the scheme which replace the state second pension). After 5 April 2015 any remaining issues have to be fixed between HMRC and the member directly. In order to make that easier (for HMRC), there is a *de minimis* amount, below which HMRC will not pay any underpaid rebate.

If you already have a Contracted-Out Money Purchase scheme, the contracting out came to an end in April 2012. You will have had to tell the members and you will have had to provide some minimum information.

RPI to CPI: implications for staff transfers from the public to the private sector
You may have some employees who have been transferred in from government or local government employment, and in some ways you have to replicate their public sector pension rights. One of their rights is to have their benefits index-linked, but the question is: which index? In 2011 the government changed the rules so that it now uses the consumer prices index (CPI) rather than the usually more generous retail prices index (RPI). This has

made it difficult to work out what to do, especially because the Government Actuary's Department (GAD) – the body that fixes the rules for public sector pensions – said that it would not issue bulk transfer terms or start new broad comparability testing until the issues arising from the CPI changes have been worked through. This makes many public-to-private outsourcing exercises involving the transfer of staff rather difficult to plan.

Normally, when you take on transfers of employment from the public sector, the government policy is to provide a level of protection for future pension provision for the staff – the so-called 'Fair Deal'. Employees either transfer to your scheme or remain within their existing public service pension scheme. If they transfer, employees have the option to request that the benefits they have already built up in the public service pension scheme be transferred to your pension arrangement by way of a 'bulk transfer'. Until the details of how the government will implement the RPI/CPI changes (which are likely to reduce transfer values) become clear, if you are involved in any outsourcing project involving a bulk transfer of pension rights you need to think twice about taking them on.

The GAD announcement where bulk transfer terms have been agreed

For certain public service schemes (eg the NHS Pension Scheme), GAD sets the bulk transfer terms; in most cases, GAD also determines whether the pension arrangements into which the bulk transfer will be paid offer 'broadly comparable' benefits. Where a contract award is imminent and bulk transfer terms have been offered and accepted, these are normally honoured based on a RPI equivalence. GAD usually considers pension arrangements on a case-by-case basis with the relevant public service schemes and awarding department in the short term. GAD is likely to require any submissions to it to discuss in detail how CPI issues will be dealt with. You may need to consider postponing the transfer until there is greater clarity from GAD about how the changes will work in practice and, in particular, what bulk transfer terms are offered. If proposed bulk transfer terms are unknown, you cannot accurately quantify the pensions cost associated with a bid.

Divorce

Pension systems were originally designed before divorce became widespread. Nowadays, around half of all marriages end in divorce, and civil partnerships, introduced in 2004, are also beginning to develop a similar track record. Accordingly, major reforms have been introduced to cope with the impact of divorce on pension rights. The legislation (as ever) is astonishingly complex[2] but can be summarised as follows.

■ The basic state pension cannot be divided between divorcing couples.
■ The state second pension can be divided – but only with a court order.
■ Private pensions can be dealt with in one of three main ways:

1. attachment: an order of the court that when the pension or other benefits begin to be paid, some or all of them are paid direct to the former spouse from the pension fund
2. set-off: an order of the court (usually) that other assets of the marriage are re-allocated to take into account the fact that one partner has a pension and the other does not, so that the partner without a pension takes perhaps more of the value of the home
3. sharing (formerly called splitting): an order of the court directing some or all of one partner's pension rights to be put in the name of the other partner.

This is not the place to discuss the pros and cons of such orders for the divorcing couple (including civil partners) but, so far as you are concerned, it poses a policy question. The pension has been put in place for the benefit of the employee, not the benefit of the employee's former partner. It is hardly a good use of scarce resources for you to spend a great deal on pensions for non-connected people. Accordingly, in due course you will need to make a decision (with the trustees) on whether you wish to continue to manage the pension rights for the former spouse or require them (even if it results in poor value for money for them) to move their pension rights elsewhere. Secondly, you will need to explore whether you should charge for providing information and implementing the court order in due course. There are National Association of Pension Fund (NAPF) guidelines on reasonable amounts to charge, and they are surprisingly high.[3]

COMMUNICATION

All good employers pride themselves on good communication with their employees, and you will be no exception, but explaining about pension arrangements is in theory at least 'selling financial services', and in principle you need to be authorised, probably by the Financial Services Authority.

In practice, the FSA has hinted very strongly that it will not attempt to impose its rules on employers who market their pension schemes to staff. Over the last 10 or 15 years, also in practice, there has never been a case in which it has attempted to do so. A couple of years ago the NAPF produced a study exploring what should be done to make your life easier when communicating pensions to the workforce.[4] Indeed, the Pensions Regulator has also issued a guide to the legal position.[5] In some ways it is quite a useful document, which operates using a question and answer technique. It uses many words to say rather little – and qualifies most of what it says. Most importantly, it does not make the immunity of employers from regulation as clear as it should, since the crucial statement is rather hidden by the length of the document. It is clear that the joint exercise, admirable as it was, has made it harder to send a clear message to employers that they have nothing to fear in selling their scheme to members. The true position is quite straightforward.

- If you have an occupational pension scheme, whether DC or DB, it is not regulated by the FSA.
- You can say what you want about your occupational scheme provided it is not misleading.
- If you have a (group) personal pension scheme, in theory it is probably advisable that an FSA-regulated body market it; in practice, no employer has been criticised by a regulator in over 15 years for a breach.

The regulator's guide is probably more suited as a simple guide for advisers than for you. The judges are much more relaxed than even regulators and, with some rare exceptions, they have made it clear that they will exonerate you as an employer from complaints about the provision of information (or lack of provision).

CHAPTER 4
PENSION ARRANGEMENTS
FOR THE GENERAL
WORKFORCE

We would all like a decent pension, payable at an early age until we die. Rather like we'd like a cottage in Provence and, subject to taste, Brad Pitt or Angelina Jolie to prepare our soothing unguents as we enter into gentle decline.

For most of us, these may be dreams too far but, with some help from an employer, at least some of these ambitions may be realised. Employers can help, because very few of us have the resource, either financial or practical, to organise financial provision for our own retirement.

There are two essential facts about pension provision for most people.

1. It is more efficient to provide it collectively rather than individually.
2. It is more efficient to have it provided through the employer.

The costs of running pension schemes have increased greatly because you need to comply with the complicated legislation, and increased costs can lead to much reduced benefits. It is sensible, therefore, to have pension arrangements provided through a group, where the costs can be shared and the scheme can afford to hire people to act on behalf of the members rather than the providers. A 1% increase in administrative costs can reduce benefits by 25%, so cost management in pensions is critical – as are investment returns. Pension provision through the company seems to offer by far the best value.

However, you have to make some critical decisions when designing your scheme for the general workforce.

- **Collective or individual provision:** should you have a company workplace pension scheme, or have it provided as a collection of individual personal pension arrangements?
- **Trust- or contract-based:** should you set up a company scheme with trustees, or just sign a contract with one of the providers and let them manage everything?
- **Level of contributions:** should you simply match the levels required by law (ie your 3% contributions, in which case it might be best simply to join the NEST scheme) or try to do something better, in which case you need your own scheme?
- **Level of benefits** (especially in defined benefit arrangements): should you try to target benefits (eg a pension of half-salary at retirement age), or just leave it to chance as to what the contributions might buy at retirement?
- **Advisers needed:** should you simply join the government's NEST scheme, or set one up on your own? And if so, do you need lawyers, accountants, actuaries, pension consultants and investment managers?

WHAT SHOULD EMPLOYERS PROVIDE?

Before implementing a scheme, you need to consider what resources you have on hand, and whether that resource is available in-house (eg a pension scheme manager, normally available nowadays only to the larger companies) or if external help should be brought in. Lawyers, actuaries and pension consultants can all offer you good advice on how to choose a pension scheme (or a range of schemes) suitable for your workforce.

The first issue is how much pension (or what level of contribution) is the right amount.

- It is a waste of your resources to provide a level of pension that is too high.
- It is pointless (and counter-productive) to provide too low a pension; it doesn't grant a retirement income of any consequence, it irritates the workforce and it still costs you money.

Designing a scheme that is cost-effective means looking at what the customers (your employees) want or need, depending on whether:

- they are on very low incomes
- they are going to rely on other income in retirement (eg a spouse)
- they are going to move abroad
- most of them really do not want to save for retirement.

In these cases, it might be best to walk away from the whole idea or only put in a skeleton scheme. However, most people generally would like help in organising how they are going to manage once they stop work, so if you put in a decent scheme – and tell people about it – you will become very popular.

Design, therefore, includes thinking about:

- the level of target pension for each employee
- whether different groups of employees are looking for different outcomes
- whether there should be survivor's pensions (ie for civil partners or widows and widowers)
- whether there should be life insurance cover built in (this gives, roughly, two or three times the annual salary if they die before retirement)
- whether they should have any choice in the selection of investments
- what kind of trustee arrangements there should be (employees in workplace pension schemes have a right to appoint up to one-third of the trustee board)
- what kind of dispute resolution system there should be
- what kind of inflation protection (if any) is thought sensible
- what the right to transfer rights out of the scheme should involve
- whether you should accept pension rights from other schemes.

Once you have worked out the kind of scheme you want to provide, you can then move on to explore what it all might cost.

System

That cost will vary according to your choice of pension system, ie whether you choose:

- a salary-related system
- a contribution-related system.

Salary-related system

Salary-related systems are commonly called final salary systems or, using US terminology, defined benefit (DB) systems.

Originally, defined benefit systems tried to promise (or at least use their best endeavours, without a formal promise) to pay a pension linked in some way to the level of salary enjoyed by the employee. This might involve attempting to provide, say, half the salary from retirement until death (reduced if the employee did not have a full career with the employer).

Sometimes these are called 1/60th schemes, ie they provide 1/60 of the salary for each year the employee worked for the company. If he or she worked for 40 years, it would provide forty-sixtieths, (the same as two-thirds) of salary. Nowadays, you will find it hard (unless you are a very successful company) to provide such arrangements, due to the following reasons.

■ You have to index-link the benefits against inflation, which broadly doubles the costs.
■ You have to fund them in a way which is expensive and may not suit your company (ie if the value of the funds held falls, you have to make added contributions to make up any deficit).
■ They may have an adverse consequence on your company balance sheet (the values of the funds and of the liabilities have to be put on there).
■ You have to make up any shortfall (commonly called a deficit) within an improbably short time, thus badly affecting your company cash flow and profitability (an ability to raise capital or restructure the company).
■ You have to comply with expensive governance arrangements.
■ You will find it difficult to change the scheme if it is found to be too costly.

In other words, the risks of such a system, if the investments do not produce the amounts necessary to pay the benefits, are almost all borne by the company. In addition to the risks you also have:

■ unmanageable future inflation
■ unmanageable future returns
■ unmanageable tax changes
■ unmanageable mortality changes.

These combine to make this type of provision a challenge. This means that very few companies these days establish such schemes, and the few examples that exist are usually connected with promises that employers have to make to replicate government pension arrangements for their own staff when they take on a workforce from the public sector.

Contribution-related system

Given the drawbacks of defined benefit systems, it is very probable that you will choose to set up a defined contribution scheme (also called a contribution-related or 'money purchase' scheme). This is simply a form of savings account into which you and your employees (usually) place money, which is invested as best as the trustees can. They then usually buy an annuity with the money when the employee retires.

With these plans the employee shoulders almost all the risks, which include:

■ the risk that longevity will increase and therefore the sums saved will have to last a longer time

- the risk that the investments may fall in value at the time they are sold to buy an annuity at retirement
- the risk that tax rates may change
- the risk that the asset manager may perform worse than expected and or planned
- the risk that annuity rates will be unattractive just at the time they have to be bought
- the risk that administrative costs may rise to meet increased compliance and regulatory costs
- the risk that inflation will diminish the value of the benefits over time and that this fall is not countered by increases in nominal value. Inflation is an insidious destroyer of value. Firstly, the official inflation statistics do not seem to reflect what is actually happening to the value of money; secondly, the indices include things which do not reflect the needs of pensioners; and thirdly, even small inflation rates (eg 3% pa) can destroy value in a short period of time. For example, an inflation rate of 3% pa destroys about 35% of a fixed pension's value in 10 years, and 70% in 20 years. Given that a pension might be expected to be paid for around 30 years, in many cases it means that inflation is often an underestimated risk.

All these risks are the reason why defined contribution schemes, called money purchase plans at the time, were largely abandoned at the end of the Second World War when inflation surged, and schemes moved to defined benefit as a solution.

Using advisers

You can undoubtedly organise pension provision for your employees in a much cheaper and better way than they can. The main reason is that it is cheaper to organise the skilled advice that is necessary to establish a pensions system; also, it takes time to buy an individual pensions contract, and the adviser needs to undertake an expensive analysis for each client to meet the demands of the Financial Services Authority (which is expensive regulatory overkill).

Pensions should not, in theory, be that complicated to sort out; it is simply saving for old age (the only real unknown being how long our old age will be, which is why 'pensions' are not quite just 'savings'). But the legislation, regulation and tax systems make that simple objective hard to achieve in practice.

It is easier for you to find an adviser who will help to design the scheme, organise the administration, report to the tax authorities and organise the benefits collectively. Before implementing a scheme, you need to consider:

- what technical resources you have available
- whether the resources are available in-house (eg with a pension scheme manager, normally available nowadays only to the larger companies) or whether external help should be brought in. Lawyers, actuaries and pension consultants can all offer you good advice on how to decide on a pension scheme (or a range of schemes) suitable for your workforce.

Almost all advisers will normally conclude that some form of collective provision is a better bet. There are several varieties – and some hybrid varieties:

- defined benefit workplace scheme
- defined contribution workplace scheme
- group personal pension plans.

The first two (workplace schemes) achieve savings through the operation of trustees, who look after the interests of members and can remain on staff even if your company stops trading. Group personal pensions (GPP) are simply a collection of individual pension arrangements, one for each employee, where the provider (maybe an insurance company) offers a discount for volume, mostly on the administration and investment charges. Although there are no trustee arrangements in GPPs, you could set up a mock-trustee board which could operate as a trustee board to protect members.

COSTS
Costs can be crucial. The government's overheads were intended to be, for its own NEST scheme, about 0.30% of contributions; in fact, it is likely to cost much more than that. But high administration costs can double the costs of a scheme – or, in other words, halve the benefits. Managing costs, therefore, is important, and paying for an adviser to help you cut costs may sound counter-intuitive but is a wise spend.

Costs, of course, involve both:

■ contribution costs
■ administration costs.

Contributions
Your contributions and the contributions that your employees make will influence the value of the scheme. You have a wide range of options (provided that, in order to meet the auto-enrolment rules, you eventually pay 3% minimum), and you can have virtually any mix you want.

■ **Age.** The contributions could be adjusted according to age: older people usually have more disposable income and a greater wish to fund their retirement, so you might have a minimum of 3% for those employees under, say, 35, and then roughly 5% for those from 35–55, and around 7% after that. There are two forms of discrimination that must be avoided when doing this: do not become involved in age or gender discrimination, and do not build a system which might prejudice you against hiring older workers.
■ **Length of service.** You could add contribution rates for longer-serving employees, again avoiding any suggestion of age discrimination but acting as an incentive for workers not to move, thus saving your recruitment costs and adding to employee satisfaction and happiness.
■ **Profitability.** You might want to link contributions to the profitability of your company, which would give a kind of tax-free bonus when the company could afford it.
■ **Need.** Different staff will have different needs. There is no law against giving different levels of contributions to different people (unlike the US at one time) and it might be a sensible use of company money, provided it doesn't give rise to jealousy among your employees.
■ **Longevity.** It might be possible to vary the contributions according to changes in national longevity statistics – or perhaps vary the age at which the pension can be drawn.

Administration

Regulation
If your pension scheme is to enjoy tax neutrality (ie not pay double tax), it needs to be registered with HMRC. This is not difficult to do. It will also automatically be registered

with the Pensions Regulator, which publishes guidance notes on the good administration of defined contribution schemes. In fact, with some exceptions, the Pensions Regulator has little to do with defined contribution schemes.

Record-keeping
One of the biggest challenges you face is keeping track of the contributions and making sure they are paid on time and to the right pension provider or investment manager. The insurer or other pension provider may well do this for you, although the track record of many providers, especially when dealing with small amounts, is rather mixed. Alternatively, you might find a dedicated administrator who would do it for you (sometimes a service offered by pension consultants or actuaries).

Communication
There is little point in you spending a lot of money on a pension scheme if the employees don't realise what a bargain they are getting. The money you spend is not only to help them in their retirement, but it also lets them have a warm and cuddly feeling about you. Put in a budget (which need not be large) for telling them – and also warning them that it may not be enough to retire on. Communication is looked at in detail on page 77.

Tax
Unless the scheme is tax efficient (ie it gives tax relief on the contributions and build-up), it is unacceptably expensive. The tax rules on the design of pension schemes are insane and make it hard to provide decent pensions for the higher paid. This is not a technical book on the taxation of pensions, but the general rule of thumb is that it is not efficient to provide a pension in respect to a salary over £100,000 pa, or a pension of more than £70,000 pa through an HMRC registered scheme.

Risk
The risks of a defined benefit scheme are your risks: investment, life expectancy and regulation, but you are best equipped to manage them. The risks of defined contribution or GPP schemes are broadly those of the workforce, ie those least prepared to take them on. The incentives are wrongly designed in the legislation, but there is little you can do about it, so just accept that the system is unfair and wrong, and move on.

Benefits
Some benefits are automatic (eg if you get to 65 you will get a pension) and some are discretionary (eg if the trustees think it right, they will give a death benefit to your spouse but not to your unmarried partner). To some extent, though, all are contingent; you will get different benefits depending on when you die and how long you live – and indeed you might get nothing after 40 years of contributions. That is the nature of a pension scheme; it is designed to protect you if you live too long, and if you die too soon you do not need a pension.

CONTRACT OR TRUST
Some schemes (including NEST itself) are organised as a trust, whereas others simply sign a contract with a provider. Each method of organisation has its adherents, and although for several years, for good reasons, there seems to have been a move away from trusts, there now seems to be something of a turn the other way, as the shortcomings of contracts become more evident. In the end, you will probably decide on the

basis of size; if you have a small scheme, say fewer than 250 members, you may elect for a contract-based system. If you have a larger scheme the attraction may be for a trust. The main factors you need to think about will be cost and governance.

Trust-based schemes became more popular even for smaller schemes in the 1960s, as the drawbacks of one-stop-shopping became evident. These included lack of transparency, hidden costs and poor investment performance – and the nightmare of being locked into a contract.

However, over the last few years trust-based schemes, even for defined contribution arrangements, have been hit by challenges of their own. A trust-based scheme is a traditional occupational pension run and governed by a board of trustees, who take responsibility and liability for the scheme and the benefits it provides. A contract-based scheme – such as a group SIPP or group personal pension – is set up so that members have their own contract with the scheme provider.

Whether under a trust-based or contract-based scheme, the employer is obliged to make the pension available, and deduct and pay contributions on time. Under a trust-based scheme the trustee has both additional responsibility for and a better ability to control:

- the administration of the scheme
- the overall investment of the scheme
- member communication
- ensuring the scheme is governed correctly
- meeting certain liabilities towards members.

So as far as costs and charges are concerned, if your company is a small one it is probably inefficient to have to be directly responsible for:

- investment management
- appointing, paying and training trustees
- scheme accounts
- scheme auditing
- administration: in-house or third party
- trustee indemnity insurance
- regulatory levies
- communications.

It is important to realise that most of these costs (as well as others, such as different regulatory costs) still apply, though they are hidden, in the costs of contract-based schemes. In addition, the costs of many contract-based schemes are designed to cope with taking on individual contracts and do not give the economies of scale on costs that trust-based schemes do.

Responsibility for investments

Trustees, even in DC schemes, retain responsibility for certain aspects of investments, including the fund options they make available to members and the scheme investment overall, and must avoid excess investment in the parent company. This may be a concern for you, although in practice the liabilities are minimal, especially if the documentation is properly drafted, and the ability to help individuals make default choices and move out of failing providers and investment managers can be considerable. Whether trust or contract, you need to make sure that from time to time (perhaps every couple of years) you review:

■ **lifestyling:** the gradual change of the investment mix to meet changing needs as members move towards retirement age
■ **suitability:** any default investment arrangements.

Deferred members

Employees who no longer work for you

Even the best run companies (even yours) have staff turnover, and it is usually inefficient for you to have to manage the pension arrangements of staff who have left you. In practice, you can arrange for such staff to have their rights transferred elsewhere, refund their contributions or manage them cost-effectively. You can spend time managing deferred membership in order to:

■ reduce the size of the potential liability faced by your company (where the scheme is a defined benefit one)
■ minimise administrative costs
■ reduce charges based on member numbers, such as the Pensions Regulator levy.

Sometimes the effort is not worth the cost, though, and similar costs of contract-based schemes are hidden in the charges.

■ Trust-based schemes can refund employee contributions to members and recover employer contributions, which can mean considerable savings if your staff turnover is high. Refunds of member contributions are allowed in cases where the member leaves the scheme in the first two years of service; in addition, members whose pots are trivial can take up to £2,000 in cash without taking other pensions into account.
■ On the other hand, under a contract-based scheme there are no deferred members; your staff take their plan with them when they leave and you do not need to keep their pension records.

Duties at retirement

When you retire, your scheme should normally buy an annuity (or make an internal reserve for an annuity). It is normally much more efficient **not** to buy an annuity from an insurance company (since insurance company regulation makes them buy inappropriate investments and makes them keep expensive reserves), although you might prefer not to be in the business of annuities and insist that external annuities are bought, either in the name of the scheme or in the name of the member.

If you buy an annuity in the name of a member you should normally shop around, usually taking professional advice from a broker.

Flexible retirement options

You are no longer able to sack your staff just because they are old or even because they have reached the state retirement age. A pension system is a useful way (if you want to) of encouraging people to move on. However, you can also arrange for them to work part time (or even full time) and take a pension at the same time.

For wealthier employees, there is no longer a need to buy an annuity. Some employees may want to manage their own retirement pots and have a 'self-managed annuity', known as income drawdown. This can be expensive and has its own risks, which are not always understood (there are no guarantees, for example, and the fund value can fall), but are very attractive to independent financial advisers. They can be useful for higher paid people, who may want to transfer their rights to another arrangement when they leave.

Higher earners

The next chapter explores some options for higher earners in greater detail. Trust-based schemes allow contributions to be made via a net pay arrangement so members receive full tax relief at source. This is a simple way for higher-rate taxpayers to reclaim their relief, and for most people it is easy to understand. Higher-rate tax relief through contract-based schemes is achieved in a different way, as payments to the pension are made after tax and National Insurance have been deducted. Basic-rate tax relief (20%) is then claimed by the provider, and higher and additional rate taxpayers claim any extra relief via their tax return or by an adjustment to their tax code.

Higher earners (which converseley this also includes moderate earners) are now only given tax relief on pension contributions up to £50,000 a year; this affects people particularly in defined benefit schemes who are given a pay rise which may trigger a notional contribution of over £50,000 inadvertently. Special planning is required.

Regulatory arbitrage

Your scheme must provide statements to members whose contributions or deemed contributions to their pension schemes exceed £50,000, so that they can complete the member's tax return. You will need to record if the scheme has a pension input period that is not the same as the tax year, and (rarely) schemes can be fined if they do not meet the requirements. You might instead choose to use a salary sacrifice arrangement to achieve the same effective tax benefits as a net pay arrangement, although salary sacrifice needs to be carefully planned to avoid unintended tax consequences for higher earners.

Governance, financial education and empowerment

If you decide to use a trust system, many employees feel more comfortable when someone is looking after their interests, helping to negotiate on their behalf, searching the market for best terms and handling communications through the company. Most employees (although there are exceptions) prefer to have someone else make investment decisions on their behalf; few employees wish to be their own investment managers, and they rarely have the time, experience or inclination – and although they should, they don't really want to spend the time being educated.

Table 9: Pros and cons of trust-based and contract-based schemes

Benefits	Trust-based DC	Contract-based DC
Employer able to contribute	Y	Y
Employee able to contribute	Y	Y
Income tax relief for member	Y	Y
Corporation tax relief for employer	Y	Y
Branding of literature, website and joining forms	Y	Y
Member guidance and support	Y	Maybe
Ongoing employer governance	Y	Maybe

Continued on next page

Continued from previous page

Benefits	Trust-based DC	Contract-based DC
Choice of investment funds and default options	Y	Maybe
Portability if member leaves service	Y	Maybe
Refunds possible within 2 years' service	Y	N
Higher rate tax relief at source on member contributions	Y	N
Access to institutional fund charges	Y	N
Liabilities and duties		
Board of trustees required (including member-nominated trustees)	Y	N
Overall trustee obligations and liabilities	Y	Maybe
Trustee/employer pays Pensions Regulator levy	Maybe	N
Professional fees: legal actuarial accounting	Y	Maybe/hidden
Trustee indemnity insurance/cover	Y	N/maybe
Trustee responsible and liable for investments	Y	Maybe
Trustees responsible and liable for annuities	Maybe	N
Trustees required to monitor collective funds to avoid 5% self-investment rule	Y	N/A
Deferred members	Y	N

(Based on a table prepared by Hargreaves Lansdown)

INVESTMENTS

Although investments are dealt with elsewhere (see page 115), it is handy to mention that they can make a significant difference to benefits values at retirement age, especially in defined contribution schemes.

In practice, you will be guided by investment consultants, pension consultants or the pension provider, but it always helps to have a general idea of the options that will be discussed. These include the following.

Passive investments

Passive investments (sometimes known as 'tracker' investments) are those which are simply invested according to the size of asset in the market; for example, if BP shares represent 5% of the stock market, the investment portfolio (basket of investments) will include BP shares, representing 5% of the total. As share prices rise and fall, the investment manager's computer will continually adjust the percentages of different shares in the portfolio to match their importance in the market. The value of the pot will fluctuate as the market fluctuates, rising and falling with it, but the managers do not have decisions to make as to whether to buy or sell shares.

Active investments

Active investments operate where your asset managers decide to buy or sell according to how well they think the investments will do in the market. If they target to outperform the market (which they ought to be able to do using their intelligence and experience) such outperformance is known as 'alpha'. Some believe that, on average, fund managers can never outperform the market or that, if they do so, it is simply an accident; others think that experience tells.

Lifestyle investments

Lifestyle investments set out a predetermined policy of switching from higher-return, higher risk investments (usually equities or shares) into lower-return, lower risk invest- ments (usually known as bonds or income-bearing investments) as the scheme member approaches retirement. The theory is that, by retirement age, as the need for flow of income crystallises, and only bonds can guarantee that, that flow of income will continue regardless of the rise and fall of the market. In fact, such a policy can be undermined by the 'reinvestment risk', ie when the bond is repaid by the government or the company, the rates of interest at the time are lower, thus making it harder to find the right level of income.

Diversification

Investment risks – shares not keeping their value, bonds not giving the interest you need or performance being less than it should be – may make the provision of pensions seem too complicated, too risky and too expensive to be bothered with. In fact, industry skills are used to manage these risks and, while they cannot guarantee the rate of returns or security, by diversifying into lots of different investments they make the risks usually manageable.

Diversification is often underestimated as a risk manager, and it is also much easier to diversify – and to take manageable risks – if the pot is larger. Individuals cannot afford this advice or take the spread of risk; when individuals invest they are usually forced to invest in cash or bonds, which may be less volatile but usually offer lower returns. Low- er returns (with lower risks) also mean lower benefits for the same amount of money. The balance between risk and reward is much easier to manage with larger sums, and larger groups of investors, than as individuals. This is why company schemes are so attractive, especially where compared with individual personal pensions.

Default options

The philosophy behind much of the government's present pension policy is based on default options. The idea comes from behavioural economics, especially the inertia that most of us experience when trying to make decisions about pension provision. For example, the auto-enrolment system (see page 29) is voluntary – but all employees have to opt out, rather than opt in: they have to make a positive decision not to join and, without sufficient incentive, few of us do it.

Similarly, in terms of investments, few of us are motivated to make decisions about the investments we should make to support our pensions. There are several reasons for this, including the following.

- Few of us have the knowledge or interest in investment matters to make a decision.
- Even fewer of us have specialist investment skills to make pension investments.
- Even fewer are willing to actually make decisions, even if we had the knowledge and information.

Therefore, it is often sensible to have in place a system which makes the decision on behalf of the members, who can, however, opt out of it or make different decisions about it.

In practice, many providers offer 'lifestyle options' (lifestyle investments), which are sometimes justifiably considered to be rather crude but work well enough for most of us most of the time – and, in any event, are preferable to what we would do if we made our own decisions. In simple terms, the default investment options automatically balance investments towards bonds as opposed to equities as we get older and closer to retirement age, thus making it more likely that we will have enough money to buy an adequate annuity.

HOW MUCH SHOULD BE CONTRIBUTED?

Very few of us put in enough to provide for our retirement. There are some rules of thumb, however, which you should try to follow. You can start by having a look at this website (and there are others, too, such as moneyover55.about.com) which helps you do your own calculations: money.guardian.co.uk/calculator/form/0,,603163,00.html.

If you want to save enough to provide an income of roughly half your salary at retirement at 65, a useful rule of thumb might be that you need to put away:

■ at the age of 21, around 10% of salary for 44 years
■ at the age of 30, around 18% of salary for 35 years
■ at the age of 40, around 26% of salary for 25 years
■ at the age of 50, around 40% of salary for 15 years.

This guidelines ignores inflation and state pensions. In practice, few of us are able to afford to do this, nor can we come close to the goal of putting away 30% whatever our age. However, the table shows the power of compound interest and the value of starting early.

If you want an income of £10,000 pa at retirement at age 65 you probably need to have around £200,000 saved in your kitty. However, very few of us can manage to build up that amount; all you can do as a facilitator is help your employees save as much as they can, reduce their costs as much as you can and default them into investments which maintain a balance between risk and return.

All these numbers are rough and ready; use one of the calculators available on the web to figure out your own circumstances.

INTEGRATION WITH THE STATE SCHEME

The state scheme benefits are complex and described in Chapter 1. At one time, it was sometimes cost-effective to provide at least the state second pension through your company pension scheme, as the deal was that the government let you pay a lower National Insurance contribution (ie contracting out).

That deal is still available for a while if your scheme is a defined benefit scheme, but the general consensus is that contracting out is a 'mug's game'.

■ There is a great deal of extra administration.
■ The reduction in National Insurance contributions is not worth the extra you have to pay into the scheme.

However, it is also sensible to take into account that the state will be paying a pension which, to lower paid staff, will be a major percentage of their working income. This means that for them to join an expensive company pension fund may be simply to provide more income in retirement than is appropriate.

ADMINISTRATION

Administering pension schemes can be difficult and complicated, not so much because pensions are complicated (they are not) but because the regulations are excessive. Few companies, apart from the largest, administer their own pension arrangements, even if they manage their own payrolls, and there are innumerable pension administrators, including insurers (the way in which you can select an administrator is set out in Chapter 6).

COMMUNICATION IN PRACTICE

It may seem an extravagance to spend money telling the workforce what a great deal your new company pension scheme offers, because of the following reasons.

- The communication exercise may cost money (which may not have been budgeted for in the original specification, or there may not be a resource to manage the communication exercise).
- The more people that join the scheme, in most cases, the more it will cost the company. It is in the finance director's interest to see that as few employees join the scheme as possible.

However, introducing a scheme and then ensuring that few employees join rather defeats the purpose of the exercise.

- Under the NEST system, there has to be a scheme anyway, so the company has to pay at least 3% of payroll in most cases, whatever the success or otherwise of a pension plan.
- Once it has been decided that it is in the company's interests to provide a scheme (for all sorts of commercial, paternalistic or competitive reasons), it seems an expensive exercise not to point out to the workforce the benefits they can obtain at the expense of the company. For most of them, especially if they are longer-term employees, it will be the most valuable asset they will possess apart from their house, and one of the most useful.

Pensions are probably the most valuable benefit an employer can offer, although employees might not realise it. Since people are easily turned off by the language used and the way the information is presented, many of them don't realise the huge investment their employer is making on their behalf and, perhaps more importantly, what their likely retirement income is going to be. Communication systems should be designed to give employees clearly presented and easy-to-understand information, including communication from the employer alongside scheme details and a 'plain English' statement of what their likely retirement income will be (dynamically updated). Some systems allow employees to enter details of any other pensions they have, which makes sure that the estimated retirement income is as accurate as possible, and often include a forecasting tool to show them what will happen if they alter their contributions.

You should give your employees:

- details of the company scheme, in short form, with access (perhaps on the web) to the full rules
- a 'plain English' statement of what the benefits are likely to be worth
- an opportunity to test 'what if' scenarios (eg if the contributions were increased)
- an opportunity to aggregate personal pensions from different sources

■ an opportunity to contact an independent financial adviser, perhaps paid for or partly paid for by the employer.

A good system should:

■ allow, where appropriate, the simple establishment of both defined contribution and defined benefit schemes
■ allow the retention of editorial control to allow changes to the arrangements as external circumstances change
■ allow you to provide straightforward definition of rules based on length of service, age, etc where applicable
■ allow you to amend the configuration of a forecasting tool, if provided
■ give you an opportunity to monitor how many employees are using the system and what the costs are
■ allow you to provide the HR or payroll department with appropriate access to each employee's information, for accounting and other purposes
■ involve a simple system to allow the proper management of joiners and leavers
■ involve an integration with payroll and HR systems
■ allow the provision of scheme booklets with printed or email distribution.

REASONS TO COMMUNICATE

Why should you bother giving your employees information about pensions? In theory, it might be against the law and you might get it wrong. In fact, employees welcome advice from a source they trust (as opposed to an insurance company, financial adviser or the government) and with luck the following will take place.

■ They will recognise the value of the scheme as part of the employment package you offer.
■ Your employees will have a better understanding of pensions, which will lead to better retirement planning on their part and easier workforce management for you.
■ Employees in defined contribution (DC) schemes will have a better understanding of how their decisions – such as how much to contribute, what investment funds to choose, how to draw their benefits at retirement – will affect the size of their retirement fund.
■ Problems which might arise further down the line as a result of misunderstandings now will be avoided.

The rules relating to telling your staff about pensions are very simple. You can tell them:

■ how they can join
■ how much it will cost them
■ what benefits the scheme provides
■ the facts about the scheme and pensions in general. For example, if it is a defined contribution scheme, let them know:

  ☐ how much money they and you have paid into the scheme
  ☐ how the investments have performed
  ☐ how much of this money has been used to pay any charges – this will influence the value of their fund at retirement
  ☐ that their fund at retirement is used to provide their pension income

■ whether you as the employer, will pay a contribution to the scheme, how much you pay and that, if they choose not to join the scheme, they lose out on this contribution from you

- that they receive tax relief on their contributions to the scheme, and explain the positive effect this has on the amounts actually being invested into their pensions
- by organising a presentation about the scheme. If your scheme provider does not offer this, the Money Advice Service (once known as Consumer Financial Education Body (CFEB) and a government-funded organisation), TPAS (The Pensions Advisory Service, another government-funded service) or PENSIONSFORCE (the National Association of Pension Fund's company pensions information service) may be able to visit your workplace, normally free of charge. Look at:

  - ☐ www.moneyadviceservice.org.uk/about
  - ☐ www.pensionsadvisoryservice.org.uk
  - ☐ www.pensionsforce.co.uk.

You can also:

- give them documents from the scheme or pensions company
- explain the tax reliefs that are available and the limits on pension contributions you make to their pension
- refer them to TPAS, an independent organisation that gives members of the public information and guidance on pensions (their website at www. pensionsadvisoryservice.org.uk provides general information on occupational, personal and stakeholder pensions)
- refer them to the Money Advice Service www.moneyadviceservice.org.uk or 0300 500 5000
- use the guidance on stakeholder schemes, as given on the Pensions Regulator's website at www.tpr.gov.uk/stakeholder-faqs
- suggest that employees consider seeing an adviser authorised by the FSA
- pass on projections produced by the scheme, showing what benefits may be paid
- pass on any promotional material produced by the pension company
- pay a financial adviser to give your employees information and advice. (The cost of this advice, up to £150 per employee each tax year, is not classed as a benefit-in-kind for employees as long as it relates only to pensions and is not general financial and tax advice, so they will not be taxed on it.) You can claim the cost of financial advice as a business expense if that advice is provided only for the purposes of your business
- look at the guidance on effective communication for ways of passing on information. That guidance is given on the Pensions Regulator's website at www.tpr. gov.uk/effective-member-communications
- promote your occupational scheme in other ways (for example, produce your own communications, arrange presentations for staff and have sessions for members with questions about their scheme).

In theory some regulators suggest that you cannot tell your employees whether or not it's a good idea, but that is probably over-cautious.

On the other hand, **do not**:

- give individual advice to any employee
- take any commission or other benefit for introducing a scheme.

The rules are a little bit different if you communicate promotions for your personal or stakeholder scheme (or contract someone else to do so), where you have to:

- make a contribution to the scheme
- tell your employees in writing how much you contribute
- avoid receiving any direct financial benefit for promoting the scheme
- tell your employees that they can get advice from a professional financial adviser authorised by the FSA
- tell your employees in writing what remuneration they will receive for doing so if someone is contracted to communicate the promotions for you.

IS IT LEGAL TO SELL YOUR SCHEME TO EMPLOYEES?

There is, in theory, a problem with marketing your scheme to employees. Some people suggest that it might be contrary to the financial services law, because you are not an authorised person under the Financial Services and Markets Act. In fact, since the system has been operating over the last 15 years, the authorities have deliberately turned a blind eye and have issued guidance encouraging employees to communicate with their staff.

An NAPF study some years ago suggested that while 98% of employers felt they should have a role in providing information and support to their employees regarding pensions, 57% also saw the law as an obstacle that prevented them from doing so.[1]

Provided the advice given is generic rather than individual and personal, you should have no concerns about breaking the law. The Pensions Regulator and the Financial Services Authority have published a complicated guide on the issue, the bottom line of which is: do not give individual advice to members – but there is no problem in lauding how wonderful the scheme is generally.

STAKEHOLDER PENSIONS

If you have five or more employees, by law (since October 2001) you must offer them access to a pension scheme through the payroll – although you do not need to make a contribution yourself. The obligation (ie the 'stakeholder pension obligation') is being phased out as auto-enrolment begins. The law used to say that you had to offer your employees:

- an occupational pension scheme
- a personal pension scheme to which you contributed
- access to a stakeholder pension scheme, which offered low charges (see www. stakeholderhelpline.org.uk).

Since there was no requirement for you as the employer to put any money in, it was less of a pension scheme and more of a payroll deduction facility. In practice, hardly anyone used it, although if you didn't provide it there were significant financial penalties (in theory – no one seems to have had to pay a fine for failure to comply in over 10 years). From 2012 you have to use auto-enrolment and make a contribution anyway, so the system is virtually dead. It was always pretty moribund in any event.

GENERAL FINANCIAL ADVICE

It is not unreasonable for employees to ask whether it would be best:

- to increase their mortgage repayments in order to pay it off earlier, rather than paying into their pension

- whether they should top up their occupational pension with a stakeholder or personal pension, or by paying additional contributions
- whether they should transfer from another scheme to your scheme
- how much they should contribute to the pension scheme to get an adequate income in retirement
- whether they should reduce or suspend contributions.

However, do not be tempted to advise them on these issues. They will have to look on the internet, read their newspaper or use their own intelligence. Firstly, it is illegal for you to advise them, and secondly, it is highly unlikely you have the expertise.

On the other hand, if they want to know about the costs, you can:

- tell them about the contributions paid by them and by you as the employer
- pass on information about what the scheme charges are (for example, investment and administration charges) and how these are paid (for example, by you as the employer or by the members). All of this information should be in the scheme literature
- point them to the guidance on:

    □ TPAS's website at www.pensionsadvisoryservice.org.uk, if your scheme is a group personal pension scheme or stakeholder pension scheme
    □ the Pensions Regulator's website at www.tpr.gov.uk/dc-schemes-guidance.

When an employee approaches retirement

When employees approach their retirement, they often have to decide whether they should carry on working or buy an annuity and, if so, from whom.

For defined contribution (DC) schemes in particular, the scheme or pensions company must tell the member they can buy an annuity (which pays them an income for the rest of their life) from the insurance company of their choice, and that they don't have to take the one offered by the scheme. This is called the 'Open Market Option' (OMO) and means they can make sure they get the best deal.

To help your employees, you can do the following.

- Arrange for your adviser or pensions company to hold face-to-face or group meetings with them about their retirement options.
- If they have a DC pension, let them know that they can choose who provides their annuity and encourage them to shop around to get different quotes.
- Tell them about the annuity comparison tables on the Money Advice Service website at www.moneyadviceservice.org.uk, and provide a copy of *Your Guide to Retirement* and the range of printed guides produced by the Money Advice Service.
- Tell them about TPAS's annuity planner tool, which helps members choose the right type of annuity (see www.pensionsadvisory service.org.uk).
- Suggest they consider seeing a financial adviser authorised by the FSA.
- Consider providing access to an adviser.
- Remind members about information available from the pensions company (including information on the pension company's website and any website the scheme has).
- If they are members of an occupational DC scheme, make them aware of the leaflet on retirement choices, available on the Pensions Regulator's website at www.thepensionsregulator.gov.uk/docs/making-your-retirement-choices-2011.pdf.

- If you offer an occupational DC scheme, you could review the guidance on the Pensions Regulator's website at www.tpr.gov.uk/professionals/leavers-retirement-options and consider what strategies you might want to put in place to help your employees through the retirement process.
- If you offer an occupational DC scheme, consider providing a service that offers members a competitive annuity.

Occupational scheme

If your scheme is an occupational scheme and a member asks you how safe their money is in it, you can do the following.

- Explain that the scheme has trustees to look after it, and that these include people nominated by the scheme members. The scheme's assets are held separately from the business assets and the trustees must have relevant knowledge and understanding. (The Pensions Regulator's codes of practice give trustees guidance on how to run the scheme.)
- Mention that the scheme is covered by the Fraud Compensation Fund (FCF), which was introduced to provide compensation to occupational pension scheme members who suffer a loss as a result of dishonesty.
- Describe the complaints procedures your scheme has in place, and mention the Pensions Ombudsman (PO) and TPAS, who can help members who have difficulties with their scheme.
- If your scheme is a defined benefit (DB) scheme, also explain that it is covered by the Pension Protection Fund (PPF), which pays a certain level of compensation if an employer goes bust and there is not enough money in the scheme to pay benefits. Details of the fund are given on the website at www.pensionprotectionfund.org.uk.

Personal pension or stakeholder scheme

If your scheme is a group personal pension scheme or stakeholder scheme, you can do the following.

- Explain that, as the pension company running the pension scheme is authorised and regulated by the FSA, it must conduct its business in line with requirements set by the latter. This means that it must have enough resources available and proper controls in place in order to manage your employees' pensions properly in good times and bad, and pay benefits when they are due.
- Clarify that if the pension company goes bust, the Financial Services Compensation Scheme (FSCS) would be able to offer protection – either by arranging to transfer the pension fund to another pension company or by offering a certain level of compensation. More information is given on the FSCS website at www.fscs.org.uk/what-we-cover/questions-and-answers – it's best you look at that, since what the FSCS actually covers is rather uncertain.
- Mention that if a firm authorised by the FSA is involved in advising members, they might be protected by the FSCS if things go wrong and the advice was bad (see the website at www.fscs.org.uk/what-we-cover/questions-and-answers). You could also tell your employees that the Money Advice Service has issued a guide on making a complaint.
- Tell employees about any arrangements you have for looking after the scheme, such as meeting with advisers every so often or having a mock-trustee board.

DC scheme

If your scheme is a DC scheme (occupational, personal or stakeholder) in which the value of funds can rise and fall, you can suggest that members check what type of fund they invest in and decide whether it is appropriate for their circumstances (for example, many schemes offer a range of funds with different levels of risk). You should also explain that it is important for members to review regularly the funds they are invested in.

CHAPTER 5
PENSION ARRANGEMENTS
FOR THE HIGHER PAID

Pensions are not for everyone; if you are very rich, the last thing you need is a pension (with one exception). Pensions can only normally be taken in pension form, the funds have limited investment opportunities, there are strict controls on the contributions, benefits and investments, and the compliance costs are excessive. If you are rich you are better off investing your wealth in the normal way: buying and selling shares, bonds and (probably most of all) property. The money is not locked up – and you do not need the security of an income every month or year.

The only reasonable exception to this principle is where there is a risk of bankruptcy; with few exceptions, money in a pension fund is immune from the predations of a trustee in bankruptcy. Since it is possible to provide up to around £70,000 pa in a protected pension fund, keeping enough in the fund to provide a buffer against a liquidator or administrator may be useful. However, the pension, if paid, may itself be subject to collection by the trustee – but in practice most individuals are discharged from bankruptcy within a few years.

This chapter, therefore, is dedicated to exploring what options may be available to cope with the needs of the higher paid. It is hard to put a figure on what defines higher paid, but it probably applies:

- to **income over £40,000 pa**, which may not seem higher paid to many, but is regarded by HMRC as being the amount over which they worry about how much contributions are being paid
- to **income over £100,000 pa**, which reflects the maximum allowable fund in a defined benefit scheme of around £1.5m; today that will buy maybe around £70,000 a year (depending on the rates at the time, the state of the market and whether the pension should be flat or index-linked, ie inflation proofed), which is around two-thirds of £100,000 – a target which remains common in the pensions world
- to **income over £150,000 pa**, which is when the excess charges on tax relief begin to bite. Contributions in relation to salary in excess of this figure fail to gain full tax relief; this means, for example, that if only 20% tax relief is given on the contributions, and benefits are taxed at 40%, saving in a pension is not very tax efficient (allowing for the fact that the amount in the pension scheme grows tax-free).

Oddly, the tax system is generally skewed against pension provision even in relation to smaller incomes when, for the majority of lower earners, an ISA would be better value than a pension scheme. The destruction of the purity of the EET tax system for pensions (exempt on the contributions, exempt on the growth and tax on the benefits) is a flawed policy that will haunt governments and pensioners for generations to come.

CONVENTIONAL PENSION SCHEMES

Most of your senior executives will (or should) seek membership in the ordinary company pension scheme, regardless of whether it is defined benefit or defined contribution. Getting paid roughly another 5%–10% (assuming typical employer contributions) is a no-brainer, especially if the employee contributions receive tax relief so that the cash flow cost is maybe half the nominal cost. Being a member of the conventional scheme offers protection for dependants such as a spouse, life cover (ie death cover) and probably ill-health early retirement – all bundled up in the package.

However, because of the tax system, it may only provide benefits at a level which is insufficient for needs or expectations, in which case they and you will need to think about some form of unregistered pension scheme, ie a scheme for which tax relief on the employer and employee contributions is not ordinarily available. Those kinds of employees may be looking for something rather more relevant to what they need, with perhaps the right to manage their own investments.

HMRC (itself an unmelodic acronym) is given to spawning acronyms across its bailiwick, and pensions are no exception. In relation to the higher paid, acronyms have had a field day. You might want to think about three registered pension systems (ie registered with HMRC) and an unregistered system as additional options for the higher paid. These are conveniently described as:

■ SSAS: small self-administered scheme
■ SIPP: self-invested personal pension
■ GPPP: group personal pension plans
■ EFRBS: employer-funded retirement benefit scheme.

Other kinds of scheme are still around, but they are increasingly unattractive from a tax point of view and are gradually being dismembered. Examples are:

■ FURBS: funded unapproved retirement benefit schemes
■ UURBS: unfunded unregistered retirement benefit schemes.

Small self-administered scheme (SSAS)

Small self-administered pension schemes do what they say on the tin. They are an occupational pension scheme, usually set up to provide defined benefit arrangements, but unusually and exceptionally capping employer's liability for the amount of the contributions paid (ie the benefits are not guaranteed). Since they are usually limited in practice and by HMRC rules to fewer than 12 members, and because the members are also usually also the trustees of the scheme, they are exempt from many of the detailed regulations designed to protect members' interests, which makes them a little easier to manage.

The fact that the member can also (sometimes) be the director of the company, the owner of shares in the company, a member of the pension scheme and the beneficiary of the pension scheme makes a SSAS a self-contained pension unit. Within certain limits a SSAS can:

■ buy property (including the offices or warehouses of the employer)
■ make loans to the company
■ buy property overseas or in hotels or other semi-residential variety
■ buy tangibles (works of art or other things which can be touched).

The use of money in the pension fund to help the company through a tricky time, or to act as a friendly banker (which is rare to find these days), is a genuine attraction, even though the terms of borrowing have to correspond with commercial terms.

For smaller companies, there's little doubt that SSASs, used carefully, can be a creative way of funding the expansion of the company and managing its property assets.

Self-invested personal pension (SIPP)
Self-invested personal pensions are another, increasingly popular, form of pension arrangements for the higher paid. The key features of such schemes include the following.

■ They allow freedom of investment decisions by the pension scheme member, subject to limits.
■ They carry a fee, rather than hidden charges.
■ They permit the purchase of property.
■ They are personal pensions, rather than company pensions, so the employer does not need to make contributions.

Many employers now offer what are sometimes called 'company' or 'corporate' SIPPs; these offer a variety of options to different levels of employees. Junior employees (perhaps on salaries under £50,000) have their contributions and the contributions of their employer placed in a default investment account, managed by a professional investment manager. More senior staff, earning over £50,000, could be given the opportunity to select their own investments, including property, shares or more commonly collective investments. They could then decide to select high or low risk investments to suit their taste (and other expected income) – and expected retirement or pension age – and pay the costs of investments dealing themselves. Property investments are notoriously expensive to manage (because of the regulations) and the cost is rarely borne by the employer.

The corporate SIPP offers the advantage to employees of not having to change their arrangements or freeze them as they rise up the corporate ladder. Meanwhile, it is customary for the employer to bear the cost of administration of the scheme and, in relation to lower earners, the cost of investments. This makes corporate SIPPs cheaper to run for staff because of the economies of scale.

Group personal pension plans (GPPP)
These are also popular, because again (in theory at least) the compliance and regulatory overheads are lower. Such plans are again simply personal pension plans, which any individual can negotiate or buy for themselves from one of the main providers.

However, if bought by an individual these plans can involve high overheads; this is because the provider has to pay for the marketing costs of selling to individuals. Where such plans are bought in bulk by an employer, who may in addition operate a collective payment system through the payroll, the costs for the provider can be much lower and are frequently borne by the employer – the employee merely pays for any additional investment or transfer costs. These plans, however, rarely (if ever) permit the employee or member to choose their own investments, other than perhaps offering a narrow range of collective investments, such as specialised unit trusts.

Employer-funded retirement benefit scheme (EFRBS)
For employees earning over a certain amount (difficult to say, but a good rule of thumb is £100,000 pa) it may be inefficient from a tax point of view to provide pensions

through the HMRC-registered systems (ie conventional occupational pension schemes, SASSs, SIPPs, GPPPs – whether defined benefit or defined contribution).

Unregistered schemes may offer opportunities which are quite attractive. Individuals can be members of their conventional arrangements for the first part of their income and then arrange for their excess income to be made pensionable through an EFRBS. The predecessors to EFRBS – including FURBS (funded unapproved retirement benefit schemes), UURBS (unfunded unregistered retirement benefit schemes) and SUURBS (secured unfunded unapproved retirement benefit schemes) – are now no longer used or are being slowly phased out, as they are tax inefficient or inappropriate. Even EFRBS nowadays look to be increasingly unattractive, as the new (2011) rules on disguised remuneration seem to attack them profoundly.

Over the next year or two, unfunded top-up systems are likely to be available, which do not seem to attract the disapproval of the Treasury in the same fashion. In the meantime, the provision of pensions to levels over the annual allowances and lifetime allowances is probably inefficient. What does seem to be acceptable are lifetime employment contracts (at, say, a lower level), which is what the judges nowadays have instead of pensions which exceed the allowances.

QROPS, QNUPS AND MOVING OVERSEAS

The original dream of a simplified tax system, born with such hope in 2004 and implemented in 2006, was dashed just three years later when horribly complex tax reliefs were proposed (and very nearly implemented) for the higher paid. The thinking was that the higher paid enjoy disproportionate tax relief and should therefore have their tax breaks cut back in difficult times. In fact, the tax relief for pensions – even for the higher paid – is neutral. The rich might get higher tax relief when they put the payments in, but they pay higher tax when they take the pension out. (There is some distortion at the margins because some of the tax relief might be at a higher rate, but the tax is paid at a lower rate. And there is double tax relief on the lump sums. But even so . . .)

Public marketing of the constraint on the higher paid was, however, very successful. While the astonishingly dysfunctional rules were abandoned after the election in May 2010 and simpler rules introduced, they still detracted from the original simplification exercise, and they remain complicated to apply in practice.

The revised rules are now in place. In brief, the annual allowance afforded to a UK resident saving for a pension (as from April 2011) was reduced from £255,000 to £50,000. The relief is given at the taxpayer's highest marginal rate, so it could be at 50%. Where the individual exceeds the annual allowance, the excess is taxed at the highest marginal rate. Similarly, the lifetime allowance (the amount that could be accumulated in a pension pot) was reduced from £1.8m to £1.5m – and if the individual exceeds the limit, the excess is taxed at 62.5%, which is a serious deterrence.

This amounts to a double taxation, and at a very high rate, so it is no wonder that higher paid individuals have started to look at alternative methods of pension provision which aim to provide a pension over the roughly £70,000 pa that the conventional pension system can deliver.

This section explores options for employees who:

■ wish to enjoy pensions over the limit
■ wish to avoid the complexities of UK HMRC regulation
■ wish to move themselves or their pension arrangements overseas.

Qualifying Recognised Overseas Pension Scheme (QROPS)

A Qualifying Recognised Overseas Pension Scheme is one solution. Since 6 April 2006, HMRC has allowed individuals to transfer their UK pension funds to a QROPS. As a condition of being granted QROPS status, the overseas scheme must agree with HMRC to report any payments made, from the scheme to the member, for the first five complete and consecutive UK tax years of the member's overseas residency. This period is known as the 'QROPS Reporting Period', during which payments to the member must:

■ not exceed the allowable UK Government Actuary's Department (GAD) limits
■ not be made to the member before the retirement age of 55.

After the member has completed five consecutive years of non-residency, the reporting period falls away, providing significant advantages. A QROPS is useful to any individual with UK pension funds who is living or planning to live outside the UK, since it offers a number of ancillary benefits.

■ The requirement in UK schemes to purchase an annuity, while theoretically removed in 2011, still involves a number of constraints which do not apply to QROPS.
■ It may be possible to access benefits 100% tax-free, depending on the jurisdiction.
■ There are improved ways on how and when you can access your benefits.
■ There is much less constraint on choice of investments.
■ The assets can be held in the currency of your new home country, removing exchange rate risks.
■ There is a possibility of passing the balance of the pension fund to heirs upon death, free of inheritance tax or of any free-standing charge (currently 55%).
■ There may be additional tax benefits for those with funds approaching the lifetime allowance (£1.8m in tax year 2010/11, reducing to £1.5m).
■ Whilst some QROPS require you to be resident in the jurisdiction to which you wish to transfer your benefits, others have no such restriction, allowing you to choose a tax-friendly regime to suit your personal circumstances.
■ The strategy of using a QROPS in a third country can be useful for individuals in many circumstances. For example, the local regime of the migrant's new country may have similar restrictions to the UK when it comes to accessing benefits. Another example may be that the migrant's new country of residence has high levels of taxes or low levels of investment growth in their schemes.

As QROPS are available in such a wide range of jurisdictions, there is clearly a need for expert advice.

Qualifying Non-UK Pension Schemes (QNUPS)

In February 2010 QNUPS were introduced by HMRC and they are useful if you:

■ have already exceeded your QROPS period
■ wish to return to the UK.

The QNUP is based on the fact that certain types of Overseas Pension Schemes are now exempt from UK inheritance tax (IHT). The 'qualifying' part of the definition means that the Overseas Pension Scheme must meet HMRC's specific criteria for pension schemes that do not attract IHT. The schemes:

■ must be based overseas
■ need not be in countries that have signed double taxation agreements with the UK.

Prior to February 2010, there was some uncertainty about the IHT issue in relation to certain overseas pensions (which did not apply to UK registered pension). Unlike other IHT planning steps you may have been considering for other assets, when an asset is transferred into a QNUPS, the IHT protection is immediate. Accordingly, there is no need to wait for seven years after the transfer has been made to ensure immunity from IHT.

QNUPS also offer growth of retirement savings:

■ free from capital gains tax
■ with an opportunity to avoid currency uncertainty if you live abroad by fixing assets in an appropriate currency
■ with no annual or lifetime maximums, so they are suitable for high earners who receive substantial bonuses
■ with competitive fee structures which allow schemes to be available to those with a more modest pension pot
■ as long as the rules of the scheme allow, with benefits that can be taken from the age of 55
■ which can provide a loan from a QNUPS before age 55 in certain cases
■ in a scheme which can accept money that has not been earned in employment
■ with no lifetime contribution limit
■ with no maximum age at which you can make payments into the scheme
■ involving investments in residential property and assets that are traditionally associated with retirement funding
■ involving assets not normally linked to pensions, such as fine wines and antiques.

QNUPS are available to people who:

■ are UK resident
■ are resident elsewhere in the world but have retained their UK domicile status for IHT.

Domicile and residence are different concepts and need to be considered in their own rights. Whilst it is fairly straightforward to change your country of residence, changing your domicile is more difficult. Accordingly, even if you left the UK some time ago and consider yourself to have no more links to the place, you may still be domiciled there for the purposes of IHT. QNUPS are exempt from UK inheritance tax, so their major draw is that they enable savers to pass on their assets free from death duties to their heirs.

As with a UK private pension scheme, you cannot typically access benefits before the age of 55. However, it may be possible before that age to get a loan from your scheme. Depending on the rules of your QNUPS, the scheme may allow access to larger tax-free lump sums sooner than a UK pension.

ANNUITIES

The point of a pension scheme is to protect against the financial disaster of living too long. While the build-up of assets in a pension scheme is important, what is equally crucial is the spending of those assets. In the trade this is called 'decumulation', and for most of the population the best way to do that is through buying an annuity.

Buying an annuity is a respectable form of gambling contract entered into with an insurance company. You give them some money as a lump sum, and they pay it back to you in dribs and drabs until you die. They hope you die soon. You hope to live forever.

This is the reason why pension schemes are treated by the taxman differently from savings. Unlike most savings, while the taxman gives tax relief on the build-up, he gets his tax back in the end when the pension (or annuity) is paid. HMRC therefore try to make sure that the money is not used for other purposes – and especially not as a way of passing on money to the next generation.

The government made clear in its December 2006 Pre-Budget Report that it would act to prevent pension savings (their phrase, even though it is a contradiction in terms) from being used other than as intended. The purpose of tax-neutral (or 'privileged' as they call it) pension savings is to produce an income in retirement, and is not a mechanism to accumulate tax-relieved capital that can be passed down on death.[1]

Alternatives to annuities
Alternatively secured pensions (ASPs) were introduced some years ago (the government said, not exactly correctly, in order to meet the needs of those with principled religious objections to annuitisation). In order to ensure that annuities or decumulation systems matched the policy intention that tax-relieved pension saving should be used to secure an income in retirement, there are now changes to the old ASP rules. Conventional annuities operate on a risk-pooling basis to provide a secure income in retirement for scheme members.

However, when arrangements were introduced to pass down tax-neutral pension savings to the next generation, the government objected. So now any leftover ASP funds are subject to inheritance and pensions tax (at quite a high rate). In particular, the objections are related to circumstances where:

- a member dies with a scheme pension or annuity in payment
- arrangements have been put in place that seek to increase the rights of another person as a consequence of the death of a member (or a dependant), except in the form of authorised dependants' benefits
- the other person that benefits from the increase in rights was connected with the deceased.[2]

EARLY ACCESS TO PENSION SAVINGS
In the coalition agreement, the current government pledged to explore the potential to give you greater flexibility in accessing part of your private pension fund early. The idea was that if you could gain access to your fund earlier than your normal retirement date, perhaps for education or housing (as happens with some schemes in the USA), you might be more encouraged to put money into a pension scheme in the first place.[3]

At the time of writing no formal proposals have been made.

DISGUISED REMUNERATION
Draft legislation on 'disguised remuneration' and enacted in the Finance Act 2011 is intended to prevent the use of arrangements such as remuneration trusts and

employer-funded retirement benefit schemes (EFRBS) to provide benefits with tax advantages, particularly to high earners.

Outline of the rules

The legislation is deliberately drafted to start with a very wide net and then to exclude by specific provisions. It is very complicated, and normally you would be best advised not to try to understand it yourself, although for reference and completeness some of the details are set out below. For example, it incidentally catches approved share plans and registered pensions, so that specific wording has had to be devised to try to exclude them. There is no general exclusion for arrangements which are purely commercial and have no tax avoidance motive.

The legislation provides for an income tax charge (collected under PAYE) to arise broadly where there are arrangements, using a trust or other vehicle, which will result in a benefit to an employee as reward or recognition in connection with employment. This applies in the following circumstances.

- Where a sum of money or an asset, held by a trust or other intermediary, is earmarked (however informally) for use as part of the arrangements. The amount of money or value of the asset is treated as a payment of income by the employer to the employee for PAYE purposes. (The obligation to account for PAYE remains with the employer, even though the trust/intermediary takes the relevant step in the arrangements.)
- Where a trust/intermediary makes a payment, transfers an asset, takes a step whereby shares/securities or share options are acquired, and provides a loan or grants a lease to an employee, the amount paid or market value of the asset transferred or acquired will be treated as a payment of income by the employer to the employee for PAYE purposes. (In relation to a loan, the full capital value of the loan – not just the amount of the benefit – is subject to tax.)
- Where an asset is 'made available' to an employee by a trust/intermediary, for the employee to benefit from or to use as if his own, the value of the asset is treated as a payment of income by the employer to the employee for PAYE purposes.

Employee taxation

Provisions were introduced to apply National Insurance contributions to these amounts; there are also particular provisions in relation to tax residence and the remittance basis. Areas currently caught (but which may be likely to be ultimately excluded) include straightforward share plan arrangements, arrangements to defer cash bonuses for regulatory reasons, arrangements put in place to protect employees from the insolvency of their employer and some overseas pension plans.

New arrangements

For employers considering any new arrangement involving a trust (or any other third party holding shares or cash, or providing some benefit to staff), it is normally preferable to delay implementing such arrangements until the position is clearer. This includes all employers seeking arrangements to top up (over the £50,000 annual allowance from 6 April 2011) or work alongside registered pensions (including EFRBS).

Existing arrangements

For employers with an existing EFRBS or cash-funded employee benefit trust, it might be best to take no new steps (so no new sub-funds should be created or informal allocations and new loans made) until the position is clearer, including on the anti-forestalling rules. It seems that any new step under existing arrangements may be a 'relevant step' for the purposes of the new rules. This includes where steps have already been taken, such as loans being made or assets being made available.

Where existing arrangements fall foul of the new rules (as they are currently drafted), it may be possible to unwind them in certain circumstances, without adverse consequences, under the anti-forestalling rules. However, employers should not act in haste until the final form of the legislation becomes clearer.

Implications for share plans

In terms of employee share plans, there are a number of specific exemptions. However, the draft legislation is widely drafted and, as it currently stands, it would potentially affect certain commonly used share plan arrangements where an employee trust is involved. HMRC has indicated that this is not its intention and further published guidance is awaited.

Exemptions

There are specific exemptions for any step taken under an HMRC-approved share plan or an arrangement to grant certain options. There are also specific exemptions for the acquisition of forfeitable shares or the grant of share options. In addition, where an income tax charge arises on the lifting of restrictions (such as on 'vesting' of forfeitable shares), or on the exercise of a share option, the new rules will not apply.

Concerns

The legislation is widely drafted and, as it currently stands, appears to catch arrangements which do not have tax avoidance as part of their aim – in other words, it catches more than just 'disguised' remuneration and extends to other remuneration which is always intended to be fully taxable. At present, where a trust or other intermediary is involved in the operation of share plan arrangement, such as a long-term incentive plan (LTIP) or deferred bonus plan, it seems the new rules may potentially apply.

For example, companies commonly fund employee trusts to acquire shares in the market, and the trust agrees to use those shares to satisfy awards at maturity. In such circumstances, it is always intended that the employee will be subject to income tax and National Insurance contributions on maturity of the awards. However, the legislation as currently drafted may impose a tax charge on award holders when shares are acquired or 'earmarked' by the trust – notwithstanding that there may be conditions attached to any subsequent transfer of those shares by the trust to the award holder.

There seems to be little rationale for this; there could be an upfront tax charge when a share plan award (of whatever type, and whether or not subject to performance conditions) is made, just because the shares are to be sourced via an employee trust, in circumstances where there would not be such a charge if the company planned to satisfy the awards directly by issuing new shares.

This would often have an impact upon arrangements for the deferral of bonus awards into shares – and this seems at odds with corporate governance pressures to defer bonuses into shares and subject them to claw back conditions or 'performance adjustment'.

What should employers be doing?

If you use trusts in the operation and administration of your share plan arrangements, you need to be aware of these new rules and their potential impact. In straightforward situations where there is no tax avoidance intention, it is expected that HMRC will issue a relaxation.

EFRBS and unfunded EFRBS

Since funded pensions for the higher paid have been so comprehensively attacked, some pension scheme designers are examining the prospects for unfunded pension systems. The advantage of these is that they operate well across borders, they are much cheaper to operate (no need for PPF levies or compliance with regulatory requirements) and they offer employers substantial savings, as the funds that would normally be placed within a fund can be used internally with invariably higher rates of return.

The system is not new; in fact, it resembles the original pension schemes established at the end of the 19th century, and indeed funded pensions were rare until the Finance Act 1921 made them feasible.

The downside, of course, is that there is no guarantee that the company will still be around when the pension needs to be paid, so there is a risk that the individual will not be protected. There are solutions to this in other countries such as Germany and Sweden, and it is expected that UK solutions will be available shortly.

CHAPTER 6
GETTING ADVICE

It was Adam Smith who explained a couple hundred years ago that the reason why mankind has advanced so rapidly was the development of specialisation. It is infinitely more efficient for a person to specialise in making swords, ploughshares or, in Adam Smith's famous example, pins than for each of us to do everything ourselves. *The Good Life* might be fine as an old sitcom, but it would be foolish and possibly dangerous for each of us to grow our own food, weave our own clothing and build our own cars – even if we could.

Instead of this, we use experts. The difficulty for most of us, in practice, is not only finding the experts but knowing what kind of expert is needed, and then how to judge if they are actually any good.

In order to set up a decent pension scheme (or maybe a variety of schemes), it might be necessary to hire a variety of experts: firstly, to evaluate the position of the company and to implement the decisions ultimately taken, and then to keep a watching brief and manage the day to day administration. One way is to appoint a clerk of works, ie one person who will co-ordinate the project. Another way is to hold formal evaluations of each type of adviser.

The next sections explore the different types of advisers needed for the efficient establishment and running of schemes. Not all forms of advisers may be needed in all cases; sometimes you may have in-house expertise, and sometimes one adviser can combine two or more specialities.

The list of professions includes:

- accountant
- actuary
- administrator
- independent financial adviser (IFA)
- investment consultant
- investment manager
- lawyer
- pensions manager
- trustee.

There is now an increasing number of specialist or pensions-specific qualifications for some of these specialisations.

ACCOUNTANTS

The accounting standards introduced over the last 20 years relating to company pension plans have been fiercely debated, with some arguing that they have introduced transparency and others suggesting that, on the contrary, they have been misleading. What is certain is that, instead of simply being descriptive, they have altered behaviour and made employer-sponsors withdraw the provision of defined benefit arrangements. This has happened because the standards of disclosure of pension liabilities in company accounts have obliged companies to include pension liabilities and assets in their own balance sheet (rather than being relegated to a note in the accounts) and because of the requirement to 'mark to market', ie take a snapshot valuation of the assets and liabilities at the year end, rather than smoothing them over the roughly 60 years half-life of a pension plan. This has introduced astonishing volatility into company accounts, making the life of the finance director hard; it has also made it more difficult to raise finance and avoid breaching banking covenants, and has driven employers to force trustees to invest in what would normally be an inappropriate portfolio. Now the accounting profession looks set to fix the problem, or at least improve the situation, but it may be too late to save most defined benefit pension schemes.

Company accounts

One of the major reasons for the decline of defined benefit schemes has been the relatively recent requirement that the surpluses and deficits of the pension funds be placed in the balance sheet of the company. The volatility of the balance sheet, which is a consequence of the rise and fall in the market value of the pension scheme investments, has made managing the finances of the company much more difficult and in some cases virtually impossible. Secondly, the way in which the liabilities of the pension fund are valued must be linked to the value of AA-rated corporate bonds, which also fluctuate according to prevailing interest rates.

The National Association of Pension Funds has been running a long-standing campaign against the absurdity of the accounting rules, but the unaccountable accounting bodies have so far resisted the pressure, being committed to a pure if unworkable view of accounting. As another consequence, pension funds themselves have been pressured into another investing more in bonds (which are less volatile and give a lower rate of return) and less in equities (which are more volatile and generally give a higher return) so that the cost of providing defined benefit pensions has risen considerably and in many cases became unaffordable.

Liabilities

The cash contribution and pension expense calculations are both often referred to as the cost of a pension plan – one as a cash outlay and the other as a reduction (or increase) in company earnings. Both are calculated using similar principles, although the rules for calculation are very different. Pension plan formulas are generally designed to tie the participants' benefits at retirement to their **salary** and/or **service** with the employer. Each employer chooses how to reflect compensation and service based on their individual business needs and the needs of their workforce. Pensions are sometimes referred to as a form of **deferred salary**; members exchange income now for pensions tomorrow.

Both the pension funding rules and pension accounting rules require that the cost of that deferred compensation be recognised as it is earned. An actuary takes the plan's pension formula and determines how to reflect the cost of the plan over each participant's working lifetime. There are three basic principles used.

1. Active participants earn new benefits each year. Actuaries call that the **normal cost**. The normal cost is always reflected in the cash and accounting cost of the plan.
2. Actuaries must consider the difference between the **actuarial liability**, which is the value of benefits already earned, and the assets. An unfunded liability, when the actuarial liability exceeds the assets, increases the cost. An asset surplus, when the actuarial liability is less than the assets, decreases the cost.

3. Actuaries set **assumptions** to measure the normal cost and the actuarial liability. Measuring assets is relatively easy, because the markets set a value on the equity and bond investments held in the pension trust. There is no (general) market for pension liabilities. Actuaries and plan sponsors are given very specific, and different, guidance by HMRC, the Pension Protection Fund, the Pensions Regulator, the actuarial standards bodies and several accounting standards bodies on how those assumptions are chosen, who chooses them and what conditions they must reflect.

Set out below are some notes on:

■ how assumptions are usually selected
■ how the actuarial liabilities are typically calculated
■ how funding rules use the actuarial liabilities to determine cash contributions
■ how accounting rules use the actuarial valuations to determine pension expense.

ACTUARIES

For defined benefit schemes, the advice of an actuary is essential (and indeed required by law). It is generally considered that the advice of an actuary in relation to the management of a defined contribution scheme is much less necessary and in some cases pointless.

The actuary will help to guide you (and the board and the trustees) through the expected costs of providing a defined benefit – and what the benefits might be of delivering fixed contributions. He or she can also advise on investments and maybe help select other advisers.

Much depends on the assumptions made by the actuary in performing their calculations, some of which can be agreed with you, and some of which they are constrained by their regulators in agreeing.

Actuarial assumptions

Actuaries have to make assumptions on a wide range of factors, about all of which they are bound to be wrong. These might include future rates of tax, inflation, interest rates, or mortality or investment return. Pension benefits are paid far out into the future, but how and when they'll be paid is uncertain.

■ Someone retiring at 70 expects payments for the rest of their (and perhaps their spouse's) lifetime; with some exceptions they (and you) will not know how long they will live or how long their spouse might survive them.
■ Someone working for your company today will, each year they work, earn additional benefits, and when they retire they will receive payments for the rest of their lifetime. It is unlikely either you or them will know how long they will work for the company or stay in the scheme.
■ Nobody will know for certain how their pay might increase, or when exactly they might retire and start to draw benefits (or become sick and draw benefits earlier than expected), or how long they and their spouse will live in retirement.

Both pension funding and accounting require assumptions to be made about the future. These are called **actuarial assumptions** and they, along with current plan participant data and the benefit formula described in the pension plan, are used to project future benefits. Those assumptions are controlled, especially in defined benefit schemes:

- for pension funding issues, by the rules of the scheme and the trustees, and the guidance notes issued by the actuary's regulator
- for pension accounting issues, by the company acting on the advice of the actuary. Actuarial assumptions for pension accounting are also generally reviewed and approved by the company's external auditors in their general auditing of a company's financial statements – much to the disgust of the actuary.

There are two primary types of assumptions selected:

- **economic assumptions**, which might deal with current interest rates, salary increases, inflation and investment markets, and how market forces might affect the cost of the plan
- **demographic assumptions** about the particular membership of the scheme, the lifestyle behaviour of its members and life expectancy.

There are several key actuarial assumptions which can transform the expected costs and benefits of any particular plan, and they include the following.

Interest rate

For pension funding, an assumption on prevailing interest rates is used to discount future benefits to determine plan liabilities, and it involves a reasonable expectation of the future rate of return on the pension plan's assets. It is sometimes called the **valuation interest rate**. Different plans will have different valuation interest rates, reflecting different investment strategies and varying opinions of future rates of return. It is often used as a long-term reflection of plan assets and liabilities.

Discount rate

This is the interest rate as used in pension accounting, and it normally reflects either the market rates currently used to pay the benefits, or the rates of return expected on high quality fixed income securities at a particular date.

Also involved in the calculations are the assumptions described below.

- **Salary assumptions**, which have to take into account the nature of the company and the workforce, and consider expected inflation, productivity, seniority, promotion and other factors that affect wages or salaries.
- **Inflation assumptions**, which include any HMRC limitations on benefits, and whether the index used to protect benefits is the Consumer Price Index (CPI) or the Retail Price Index (RPI).
- **Demographic assumptions**, which include whether the workforce has a higher percentage of smokers (or others with a lower than normal life expectancy) or higher paid people (who tend to have a longer than normal life expectancy). Actuaries use rates (probabilities) to model the uncertainty of participant behaviour. For example, since some participants will retire early – some will retire at 65 and some will work to age 70 – an actuary might assume that each individual has some probability of retiring early, at 65. Sometimes assumptions will be the same for many plans.

Typical demographic assumptions include:

- **withdrawal or termination assumptions:** how long will participants continue to work for this employer?
- **mortality assumptions:** how long will people live?
- **retirement assumptions:** when will participants retire and begin receiving benefits?

■ **disability assumptions:** will participants become disabled and no longer be able to work?

A pension plan's liabilities can be calculated in a variety of different ways, but in each case the following is true.

■ The actuary calculates the expected future pension payments for each participant in the plan, using the company's participant data and plan provisions. These future benefit payments consider the individual's compensation and service history, and when that individual might be expected to die, quit, become disabled or retire.
■ Each future payment is discounted from the date of payment to the present using the actuarial assumptions. The discounted rate is the **present value of future benefits** and represents the present value of all benefits expected to be paid from the plan to current plan participants.
■ If assumptions were correct (which they never are), you could theoretically set aside the predicted amount of money in a scheme today, and it would cover payments from the plan, including those for service not yet rendered. The amount includes future service the participant is expected to earn and future pay increases.

However, the tax rules do not allow you to put the cost of unearned future service in your balance sheet; it would be equivalent to recognising a cost of remuneration before it is actually paid. In practice, the actuaries often split the liabilities (in defined benefit schemes) into three elements.

1. **Technical liabilities:** the portion of the liability that is attributed to your employees' past service. There are different methods used to calculate the liability, but it always simply reflects past service. Sometimes the technical liabilities reflect expected future pay increases, because many pension plans are designed so that the retirement benefit is based on the pay at retirement. In order to allow you to recognise the cost of the scheme gradually over the member's lifetime, the actuary considers the portion of the future benefit due to past service to already include expected future pay increases.
2. **Annual costs:** the element of the liabilities that is attributed to the current year of service. This is the current value of the remuneration that is being deferred for the year; it may reflect expected future pay increases.
3. **Future costs:** the element of the liabilities that is attributed to future years of service; it covers remuneration that has not yet been earned. This number is usually not disclosed.

ADMINISTRATORS

You almost certainly do not want to do your own administration (ie keep all the records, perform all the calculations and carry out the compliance requirements), unless you run a very large company. The usual plan is to outsource it either to the pension provider (such as the insurance company) or to a specialist administrator. Administrators come in many varieties – small, specialist and large – and some of them write their own software, which these days needs to be astonishingly complex.

Before you outsource, you need to think about what you want them to do, and in theory your first task is to write a job specification. That is easier said than done, since it is improbable you are familiar with, for example, all the reporting requirements. You will often be guided by a supplier, and there is also a semi-trade body which keeps an eye on administrators, attempts to set standards and organises training: the Pensions Administration Standards Association (PASA; see www.pasa-uk.com).

PASA offers advice on a wide set of issues, including a General Statement of Administration Standards (GSAS). The GSAS was developed following consultation with the pensions industry so that customers and their administrators could have a statement of the standards by which they were expected to conduct business. In the meantime, the Pensions Regulator has also issued guidance on administration standards, especially in relation to defined contribution systems.[1]

The GSAS standard applies to the administration of trust-based occupational pension schemes and their public sector equivalents (ie not contract-based schemes, run mostly by insurance companies) or personal pensions, and it focuses on the key relationship between trustees (or their equivalent) and administrators. You could also use it as a checklist for other pension service suppliers. Several administration service providers have now indicated that they propose to adhere to the statement.

There is also a statement of principles and a checklist. The principles underpin the standard but do not form part of a detailed job specification; they are mostly aspirational, but they do set out eight objectives for an employer-sponsor.

1. Have clear, well-understood objectives for the scheme and for the administration service.
2. Ensure open, honest and comprehensive communication between trustees and administrators, and vice versa.
3. Use a range of appropriate measures to ensure a full understanding of the service provided.
4. Monitor the quality of the data held and supplied to the administrators.
5. Make sure that all roles and responsibilities are clear and fully understood.
6. Consider the views of the members as to the quality of the service offered and the service that they require.
7. Ensure regular reporting of appropriate measures and events to enhance the understanding of the service.
8. Agree on service development plans to either maintain the level of service or to improve it in the future.

INDEPENDENT FINANCIAL ADVISERS (IFA)

If you decide to organise a group personal pension plan (see Chapter 5) or offer a special deal to members of a defined pension plan to take money in exchange for leaving the scheme, you may need to find an independent financial adviser (IFA) to advise members or potential members to either join a personal scheme or transfer rights from a defined benefit scheme under an incentive programme.

The reason is that while an occupational scheme is not regarded as a 'financial product' under the Financial Services and Markets Act 2000, a personal pension is – don't ask why. Although there is no legal requirement for a company to advise a member on whether he or she should decide to leave an occupational scheme (and whether to take a transfer with them), the Pensions Regulator has threatened schemes and their sponsor companies unless they do arrange for employee members to take advice before they lose their rights under a scheme.

Some advisers suggest that there may be administrative and other savings in persuading members to leave a DB plan – and indeed there may be. The question to ask is whether the costs of providing advice, the likelihood of only a small percentage of members taking the option, and the costs of an enhancement to transfer values are worth the exercise. That is not always so clear (although the finance director may like the exercise because it allows him or her to dress the balance sheet), and it is not always clear whether the company is getting value for money. When organising a buy-out of members' rights, there are guides you can consult issued by the Pensions Regulator.[2]

Finding an IFA

Many larger firms of consultants have facilities which can arrange IFA advice around the country if your employee members are spread far apart. The alternative is to choose a local firm who can come in and run 'surgeries' – and issue letters to members which are intended to protect your interests as much as those of your employees. You do not want members/employees coming back with complaints in years to come that in hindsight they took the wrong decision – or, even worse, issuing court proceedings or complaining that you have committed a criminal act by advising on financial matters without authorisation.

Often the best way to find a good IFA is by personal recommendation; in any event, check with the Financial Services Authority that the adviser is authorised (FSA: 020 7066 5256; www.fsa.gov.uk/fsaregister/). Alternatively, IFA Promotion allows you to specify whether you would prefer commission- or fee-based advisers (although soon enough all advisers will be fee-based); you can contact them on 0800 085 3250 (www.unbiased. co.uk). There are other organisations that offer specialist fee-based IFAs, including the Institute of Financial Planning (0117 945 2470; www.financialplanning.org.uk).

If you are planning a campaign to try to get members of your old defined benefit scheme to take their rights elsewhere (for example, by offering them enhanced transfer values) you will almost certainly need to retain an IFA to give the employees some independent advice.

INVESTMENT CONSULTANTS

Investment consultants include a wide range of practitioners, from the one-man advice house (not to be sneezed at; some of the finest and most experienced advisers are one-man bands) to the very large consultancies (including Towers Watson, Mercers, Aon Hewitt) and the in-betweeners (such as Lane Clark Peacock, Punter Southall or Barnett Waddingham). They will help you and the trustees, if any, to ensure that you are diversified and that you are in appropriate investments, bearing in mind:

■ the risks
■ the needs of the members.

Remember, however, that even the best ones are prisoners of the system. Due to accounting requirements and the imprecations of the regulators and their own supervisors, they will tend to go for safer investments. That reduces their own risks, but it means that either the contributions need to go up or the benefits will be lower than they would otherwise be.

Occupational schemes, by law, are required to take investment advice from someone who is regarded as appropriate. The law, however, does not require the adviser to be qualified, or even any good.

INVESTMENT MANAGERS

The law also stops you making day-to-day investment decisions on behalf of others, so you are going to need an investment manager to manage the money, which will probably grow rather quicker in amount than you expected. Finding an investment manager is not hard; the biggest problem is fighting them off once they have heard you are in the market. Sometimes your provider will bundle the investment element into the whole package; sometimes you will have to find your own, or a selection of them to perform different tasks.

You can use your investment or actuarial consultant to produce a shortlist of candidates, and then select the ones you like the most or dislike the least. It is virtually impossible to predict how any of them will perform in the future, and some pension funds select 'index-trackers' which, for a very low fee, do not pretend to have any expertise at all but simply buy shares in the stock market proportionate to their size in the stock market.

Paying an investment manager according to results is probably the best way but, in practice, it is hard to do, since the measuring rods can always be adjusted to suit the manager.

LAWYERS

Lawyers who know how to set up pension arrangements are rare but possible to find, especially if your company is close to a major metropolis. There are now around 1,000 members of the Association of Pension Lawyers (APL), almost all of whom work full time on pensions issues, and many of whom specialise even further within the field. The APL (www.apl.org.uk) will *in extremis* find a lawyer for you.

Whilst there is no shortage of lawyers, there are some main questions which need to be addressed before hiring one.

- What do you want them to do? Lawyers can draft the documents, advise you on how to keep out of the courts, ensure the scheme enjoys the tax neutrality of pension funds and make sure that the members do not contribute more than the tax authorities say they should.
- How do you want to pay them? Lawyers can charge either by the hour or with a fixed fee. Modern practice is to move towards fixed fees where possible.
- How do you want them to interact with your other advisers? Lawyers, like other advisers, can work in a vacuum or preferably in concert with the other advisers. But if there is a concert there needs to be a conductor – and ideally it should be you. It saves money and time.

PENSIONS MANAGERS

If your scheme is fairly large, it might be sensible to employ a pensions manager; it might be useful to use a part-timer if the scheme is modest or a full-time manager for a larger plan. Pension scheme managers can create substantial savings by negotiating fees and making sure that contractors perform their roles; they can act as trustee secretaries and make reports to management. The Pensions Management Institute runs a range of training programmes and qualifications (www.pensions-pmi.org.uk); it also publishes a useful magazine and arranges good-value seminars and lectures.

TRUSTEES

The issue of whether the scheme should be trust-based or contract-based was explored earlier in Chapter 4, if you decide to have a trust-based scheme, you will need to find trustees for the scheme.

The law says that at least a third of the trustees should be nominated by members of the scheme – unless the members fail to do so. That shouldn't be a problem for you; all trustees have an obligation to put their own interests after the interests of the members of the scheme.

There are urban myths about being a trustee; here are some examples.

- It is very risky: the scheme should contain indemnities from both the scheme and the company, and arrange for insurance and exemption from liability. *The risks of being a trustee are manageable and low*.
- It involves substantial amounts of work: most of the work of running a scheme should be carried out by the experts, the administrators and managers. *Being a trustee is a non-executive role and should only take a modest amount of time if run properly*.
- The conflicts of interest make it inadvisable for company directors, and especially finance directors, to be a trustee: schemes are designed to cope with conflicts and *there is nothing wrong with conflicts, provided they are disclosed and managed sensibly*.

So you should think very positively about being a trustee (a guide to trusteeship is published elsewhere).[3]

CHAPTER 7
RISKS

In a well-known law case in the US in 2010, it was made clear that even in the best-run pension arrangements, accidents happen.[1] When things go wrong in pension cases, it can prove expensive. A small drafting error in a US telecoms company pension plan could have cost around $1.5bn, for example. There are other things that can go wrong; Murphy's Law has a special schedule for pension arrangements.

There is however, little to be frightened of if things go wrong; indeed, the law in particular accepts that, from time to time, that will be the case, and it is in the nature of business itself that there are risks: tax changes, currency changes, regulatory changes, counterparty failures, health and safety accidents, and many others. Most businesses cope pretty well with such risks.

This chapter explains how things can go wrong in pensions, and what to do to try to limit the exposure of the individuals and companies involved with pension arrangements. With a little common sense, and a little care, most if not all of these risks can be reasonably well managed.

The risks include:

■ financial risks:

  ☐ the employer's covenant
  ☐ investments

■ regulatory and legislative risks:

  ☐ the Pensions Regulator (TPR)
  ☐ Pension Protection Fund (PPF)

■ trustee risks:

  ☐ breach of trust.

There are several ways in which the risks can be managed, including:

■ insurance
■ exemption clauses
■ statutory exemptions
■ employer's indemnities
■ scheme indemnities
■ investment management.

FINANCIAL RISKS

The 'employer covenant'

One of the first risks to manage is that of the sponsor. If you fall on hard times, you may struggle to make the contributions to a defined contribution plan – and struggle even more to make up any deficits in respect of past obligations to a defined benefit plan.

The promise to pay contributions to a pension plan is at present described as 'the employer covenant', and the strength of the covenant is now considered to be a major concern both for employers and trustees – as well as for members. Covenant is just a fancy word for 'promise' and when most of these schemes were set up, few employers made a promise; they simply undertook to do their best if they could.

The Pensions Regulator describes the covenant as an 'employer's legal obligation to fund the pension scheme now and in the future', remarking that 'the strength of it depends upon the robustness of the legal agreements in place and the likelihood that the employer can meet them'. Nowadays the covenant includes:

- statutory obligations
- obligations to make payments under a payment schedule put in place for a scheme
- any other unsecured promises to provide future support to the scheme.

The Regulator has published guidance on monitoring employer support, and setting out standard practice which the Regulator expects trustees to follow in assessing, monitoring and taking action in relation to the employer's covenant.[2] Whether the guidance strikes the right balance between specifying a process for monitoring covenant and imposing disproportionate or unnecessary costs on trustees/employers is a matter which is unsettled. The guidance represents a significant change in approach and an additional burden of responsibility for the majority of trustees. The guidance, enforceable almost as law, suggests that 'monitoring the covenant can be as important as monitoring investment performance', although few trustees give equal weighting to the issues – and possibly rightly so.

Investment risks

Investments are a by-product of a pension plan; the point of a plan is to provide benefits, and many plans (especially in the public sector but also private plans) have no assets at all. In the public sector, for example, the civil service and other pension plans have no investments because the benefits are paid out of taxation. In the private sector, UURBS (unfunded unregistered retirement benefit schemes) are less attractive than they used to be, both because of additional tax obligations and because, if the company goes bust, the plan is only an ordinary creditor so the members will only recover a percentage of their expectations. There is no need to have investments in order to have a pension plan, however. The reason for the assets in the private sector is to ensure that there is something to pay the benefits if the employer's covenant fails.

The management of the investments is important. It is illegal in most cases for the trustees to manage the investments themselves,[3] so investment managers are appointed. Trustees' (and employers') risks are managed by appointing investment managers on the advice of investment consultants (who might be the actuaries), adopting an investment plan which takes into account the particular risks of the scheme. For example, if a plan is closed to new members, and the ratio of older members to newer members is high, it is conventional wisdom to have more bonds than equities in the investment portfolio, so that the risks of the investment falling in value are reduced, and the cash flow to the plan can be assured, so that the money is available to pay benefits.

LDI (liability driven investment)

LDI is a fancy term for sensible investing according to the liabilities of the plan. In more recent times, LDI has been falling into disrepute because, although in theory the investment models look attractive and the risks of market variations are much reduced, there are other risks. In particular there is a risk that when the bond matures (ie the lender pays back the money), the interest rate at which the new money can be invested is lower (or higher) than before, so that in fact the value of the fund as a whole is much affected – and the problem is made worse if there is inflation, because the new interest rates may be lower than inflation rates.

Many investment advisers offer LDI as a solution to the investing problem; but adopting a pure LDI solution disregards other risks – and inflates the price of protection.

In particular, employers may wish the pension fund (which has a legal duty to consult employers before agreeing its investment policy) to invest in more risky investments, which should have a targeted higher return, to reduce the costs of its contributions. If the bet does not pay off in time, however, and the employer fails before the investment returns emerge, it may make the fund insolvent so that it is forced to enter the Pension Protection Fund. The Pensions Regulator, which is charged with the duty of ensuring that as few pension funds as possible go into the PPF, is encouraging pension funds to avoid higher risk investment strategies, although no one, least of all actuaries or regulators, is quite certain what investments in the current circumstances are more or less risky.[4]

COMPLIANCE RISKS

The Pensions Regulator and risk management

The Pensions Regulator has issued lengthy and prescriptive guidance on risk management, much of which is in practice not achievable. Its bottom line is that it is keen to see that both trustees and employers are proactive in ensuring that there is adequate security for the scheme. The recommendations set out in the guidance include the following.

- **Devise a trustee framework** for review. Trustees should build a framework for assessing and reviewing the employer covenant, including regular monitoring. The monitoring plans will vary from scheme to scheme, but it is good practice to include key business performance measures and a plan of action in the event that those performance measures are not met. Such plans could include calling on contingent assets or looking for increased funding. In practice, a framework for a smaller scheme might be quite short.
- **Prepare a full covenant review** once every three years. A full review of the employer's covenant should be completed before each scheme's specific funding valuation, ie usually once every three years. Such a review for smaller schemes might simply involve a chat with the firm's accountant; for larger schemes or companies, there might be a need to commission a specialist to prepare a formal review.
- **Monitor the covenant briefly every year.** It will usually be appropriate to review the covenant annually once the financial results and annual plans of the sponsoring employer are known.
- **Prepare a meeting agenda.** Most trustees should have a standing item on their meeting agendas to discuss the sponsoring employer's covenant, without obsessing about it. Trustees have a system for checking whether there have been any company events since their previous meeting (and that there are no events planned in advance of the next meeting) which may affect the strength of the covenant. Usually, this is done by asking the chief executive or finance director to complete a *pro forma* certifying there are no changes – or if there are, what they are and how they might affect the ability of the company to support the scheme.

- **Have a Plan B if the covenant deteriorates.** If the covenant remains strong or consistent, trustees can simply note the position at each trustee meeting; but if the company hits bad times, trustees may need to have some ideas about what to do. This is of course a counsel of perfection. In practice, if the company is doing well, the trustees do not need to ensure additional financial support for the plan – and if the company is doing badly it is often in no position to make additional provision, perhaps by way of higher contributions or additional security.
- **Be prepared to revise the monitoring plan.** Trustees should be prepared to think laterally and outside the approved plan, where necessary. They could, for example, bring forward the next actuarial valuation, or adjust the valuation assumptions in view of the weak covenant, or realign the investment portfolio in line with the weaker covenant. In practice, the cost of doing so may exceed the benefit, and the Regulator's standing invitation to discuss matters does not always result in a practical outcome.
- **Employers and trustees should work together.** Before the current regulatory regime, trustees and employers commonly worked towards a single objective. The Regulator's guidance implores the trustees to continue this approach; even though at the same time the Regulator expects trustees to adopt a confrontational and commercial attitude when negotiating terms with the employer. It is sensible in practice for trustees to sign a confidentiality agreement with the employer to allow commercial information to be released to them without prejudicing the commercial interests of the company. Trustees should take advice on how to manage sensitive information, given simply for the purpose of understanding whether and, if yes, how much the company can afford by way of contributions or deficit reduction.
- **Query the advice.** Trustees are expected to ask probing questions and consider whether and when professional advice is appropriate. Trustees should ask these questions to enable them to understand the employer covenant, and they should assess whether they have individuals (without a conflict of interest) on the trustee board with adequate expertise to assess the covenant or whether they need to employ professional covenant assessors. The type of skills required include the ability to understand the employer's group structure and legal obligations between members of the group, and having the necessary experience to analyse and understand the information that predicts future change to company performance.
- **Act proportionately.** Trustees and employers should act proportionately in approaching covenant assessment and monitoring. Nothing in the guidance is intended to produce cost to the scheme that is disproportionate to the related benefit.

The guidance is simply that – not law or prescription. Much of it is impractical or aspirational, rather than implementable (and designed to cover the Regulator's back) so it needs to be taken with a pinch of salt; but it might be useful as a reminder of some of the options available.

Pension Protection Fund (PPF)
The Pension Protection Fund is an imperfect animal: it protects only defined benefit schemes, and then only when the employer becomes insolvent in certain ways.

There are two main risks for trustees and employers. The first is that the scheme is managed in such a way that the PPF cover fails, for example because at some earlier stage a deal was made between the employer and trustees to reduce the employer's debt in exchange for a share of the company, so that the PPF may repudiate any claim. The second risk is the levy rising to unmanageable proportions.

The Pension Protection Fund was set up in April 2005, to protect members of eligible defined benefit and hybrid pension schemes when the sponsoring employer goes bust and the scheme cannot afford to pay members' benefits (at PPF levels of compensation – around a maximum of £30,000 and no more than 90% of benefits). It excludes benefits from defined contribution schemes. There are major public policy issues with the PPF, which are listed below.

- It raises funds from solvent employers to support benefits promised by insolvent employers.
- It raises funds on a diminishing tax base to pay for benefits from an expanding number of insolvent funds.
- It does not protect certain defined benefit schemes which have been reconstructed in a certain way, so members may get a shock when they realise that, although they thought they were protected, they were not.

The PPF was established as a public corporation, nominally independent from government (although closely controlled by the DWP in practice) under the Pensions Act 2004.

Pension protection levy

The pensions movement (more accurately, the employers sponsoring such schemes) pays an annual levy charged on schemes eligible for PPF protection (ie most defined benefit schemes); the PPF also receives income and assets from:

- recoveries of money and other assets from insolvent employers of schemes that it takes on
- taking on the assets of schemes that transfer to it
- returns on the investments acquired.

Dun & Bradstreet (D&B)

Dun & Bradstreet is the business information supplier that provides the PPF with 'Failure Scores' and associated probabilities of your insolvency. You can find out more about your Failure Score and probability of insolvency in a PPF booklet, but you need to take specialist advice about how to re-arrange your company affairs so as to reduce your levy. Simple things (like clearing county court judgments) and complex things (like using contingent assets) can save you millions.

The Pensions Regulator

The Pensions Regulator – originally intended to help protect scheme members – now also tries to reduce liabilities on the PPF. Therefore, it suffers a profound conflict of interest and sometimes struggles to manage that conflict. On the whole, it does what it can to reduce claims against the PPF, by ensuring schemes are adequately funded and preventing trustees from re-arranging benefits so as to maintain a claim against the PPF.

Calculation of pension protection levy

The levy is divided into two parts:

1. **scheme-based levy** paid by *all* schemes according to their PPF liabilities
2. **risk-based levy** calculated according to the funding level of your scheme and the probability of your insolvency.

Other levies

You have to pay some other levies as well:

- an administration levy, which covers the cost of running the PPF
- a general levy (to pay for the Regulator's own costs, which have gone up nearly three times from the original estimates and budgets)
- a fraud compensation levy. The fraud levy provides funds to a Fraud Compensation Fund (administered by the PPF, but separate from it) which meets claims or potential claims as a result of losses to schemes that are attributable to dishonesty.

You have to pay the levy the moment you get the invoice, and the PPF sends in the bailiffs if they do not receive payment within 28 days of the invoice date. Not all your defined benefit pension schemes have to pay the levies, and if you think you should not have to, you should call the 'PPF Stakeholder Support Team'.[5]

Interest on late payments
The PPF charges interest on levy payments which are not received within the 28-day time limit at 5% over base rate, which might be regarded as penal. There are cases where the interest is not charged (at the discretion of the PPF, subject to an appeal process). Information about the scheme is required to be entered into the PPF/TPR database (known as Exchange), especially if there are any changes or if the scheme is winding up.

Each year a scaling factor (1.64 in 2010/11) is applied to the levy. The levy is calculated using the scheme return and valuation information that was submitted to the Regulator on or before 5pm on 31 March of the year before. It takes into account contingent assets and deficit-reduction contributions that were correctly certified to meet the requirements of the 2010/11 determination by the 2010/11 deadlines when calculating your levy.

There are special rules dealing with the position of schemes which received a full transfer of assets and liabilities from another scheme before 1 April and did not notify the PPF of the transfer by the deadline of 5pm on 30 June. There are also special rules to deal with partial block transfers.

The funding level above which a scheme's underfunding risk is calculated as a fixed percentage of liabilities is 120%, and the funding level at which no risk-based levy is payable is 140%.

Levy calculation
In practice it is not possible to challenge the calculations made by the PPF in relation to the levy without expert help. The calculations involve:

- a section 179 valuation (ie the amount needed to pay PPF level benefits if the scheme goes into the PPF) information from your annual scheme return, submitted via the Regulator's Exchange system, and subsequent updates made on or before 5pm on 31 March of the year before
- the Failure Score, Risk Indicator or equivalent for each scheme-sponsoring employer as it stood at 5pm on 31 March 2009, provided by D&B
- where there is a Type A contingent asset, the Failure Score, risk indicator or equivalent for each guarantor as it stood at 5pm on 31 March 2009, provided by D&B
- any valid contingent assets certified for 2010/11 on or before 5pm on 31 March 2010
- any relevant deficit-reduction contributions certified on or before 5pm on 9 April 2010

■ any full block transfers, where the required information has been provided to the PPF on Exchange on or before 5pm on 30 June 2010

■ any partial block transfers that have taken place up to and including 31 March 2009, which were certified by 5pm on 30 June 2009.

The full technical specification is published by the PPF on its website (www.pension protectionfund.org.uk); it is not a pretty sight.

Failure Scores
You will almost certainly have an individual Failure Score on a 1–100 point scale, where 1 represents the businesses with the highest probability of insolvency and 100 the lowest. Each Failure Score has an associated probability of insolvency, with a factor used in the levy calculation. Any two UK businesses with the same score will also have the same probability of failure.

If you are based outside the UK
D&B assigns probabilities of insolvency to overseas Failure Scores, which bring such Failure Scores into alignment with the UK system; this involves the use of a table which converts the 100 overseas Failure Scores into a UK equivalent. D&B's international branches or associates provide a Failure Score and probability of insolvency even if you are based outside the UK. If there is in fact no Failure Score, D&B provide a 'Risk Indicator', which also corresponds to a probability of insolvency.

Industry average probabilities of insolvency
In some cases D&B cannot provide you a Failure Score or Risk Indicator, so the PPF uses an industry-average probability of insolvency to calculate the risk-based levy. This is calculated as the median probability of insolvency of all UK sponsoring employers of defined benefit schemes sharing the same 1972 Standard Industry Classification code that applies to you.

Tricks to reduce the levy
You can arrange to reduce the levy by improving the rating of your company (and reducing the risk of a call on the PPF) by:

■ using contingent assets such as parent or group company guarantees, security over cash, UK real estate and securities or letters of credit and bank guarantees
■ making deficit-reduction contributions
■ restructuring the corporate structure to appoint a stronger company as the principal employer.

Using contingent assets is complex, and it requires filling in special forms and fine-judging the PPF rules; this is a job for experts, but a rather bureaucratic and impenetrable guide is available on the PPF website.

Formal reviews
Appealing an invoice is not easy; the rules seem to be in breach of the natural principles of justice, but no one has challenged them yet. The formal review process does not cover your D&B Failure Score, which is not determined by the PPF, but by D&B. You normally have to pay interest on a levy invoice on which you have sought a review. If you are uncomfortable with the result of your formal review, you can appeal to the PPF's Reconsideration Committee and, if you are not satisfied with the reconsideration decision, to the Pension Protection Fund Ombudsman.

If the PPF finds you have overpaid the levy, they will eventually issue a credit note without interest. It seems a rather unfair system.

The invoice

If the PPF thinks you should pay some money (and it will calculate this from the annual return you will have sent to the Pensions Regulator), it will send you an annual invoice. The invoice sets out the amount of pension protection levy it thinks you should pay. It is not improbable that the invoice will be wrong, so it is critical that you, or someone who knows how the charging system works, checks that invoice.

Astonishingly, the PPF feels no obligation to provide a receipt; so, if and when you do pay the invoice, you really should check that the payment has been made and reconcile the payment with the bank statements. Double payment of levy invoices is not uncommon and can be expensive.

TRUSTEE PROTECTION

One way of controlling risks for employers and trustees is to ensure that there is proper protection for everyone, especially where defined benefit arrangements are concerned. There are several ways to manage protection, including:

- relying on advice from experts
- trustee exemption clauses
- incorporation
- insurance
- exemption clauses
- indemnity clauses.

Trustee exemption clauses

Trustee exemption clauses are a very sensible clause to put into the document which sets up the pension plan. Some people (eg the former Pensions Ombudsman) have suggested that such clauses were unfair and allowed trustees to be cavalier in protecting the interests of members. It is noticeable, however, that the Pensions Ombudsman himself cannot be sued for his (then quite frequent) mistakes, as he was given statutory immunity.

The Law Commission looked at whether such clauses were fair and reasonable, and the government in September 2010[6] accepted its relaxed approach to such clauses (ie that they should not be outlawed). The Law Commission had suggested that the government should promote a model rule of practice relating to the inclusion in trust documents of clauses limiting the liability of trustees. So far, it is not clear how soon this will be done; in the meantime, you should not rely on the government giving you the protection you need, but you ought to follow the practice set out on pages 58–59. It does not matter whether you are paid as a trustee or not (and normally, if you are employed by the company, you will not receive anything extra for your trusteeship); the liabilities are the same.

Incorporation

If the scheme is 'contract-based', ie it is simply a contract with, for example, an insurance company, there are usually no trustees – and no trustee potential liability. However, in practice the trend is towards trust-based arrangements, since they allow for better governance and provide someone to keep an eye on things and protect members' interests. Trustees can either be individuals or, increasingly these days, a director of a trust company. A trust company is cheap to set up and is hard for aggrieved members complaining about their fund performance or some breach of trust to sue. There are technical issues about conflicts of interest, and companies have to file documents with Companies House, but it is simpler to change trustees and the general consensus is that trustees should normally act through a company rather than in their individual capacity.

INSURANCE
Things in pensions can (and sometimes do) go wrong. Trustees or managers might pay the wrong person or the wrong amount. Members or others can complain or sue. It is therefore sensible to take out insurance, which can be paid for out of the funds of the scheme (if the scheme allows, and it should) or by the employer.

Sometimes the employer can include pension trustee protection in the usual directors' and officers' insurance that most companies carry. However, there are drawbacks in not having proper dedicated insurance. Firstly, many claims come in several years after the individual has left the company, and few general insurance policies continue the protection for former employees (although dedicated policies do or should do). Secondly, there are sometimes conflicts of interest between the company and the individual, or between several individuals involved in the pension scheme, and most insurance policies are not geared up to dealing well with this. Dedicated pension trustee insurance policies are supposed to give personal protection to each trustee.[7] If you are owned by an overseas company, this may offer you the protection of its overseas insurance policy; in practice, whatever the company says, claiming against an overseas policy is very hard indeed.

IN PRACTICE
Being a trustee should be a very low risk activity, provided:

- your deed and rules give you a decent exemption from liability
- the deed and the company give you an indemnity against liability
- you take advice – though not necessarily follow it
- you are a director of a company that is a trustee, rather than being an individual trustee
- there is decent insurance in place.

CHAPTER 8
INVESTMENTS

'I'm sorry, I'm not a tax specialist.'
Dame Lesley Strathie, HMRC Chief Executive, Evidence to the Public Accounts
Committee, HMRC Accounts, 16 November 2010, HC 502-ii

When they write about pensions, newspapers (and governments) often confuse pensions with savings; but the former can be paid even where there are no pots of money available or set aside. The most obvious unfunded pension scheme is that of the civil service; there are no funds or investments backing the civil service pension scheme. The pensions are paid directly by the government to its former employees from the general kitty. In the same way, there is no objection to businesses paying pensions to their employees as though they were wages, without any need to set money aside in the meantime (and in fact it is now the most tax efficient way to do it).

The difference between business and government, of course, is the fact that the former can go bust (and in theory the government cannot, or at least it has the power to tax). As soon as the tax law allowed (in 1921), therefore, businesses began to set aside money to protect the pensions interests of employees. Your employees would be pretty sick if, after they had worked diligently for 40 years and had been given the expectation that you would keep them on a reduced salary for the rest of their lives as a reward, your company went bust at the wrong time.

The funding of pensions, ie the setting aside of money to protect the expectations of the workforce against the possibility of the insolvency of the employer, is therefore now well established. But it has become easy in all the discussions about the funding of pensions to confuse the *expectation of a pension* with *the money lying behind it*.

COMMON WORRIES
In a way, pensions are not savings at all. They are a form of guarantee fund, and the money would not be needed if the employee died on his or her 65th birthday, or if the employer continued to pay a reduced salary after retirement as though the employee stayed on the payroll. The money, especially in a defined benefit scheme, is there more as a safety blanket than as a pot of cash out of which to pay the pension. Even in a defined contribution scheme, the money will not be needed if the member dies exactly at retirement age and leaves no dependants; all pension schemes, including DC schemes, are established to protect, like an insurance policy, against the risk of living too long.

However, it would be perfectly understandable, when you see the apparently large amounts of money in the pot, to identify it as a personal asset. That is especially easy in defined contribution schemes, where separate accounts are kept for each member, and the member can log on to the computer almost daily and see how much there is standing to his or her credit. The trouble is that even large sums of money, when interest rates are low, represent only a small pension (you need around £1,000 in the pension fund to pay a pension of £1 a week). The sums then do not then look quite so large, or at least not so valuable. Whether the amount of money in the kitty is a problem, and what kind of problem it is, depends on the kind of scheme involved, as shown below.

- In **defined benefit schemes**, the funding is a second order problem for most of us; the value of the fund means little. What is important is the issue of whether the pension will be paid – and how much it is (and whether the employer is in a position to meet any shortfall).
- In **defined contribution schemes**, the value of the pot can be crucial, and for scheme members it is also crucial that they can see at a glance how much the pot is worth. With a transparent system, the members can see immediately how much money there is to back their retirement (or more likely how little) and can use a pensions calculator readily available on the web to see, if they retired today, how much pension that would represent. It might encourage them to set more aside – or work a little longer.

HOW MUCH DOES £100,000 GIVE BY WAY OF PENSION?
If I am a woman, maybe £4,000 pa at age 60, and if I am a man, maybe £6,000 at age 65. Although, in theory, annuity rates for men and women should be the same . . .[1]

However, transparency of information also carries a burden and may lead to unintended consequences. The burden, of course, is that your employee worries about the fluctuations in fund values. And if their pot diminishes in value, perhaps because the stock market falls, they might become very concerned. They are unlikely to appreciate that, actually, it is probably more important to keep an eye on what interest rates are doing (because the lower the rates, the less the fund will buy by way of pension income), but if they did, it might reduce their stress levels.

In practice the two kinds of schemes cause different concerns.

- In **defined benefit schemes**, the risk of there not being enough in the kitty to support the pension is largely that of the employer – and ultimately the Pension Protection Fund if the employer fails with inadequate amounts in the kitty.
- In **defined contribution schemes**, the amount is critical; the risk of there not being enough to buy a sufficient income is that of the member and, apart from putting more money in, there is not much they can do about it.

Whether your scheme is DC or DB, the investments in funded pension systems are an important matter for consideration by your business – and the members. In practice, however, few members are dedicated investment people and will largely leave things to be sorted by the employer, which may leave you with a problem.

WHICH REGULATOR?
This depends on what type of pension scheme you have. All occupational pension schemes are regulated by the Pensions Regulator. Group personal pension schemes

and stakeholder pension schemes are regulated jointly by the Pensions Regulator and the FSA.

- The FSA focuses on regulating the pension companies as well as how the schemes are marketed and sold to employees.
- The Pensions Regulator focuses on payments made by the employer and how the scheme is run (for example, making sure records are up to date).

WHAT SHOULD YOU DO?

Cash is not an 'investment' under English law. It may be safe (or at least safer) than conventional investments, but it doesn't give much of a return, so it is sensible to invest in a range of other things, such as government securities or shares.

It is probable that you are not an investment expert – and nor are your trustees. Some may say that even professional investment managers don't know much about investment, given their overall record, but that might be overly cynical.[2] Certainly neither you nor your trustees will normally hold yourselves out as investment specialists.

On the other hand, you do not actually need to be a specialist to know what to do about investments, rather like the head of HMRC does not need to know about tax to run HMRC. You can (and should) hire people who do this kind of work, and you need to do this even if the fund is small, as the amount of money involved in a pension scheme can grow surprisingly quickly. It is reputed to have been Einstein who said that the power of compound interest was the most powerful force in the universe.

THE POWER OF COMPOUND INTEREST

Table 10 on the next page indicates the effect of compound interest on savings over 40 years. The sooner you start to save, the greater the benefit of compound interest. Compound interest is the interest earned on reinvested interest, in addition to the original amount invested.

Compare two individuals: Darren and Sabrina. Assume they are both 22 years old and have £2,000 pa of disposable income; Darren puts £2,000 pa in a personal pension for six years until he's 28, whereas Sabrina spends £2,000 pa on frivolities until she's 28.

Now assume that the pension fund earns 12% pa (say all in equities showing 7%, and 5% inflation) and that Darren puts in £2,000 pa for six years but then stops contributing. Sabrina, on the other hand, spends £2,000 per year for six years – and only then does she put £2,000 into her pension fund, and she does it until she is 65 years old. She earns the same 12% interest pa.

Table 10 below shows the value of the personal pension of both Darren and Sabrina from age 22 until they get to 65. Note that Darren has invested a total of £12,000 (ie £2,000 per year for the first six years), and Sabrina has invested £74,000 (£2,000 per year for 37 years). And assume that there is no tax to pay. Look what happens. Early saving makes sense.

Table 10: Effect of compound interest on savings over 40 years

Age	Darren, £	Sabrina, £
22	2,240	0
23	4,509	0
24	7,050	0
25	9,896	0
26	13,083	0
27	16,653	0
28	18,652	2,240
29	20,890	4,509
30	23,397	7,050
35	41,233	25,130
40	72,667	56,993
45	128,064	113,147
50	225,692	212,598
55	397,746	386,516
60	700,965	693,879
65	1,235,339	1,235,557

There are several options available on where and how to invest.

■ **If the money is directed towards NEST** then it's NEST's problem. They have set out how they intend the funds to be invested, but they have a political issue to resolve. In order to avoid criticism in the newspapers, they need to ensure that the funds never fall in value. But the kinds of investments which protect against a fall in value are also very low risk. And if they are low risk, then they usually bring a low return. And that means a lower pension. They have a difficult dilemma to resolve. But it is theirs, not yours.

■ **If the money is managed by your employees,** they need to have read the literature and have enough knowledge or desire to keep an eye on the investments chosen – and be able to arrange to reinvest if circumstances change. Although many members now have access through the web to manage their account, experience indicates it is not always as simple as it looks – and few independent financial advisers want to get involved in offering advice because the fees are so low and the risks (for the adviser) are so high.

■ **If the investment management is sub-contracted or outsourced to an insurer or asset manager,** the returns might be better. It allows them to construct a system which might be more appropriate. Most fund managers operate a kind of 'lifestyle' system which automatically switches the investments as the member ages to a selection that the general consensus thinks is appropriate. This normally involves a gentle switch over time from equity-type investments to bond-type investments, because those are seen as more stable – and, although they are also seen as slightly safer, they usually offer lower returns.

FINDING AN ASSET MANAGER

Finding an asset manager can prove challenging, but the good news is that there is no shortage of them. You and your pension fund trustees can choose an insurer or a specialist asset manager – and you (technically it is the trustees who do the choosing) can choose one manager or a variety of managers (if the amounts are large enough), or a series of specialist managers each concentrating on, say, bonds or equities. In practice, you will probably ask an investment adviser (see below) to find a decent selection of investment managers.

WHAT INVESTMENTS?

At one time, just before the Second World War, pension funds were known as 'widows and orphans funds', the terminology indicating that they had to be invested as safely as possible. That meant, in the early days, that investments were limited to mortgages and government bonds – the consequence being that much of the value of the pensions was destroyed.

Over time, pension funds were allowed to invest more widely: by the 1960s in stocks and shares (equities), then in commercial property in the 1970s, and then in overseas assets (by the 1980s) – and today virtually anything at all is legal.

There are, however, some general principles, especially where the money is invested through a pension trust.

1. There should be **diversification**, ie not all the eggs should be in one basket. This can be achieved by appointing a range of advisers and/or spreading the money into different kinds of assets. Of course, if the sums involved are small, that might be a counsel of perfection.
2. Unless the trustee is an expert, the fund should **take advice**.
3. The **assets should be looked after**. In other words, where appropriate there should be a custodian, the dividends should be collected, the tax paid and (nowadays) the votes that come with the shares (if any) should be exercised.
4. The investments should be **reviewed periodically** to see if they are appropriate.

Eggs and baskets: the quintessential diversification metaphor . . . but even lots of baskets may not protect against the Black Swan.

INVESTMENT ADVISERS

Investment advisers come in many forms, as described below.

- Many **larger actuaries and consultancies** have an investment management arm, many of which are rather good. They are probably better value for the larger pension funds, and will find reasonable investment managers and keep an eye on them.
- **Independent financial advisers** probably have lower-level knowledge, and it is hard to judge between good ones and bad ones.
- Some **individuals** act as investment advisers on a personal basis; sometimes these are former investment managers and know how to manage the contracts into which the trustees have to enter with investment managers.

In most cases the law requires trustees to take investment management advice.

INVESTMENT OPTIONS AND ISSUES

Investments need to be both diversified and appropriate, which amongst other things requires that a variety of options be investigated.

Equities

Shares quoted on a stock exchange have the benefit that they (as a class, rather than individually) represent a stake in the growth of the economy. They are expensive to hold and deal in, and their value is volatile over the shorter term, which may make then inappropriate as the fund's cash value begins to be needed when the benefits start to be paid.

Private equity

Private equity is also an investment in business but, since the shares are not quoted on a stock exchange, their value cannot always be readily realised or traded. The management costs are high, but the returns should be higher than those from ordinary shares (equities). Private equities are usually regarded as a longer-term protection against inflation.

Gilts

Gilts are government bonds; the UK government borrows money at a (usually) fixed rate and promises to pay the interest, and then, on the date fixed, pays back the capital. The return should be higher than leaving the money in cash at the bank, and the safety of the capital is the highest (although investment in the bonds of governments such as Russia or Argentina is always suspect – as is that of Greece and Portugal more recently). The values will, however, fluctuate according to the prevailing interest rates; for example, if the gilt carries an interest rate of 1%, and market interest rates move to 5%, the value of the gilt will be only a fifth of its nominal value. Bonds are sometimes regarded as 'safe', but the government can fail to pay back the money – and inflation can wreck their value. Regulators and supervisors think that pension funds should increasingly buy bonds, but some commentators, such as Lord Myners (a former adviser to the Treasury), consider them to be very risky.

Property

Property – especially residential property – was at one time considered to be a core investment for pension funds. In more recent times property has fallen slightly out of favour. Firstly, residential property has been affected for many years by rent controls. Secondly, commercial property fluctuated widely in value and was also 'illiquid', ie it could not be bought and sold very easily, so that cash might not be available to pay pensions when needed. For tax reasons, mid-ground, property unit trusts have not been available in recent years, but sub-sets of property are now being offered (such as investments in high-yield or secondary property, eg shops in less attractive areas) and are increasingly popular, as is overseas property, which also offers currency risks (ie not only does the fund buy property, but its value is affected by currency exchange rates).

Cash

Cash is always needed by pension funds to pay bills and benefits. As an investment, however, the law is uncomfortable with cash – and historically it has shown very low rates of return, although (or because) it is very low risk. It is not entirely risk-free – as the collapse of major banks, such as RBS and Lloyds, has shown – but it is the lowest of all the classes, and the investment management costs are usually the lowest of them all. Cash management (squeezing higher interest rates by moving money about to different banks) is a skilled business and important for larger pension funds with large amounts of cash.

Alternatives

Mainstream investments are usually regarded as cash, equities and bonds. Anything else (including private equity and property) is regarded as 'alternative' and sometimes viewed with suspicion by regulators and others – mostly because it is usually higher risk and illiquid. At present, alternative investments include currencies, commodities, forestry and 'hedge funds'.

Pooled and segregated

Larger pension funds can appoint managers to manage their money in a segregated pot; however, smaller funds (and larger funds investing small amounts of money in a particular asset class) usually choose to invest their money with a manager, along with other investors, and 'pool' their money together. Such pooling arrangements can be legally a little more complicated but should prove cheaper, and share risk more widely, than investing directly.

Tax

In theory, pension funds should not pay tax on their investments – provided they are used for investments and there is no suggestion that the assets are being traded or used for trade. In practice, pension funds pay VAT on investment management fees; they also pay stamp duty on stocks and shares, and property that they buy and sell, and they pay (if they are DB schemes) a levy for fraud, pensions protection and regulation. They also pay extra tax if the benefits are over a permitted level. It is important that no trading tax is paid, but in practice that rarely happens.

GOVERNANCE

Since pension funds and insurance companies control (or used to control) so much of the stock market, over recent years they have been increasingly blamed for not making sure that companies behave properly. The argument is that if the owners of companies had taken more interest, we would not have had the scandals and collapses that we have had: bankers would have had to live on sensible salaries and take sensible risks, the Madoff scandal would not have happened, and WorldCom and Enron would have been avoided.

There are now several codes of practice intended to improve governance of both companies in which pension funds invest, and the way in which pension funds should behave, including the following:

■ the stewardship code, which obliges pension funds (which invest money on behalf of other people) to pay attention to the issues that emerge from the shares they hold
■ the UK Corporate Governance Code, which sets out how companies themselves should behave
■ the United Nations Principles for Responsible Investment (UNPRI) which sets out certain ethical, social and environmental guides for investors.

There are around a dozen other codes, along the same lines and with similar objectives. Complying with them all may be a task too far if your fund is relatively modest, since there is considerable effort involved in compliance. UK law requires your fund to have a think about **proxy voting** and **social and ethical investment** – and to make a declaration about what, if anything, you intend to do about voting and ethical investment in the statement of investment principles which most pension funds are obliged to make. Your statement can suggest that these obligations should be undertaken by your investment managers – or that you are not very much interested in adopting such principles in any event.

Proxy voting

If you invest in shares you own three elements:

1. the value of the share
2. the dividend it might earn
3. the vote.

In practice, few pension funds have the time or resources to vote all their shares towards AGMs and other opportunities, which is why it is said that managers are becoming out of control in relation to their personal rewards. Proxy voting (ie the votes that come with the shares) is increasingly being encouraged for investors, and many institutional investors are now beginning to flex their muscles. By law, if you have trustees, they must declare their policy on proxy voting; in practice you and they will normally leave it to the investment managers to ensure that the managers of the companies in which you invest do not pay themselves too much, or engage in pointless takeovers – and pigs might fly.[3]

Social and ethical investment

Similarly, it is thought that social and ethical improvements could take place if pension funds devoted some of their influence to improving the activities of the companies in which they invest. Of course, pension funds are moving more towards bonds than equities (so that their influence is diminishing) in their investment portfolio, and your pension fund is unlikely to own enough of any one company to have the slightest impact on their moral behaviour – whether in the manufacture of armaments or tobacco, or their operations in a currently unfashionable jurisdiction which is the target of political activism, or in their consumption of carbon. This is not to diminish the role that activism can have; it is widely contended that apartheid was dismantled largely as a consequence of activism and pension fund disinvestment – and this might be true.

However, pension funds individually – and yours in particular – do not have much power, which is why they either delegate it to their asset managers (who may produce a statement of their activities in this field) or join one of several activist organisations.[4] However, if you run an occupational pension scheme, your trustees are required to make a statement about their policy on socially responsible investments (and they can declare they have no policy).

HOME AND OVERSEAS

At one time it was considered unpatriotic and foolish to invest anywhere outside the UK. It was thought inappropriate to invest in non-sterling assets, when benefits had to be paid as it were in pound notes. In modern terminology, the assets did not match the liabilities.

Today we know better. Investing overseas has probably been the best thing that ever happened to British pensions; and even investing in UK companies quoted on the London Stock Exchange probably exposes you to around 60% investment overseas, since so many companies earn their income from there. The distinction between UK and non-UK investments is dying – actually, it is almost dead.

RISK AND REWARD

At one time it was considered safe for what used to be called 'widows and orphans funds' (ie pension funds) to be invested only in British government bonds and mortgages on real property (ie land and buildings). In fact, history has shown that that conventional wisdom was much mistaken (although we seem to be in danger of re-inventing it), and over the years pension funds have moved from those 'safe' investments to:

- shares in companies (once considered too risky because they could go down in value)
- ownership of property, especially commercial property and offices (once considered too risky because they could not easily be sold when benefits need to be paid, ie they were 'illiquid')
- overseas investments (once considered risky because of the currency exposure).

Today other 'alternative' investments such as hedge funds, commodities, forestry and other opportunities are being accepted, at least for the larger funds.

Also being heavily marketed are 'risk-managing' investments, such as swaps and other derivatives, to protect against increases in mortality rates or inflation rates. These 'investments' are perhaps more properly treated as insurance, and it is critical to find out:

- what the premium is that you pay for that protection
- what extra continual work is needed to keep it in operation
- what the risk is of the insurer failing
- how long it lasts
- if it adds much protection when it might be covered by other investments, such as equities.

TIME FRAMES

There is a dilemma for you and your trustees. Your accountants and your regulators like to look at pensions over a three-month to one-year period, but the time horizon of most pension funds, even those which are closed to new members, is invariably very much longer – maybe up to 60 years. The kinds of investments that are needed or are appropriate for a long-term project are usually inappropriate for short-term investments. The latter are also usually more expensive because of the price needed to pay for liquidity, which is not an issue for the majority of pension funds.

There is no magic solution to this dilemma, except to take courage and common sense in both hands when thinking about the right investment mix. This is particularly important in defined contribution systems, and with some very rare exceptions (usually involving some kind of fraud) trustees and employers are not liable for making investment decisions which turn out in the short-term to be wrong. Be brave and sensible.

INVESTMENT DECISIONS

The money has to be invested. It can be invested by the trustees (if there are trustees), by the insurance company or asset managers according to instructions, or by the individual member.

Giving investment options to members is in theory a good thing to do – and the higher paid members might quite like the opportunity to choose their own salvation. However, most members would rather relinquish the effort to someone else, which is why most defined contribution schemes adopt a 'default' system. In other words, some experts choose and manage the investments on behalf of the members, and adjust them as they think fit, in particular taking into account the closeness of a member to retirement and the need to buy an annuity.

Decumulation

Decumulation is a fancy word for the process that happens when money is disinvested in order to buy an annuity. There are problems with the timing of decumulation, as it may be the wrong time in the economic cycle to move into an annuity, and trying to buy the best annuity in the market is not always easy. In practice, experts take on this job.

Self-investment

It is illegal to invest the assets in the shares of the employer (there are some minor exceptions). It is common in the US but it is considered the wrong thing to do here, despite some advantages.

Investment management agreements

By law the investment managers have to produce a formal agreement for you to sign. This can be complicated and expose you (because you are often regarded as a 'professional investor') to serious risks, especially where derivatives are involved. One of the most well-known investment managers used to issue a standard contract which provided 'this contract is of no contractual effect', which is not as daft as it sounds but may not do the job you need. You should get your lawyers to check out the contract or insist the asset managers use the industry standard approved by the National Association of Pension Funds and issued by the Investment Management Association (although curiously they seem to keep it rather a secret).

Regulation

Investment regulation makes it illegal for you or the trustees (unless you are already regulated, which is unusual) to make day-to-day decisions on investments. You are allowed (and encouraged) to set out strategic and tactical decisions but not to select individual investments – and, in any event, you are required to take formal advice from someone experienced in investment management.

CHAPTER 9
UK OR OVERSEAS?

'I call myself an innocent, but a reckless ignoramus might be more appropriate.'
Lord Brooke of Sutton Mandeville during the Pensions Bill Debate (Hansard, Lords, 15 February 2011 Col 612)

There was a time not that long ago when the UK pension system, or certainly that part of it which was the workplace pension system, was the best in the world. Visitors came from faraway countries – many of them developed states – to marvel at our simple, generous and appropriate company pension system built by employers to cover half the working population without any legal obligation to do so.

However, over the last 15 years, successive British governments have all but destroyed the corporate pension system by imposing a destructive tax system and an excessive regulatory framework. There are now other countries that have developed infrastructures which are much more attractive.

In practice, many countries are not available to UK employers as a base to place their pension arrangements, because the cross-border tax arrangements do not work; however, many EU countries have in recent years become available as a base from which to operate pension arrangements. Changing the base of a pension scheme is much easier than changing the base of a company, but it is rather similar to the way in which UK companies (such as WPP or Shire) have relocated their headquarters from London to Dublin, for example.

Why would you want to move your pension scheme abroad? The general reasons for considering relocating include:

■ reduced compliance costs
■ opportunity to run one scheme cross-border, where there are cross-border operations
■ simplified tax and reporting requirements
■ reduced administrative and adviser costs.

The opportunity to move your scheme overseas has been around since 2005, but in practice few companies have taken advantage of it. The reasons are understandable. The rules, reporting requirements and foreign regulations might be in another language (although many countries now use English for regulation). The local rules themselves may be unattractive, the UK labour and social laws still continue to apply, and you might come across problems in finding the right advice – and even if you can find it, it might be expensive.

Whilst going abroad might be difficult, there is no doubt that the UK is a very unattractive jurisdiction in which to run a pension scheme. You already know that the laws are very complicated, the tax law is very difficult and continually changing, there are difficult and unhelpful regulators, the adviser costs are high, and for defined benefit schemes there are levy costs – and in a multi-employer scheme the last man standing faces nightmare risks of having to pay the pension costs of other unconnected companies (and about which some charities in particular are very distraught).

The bottom line is that for many UK companies, of whatever size – and especially where the parent is foreign or there is a joint venture with a foreign company – overseas schemes look very attractive.

WHICH COMPANIES SHOULD LOOK AT GOING OVERSEAS?

You might only do business in the UK or you might also do business overseas.

- **If you are a multinational company** you might want to save pension costs by pooling risks or cutting administrative costs. If you have a subsidiary in one country where there are only a few people employed in the company, it may be disproportionately expensive to set up a local pension scheme, and putting them in the main employer's scheme is sensible (if it is possible).
- **If you are a company based simply in the UK** you may find it cost-effective to establish the pension scheme in another EU country.

The reason for looking overseas is not only that the UK is not user-friendly; it is also that several foreign countries have made it their business to be an attractive place of pension fund registration.

WHERE SHOULD YOU GO?

Where should you go to set up or move your pension scheme? It might be attractive to choose a country with a warm climate and decent beaches and food (ie anywhere other than the UK), but it also helps if there are suitable and effective double taxation agreements (ie an agreement between countries to recognise each other's tax reliefs).[1] In pensions matters there is no doubt that, for UK companies, you are best off with an EU country (because the European Court of Justice has made it clear that HMRC must give cross-border tax relief to contributions to other pension schemes within the EU).[2] Wherever you go, without cross-border tax relief no cross-border pension scheme is going to be attractive.

The most attractive countries at present include:

- Austria
- Belgium
- Gibraltar
- Ireland
- Luxembourg
- Malta.

The reason why these places are attractive is that many of them have decided to market themselves as pension fund centres. Most have adopted English as the language of registration, have translated their regulations into English (can you imagine the UK Pensions Regulator making its rules available in French?), have trained their staff to be welcoming, have adopted decent standards without gold-plating (ie over-engineering the rules), and have made their registration arrangements as simple and straightforward as possible.

In addition, for defined benefit (salary-related) schemes, there is no pensions levy to pay (worth an advantage of several million pounds to larger companies), no Pension Protection Fund to deal with, and much simpler compliance and accounting rules. More importantly, there is much greater freedom of pension design, and the employer has greater control over costs and management than in the UK – rather like it used to be in the UK 30 years ago.

OBSTACLES TO ESTABLISHMENT OUTSIDE THE UK

Nothing's perfect. Even though the advantages of moving out of the UK are so signifi-cant in practice, the number of employers establishing such schemes has been very modest so far and usually restricted to some of the very largest, operating for cross-border employees, such as oil company executives who continually move between different countries.

There are some disadvantages to establishing a scheme outside the UK, including the following.

- **Language:** even where the regulators work in English, there will be numerous occasions when it may be necessary to use the local language.
- **Perception:** employees and members may feel uncomfortable with having their pension rights based in another country, where they may find it difficult to enforce their rights and find their way around a foreign regulatory system.
- **Trade unions:** trade unions will similarly sometimes find it difficult to come to terms with understanding how foreign-based pension arrangements work.
- **Tax authorities:** the UK tax authorities have in recent years become obsessed with control of pension arrangements; foreign pension arrangements are largely outside their control and they may find this suspicious. They may have a point: one of the benefits of going overseas is to avoid most of the 4,000 pages of HMRC rules.
- **Protection:** the benefits of the Pension Protection Fund do not apply if the scheme is a defined benefit one.

OVERSEAS PENSION ARRANGEMENTS

You can, if you wish, establish a pension scheme in the UK for your overseas employees or contribute to a foreign scheme for UK-resident employees.

- UK schemes for non-resident employees are not very popular these days, but might be handy for some people with high net worth. These schemes are known as 's615 schemes' after the section number of the Income and Corporation Taxes Act 1988 under which they are recognised by HMRC.
- You can also get tax relief by paying into foreign pension schemes for UK-resident staff. The rules which cover this are called 'Migrant Member Relief' and deal with the number of years that, in theory, UK employees can contribute to an overseas scheme (even a non-EU scheme) and still receive tax relief on the contributions.

WHICH RULES APPLY?

Obviously, if the scheme is registered outside the UK, foreign rules apply. But UK rules still apply in such cases, as detailed in the instances below.

- The UK tax relief on contributions and the tax on benefits apply to contributions made and benefits received in the UK.
- In theory, at least (but mostly ignored in practice), UK 'social and labour law' continues to apply to UK workforces. There is some confusion about what this law is, and the Pensions Regulator publishes a list of laws (almost certainly wrong) which it considers as still applying to UK members to protect their rights.

In any event, foreign pension schemes do not have to have UK rules built in but, of course, things like equal treatment and the disclosure of the pension arrangements in the contract of employment still apply to your company in the UK. In practice, although it is unwise to disregard any law, a blind eye should be turned towards many of the regulations, and there is little legal difficulty in practice in introducing a foreign pension scheme.

SCHEME DESIGN

One of the joys of going overseas is that there is no need to think too much about the rules of HMRC and the Pensions Regulator when designing a scheme to meet the needs of members. In the past, the design of pension schemes in the UK has been driven as much by regulation as by the needs and expectations of employers and members. In the UK, HMRC sets down:

- what is permissible by way of benefits (eg pensions for members, for their dependants, for their civil partners)
- what kind of lump sums or disabled benefits can be given
- whether certain kinds of annuities are permissible
- whether certain investments are permissible.

The Pensions Regulator imposes requirements for the appointment of member-nominated trustees and rules for the reporting of pension fund investments solvency and accounts.

While similar requirements are imposed by overseas tax and regulators, by and large they are much fewer in number, the accounting rules are imposed in less onerous ways, and it is possible to design the scheme so that the risks to employers are constrained but the benefits to members are expressed in a way which the parties prefer.

The usual designs of pension schemes (discussed in Chapter 2) are available, but in addition there are:

- CDCs
- s615 schemes
- QROPS
- QNUPS.

These may be attractive to companies who are prepared to be slightly more creative.

Third-way pension schemes

CDCs
It would be sensible for many employees for you to offer a kind of 'mixed risk' scheme; employees find it hard to carry the many risks of pension schemes to which they are exposed in defined contribution schemes – and employers are scared of being exposed to the risks they see in defined benefit schemes. It may be, however, that there is a 'third way'.

Employers have been looking for several years, rather like mariners seeking the North West Passage, for such a third way.[3] Unfortunately, the government suggests that in theory it is not possible in the UK to offer one of the most popular third ways of risk sharing, known as 'collective defined contribution' or CDC schemes, which are common, for example, in the Netherlands. In the UK, pension schemes that are not purely defined contribution, ie simply savings schemes with a requirement to spend the savings on an annuity (or pension) at retirement, are regarded as defined benefit and bring with them the excess of regulation. However, pure defined contribution schemes are often not suitable for employees.

While purely defined contribution pension schemes limit the exposure of employers (unlike defined benefit arrangements, where fluctuations in stock market values or longevity expectations can involve substantial increases in costs), they have their drawbacks for members:

- the outcome is very uncertain
- the benefits are at the mercy of the investment markets
- the annuity rates vary according to interest rates prevailing at the time of retirement.

Therefore, they are forced to lean towards the safer (and thus lower return) investments, which in turn lead to lower benefits.[4]

There are many hybrids on offer as a solution, including cash balance plans,[5] but the most obvious and popular one in Europe is the CDC. The definition of CDC schemes is interpreted in different ways by different people. The DWP, which was not sympathetic to their introduction, regard it as risk sharing between members (rather than between employer and employee) and consider that it involves transferring rights between different generations of members, with the possibility (so the DWP think) for claims against the government should there be a failure of the scheme. It also considers that there is no demand for CDC within the UK.

In fact, many employers would like to return to a non-guaranteed form of pension provision, rather like the UK DB schemes of 30 years ago, and that is what a correctly designed CDC scheme can do. It manages to share investment risks between individuals and allows them to invest in a strategy that, as individuals, they find hardly possible. And it shares mortality and other risks, and allows the trustees to average out investment returns and use their discretion to attempt to provide as near as possible to a defined benefit arrangement – but without the guarantees that make such arrangements difficult if not impossible to provide.

CDC is therefore not usually available as an option in the UK, but it is available under a Belgian, Irish or Dutch arrangement.

s615 schemes

An s615 scheme is a UK pension scheme set up under trust, registered with the HMRC and with trustees resident in the UK. Neither the sponsoring employer nor the scheme's participants need have any connection with the UK; the structure is a remnant of the pre-2004 legislation but may still be appropriate for some employers.

An s615 can be either a defined benefit or a defined contribution scheme, but only individuals working wholly outside the UK may accrue benefits in it. Any UK duties, other than incidental duties, are not allowed. The test of incidental duties is based on the type of work done in the UK rather than purely the amount.

s615 schemes have advantages over UK Registered Pension Schemes because:

- the annual allowance (AA) does not apply to contributions to s615 schemes
- benefits from a s615 scheme do not count towards the lifetime allowance

- the increase in the minimum retirement age to 55 (from 2010) does not apply to a s615 scheme
- benefits can be taken entirely as a lump sum at retirement and, under Extra Statutory Concession A10, lump sum retirement benefits from s615 schemes are not subject to UK income tax.

Investment returns within an s615 scheme are largely tax-free for the trustees if the right assets are chosen.

A UK corporate tax deduction for employer contributions to an s615 scheme depends on whether the contributions meet the usual test of being exclusively for the purpose of the UK entity's trade or business. This might depend, for example, on whether the overseas duties of employees were undertaken through an overseas branch of a UK company.

Qualifying Recognised Overseas Pensions Schemes (QROPS)[6]

An individual working overseas can join an Recognised Overseas Pensions Scheme, subject to comply with any local requirements for eligibility.

The UK's Annual Allowance, Lifetime Allowance and Unauthorised Payments Charges are discussed below. In general, at the time contributions are made to, or benefits accrue in, a Recognised Overseas Pensions Scheme, these charges:

- do not apply if the employee is non-resident for UK tax purposes and has no UK taxable earnings from the employment
- do not apply if the employee is UK resident or has UK taxable employment (or self-employment) earnings, but the scheme is not an overseas pension scheme unless Migrant Member Relief, Grandfathered Corresponding Acceptance (GCA) or treaty relief is claimed
- apply to overseas pension schemes where the employee remains UK resident or has UK taxable earnings from the employment. This might affect 'commuter assignees' on short-term assignments where UK residence does not end up broken.

EU IORPS DIRECTIVE (EUROPEAN PENSIONS DIRECTIVE) AND UK-BASED CROSS-BORDER SCHEMES

Many of the opportunities now available for you to move your scheme are in place because the European Union Pensions Directive (also known as the IORPS Directive)[7] includes the concept of a cross-border pension scheme and contains provisions to regulate the operation of such a scheme. The UK included the directive's requirements in the Pensions Act 2004 and later regulations. Each EU member state has adopted similar legislation – but the detail of the legislation varies between member states and can offer advantages. However, you might want to place overseas employees in your UK scheme; if you do that you will have a 'cross-border scheme', to which special rules apply.

Definition of a cross-border pension scheme

Under UK legislation, an occupational pension scheme is a cross-border pension scheme if its main administration is in the UK and it has at least one member who is:

- employed by a 'European employer' and is a 'qualifying person', and the European employer pays or proposes to pay contributions to the scheme in respect of that member, or
- a 'qualifying self-employed person' who makes or proposes to make contributions to the scheme, or
- a widow, widower or civil partner of such a member who is entitled or will be entitled to benefits from the scheme in respect of that member.

A European employer is any employer of a qualifying person who is making or proposes to make contributions to the scheme in respect of the qualifying person. This includes not just employers who are resident in another EU member state but also a UK-resident employer. It would also include an employer established or resident outside the EU if they employed a qualifying person.

A qualifying person is an individual employed under a contract of service whose place of work under that contract is sufficiently located in an EU state other than the UK, so that the social and labour law relevant to occupational pensions of the other EU state applies to that employment. However, if the individual is a seconded worker there is an exemption: he or she will not be considered a qualifying person.

A self-employed qualifying person is a self-employed person whose place of work is sufficiently located in a member state other than the UK so that the social and labour law relevant to occupational pension schemes of that other state, rather than the UK, applies.

A seconded worker is an individual who:

- is, or was immediately prior to the commencement of the secondment, employed by an employer established in the UK and whose habitual place of work under that employment contract is the UK
- was posted before 30 December 2005 for a limited period that did not expire before that date, or was posted after 30 December 2005 for a limited period, to another member state for the purpose of providing services on behalf of his or her employer
- at the time when the posting began was expected at the end of the limited period to return to the UK to work for the original UK employer, or was expected to retire immediately on expiry of the limited period.

The Pensions Regulator has not set down any particular period of time as a 'limited period' for posting a seconded worker, although its guidance indicates that the main characteristic of the period is that it should either end on a specified date or on the occurrence of a specified event (for example, the completion of a project). Trustees will need to make an objective judgment and, where assignments are extended beyond five years, the characteristic of the limited period will need to be examined with greater rigour.

Many assignees who participate in UK pension schemes are covered by the seconded worker exemption. However, there are also a number of situations where an employee might be eligible to join or remain in a UK pension scheme but might fall outside of this exemption. For example, this would potentially include employees who:

- were recruited outside the UK
- did not have a habitual place of work in the UK prior to being 'posted' to another EU state
- are cross-border commuters or work in more than one EU state.

If there are UK scheme members who are not covered by the exemption, it will be necessary to determine which member state's social and labour law relevant to occupational pensions applies to the individual.

Additional requirements of a cross-border scheme
A cross-border scheme that has its main administration in the UK:

- must apply to the Regulator for general authorisation to accept contributions from European employers
- must apply to the Regulator for approval of a specific European employer for the relevant country. This involves a separate approval for each employer for each EU country (other than the UK) in which that employer has employees who are members of the pension scheme. Parts of the form must be completed in both English and the local language of the host country
- must ensure that it is operated in accordance with the social and labour law requirements of the other EU state. The authority in the other EU state is responsible for notifying the Regulator of these requirements, and the Regulator is responsible for notifying the pension scheme trustees or managers
- must be 'fully funded' (ie there has to be more money in the kitty than if it were simply UK-only).

The timetable for complying with these requirements varies depending on the background of the UK pension scheme, which will fall into one of the following categories.

- A pre-23 September 2005 scheme: on 22 September 2005, the scheme was already receiving contributions from a European employer in respect of a qualifying person in another EU country.
- An established scheme: the scheme has members but on 22 September 2005 it was not receiving contributions from a European employer, ie there was then nobody in the scheme working in another EU country (apart from seconded workers) who would trigger the cross-border rules.
- A new scheme: the scheme has no members.

General authorisation to accept contributions from European employers
In order to operate a cross-border scheme, an application for general authorisation must be made. This is made to the Regulator on a form signed by the trustees or managers. Authorisation is a general process and does not relate to a specific European employer or EU state. The application requires details of the UK schemes, including trustees, advisers, scheme type, funding etc. (For a pre-23 September 2005 scheme, the application must have been made by 29 March 2006). An established scheme or a new scheme must receive authorisation before the scheme can accept contributions from a European employer.

Specific approval in relation to a particular European employer
In addition to general authorisation, the scheme must also be approved in terms of the specific cross-border operation for each European employer and each EU state in which that employer has employees who are members of the scheme. Thus, if there are two companies participating in a scheme in which company A has employees working in Ireland and Spain and company B has employees working in Ireland, then two

employer/country authorisations will be needed. The applications may be made at the same time or at a later date (but not before) the application for general authorisation, and some of the application will need to be made in both English and the language of the host country. For a pre-23 September 2005 scheme the application must have been made by 29 March 2006.

An established scheme or a new scheme must receive the authorisation before the scheme can accept contributions from the European employer. The Regulator must notify the scheme whether or not the scheme has been approved within three months of receiving the application. However, the scheme may not accept contributions from the European employer for two months after receiving approval or, if sooner, until it receives further information from the Regulator regarding the law of the other EU state. This means that the time between applying to operate cross-border and being able to accept a contribution from a European employer could be up to five months.

Requirement to act consistently with the law of the other EU state

The UK scheme must continue to comply with the legal requirements and rules of the UK, and it remains under the regulation of the Regulator. In addition, the trustees are required under UK legislation to ensure that the scheme operates in a manner that is consistent with the requirements of the social and labour law of the other EU states in which it has members who are qualifying persons. Some EU states may impose special disclosure and investment requirements on the UK scheme.

The Regulator is required to contact the authority in the relevant EU state to inform it of the intention of the scheme to operate cross-border. The Regulator must do this within three months of receiving the application from the scheme for specific approval. The host country must provide details of its requirements to the Regulator within two months, and the Regulator must forward this information about the relevant social and labour laws to the scheme as soon as practicable.

The authorities in the other EU state will monitor compliance with their legal requirements and notify the Regulator of any irregularities. The latter, together with the authorities in the other state, may act to remedy any breach of the requirements. Trustees who fail to comply with this requirement may be subject to civil penalties

Funding requirements

Cross-border pension schemes are required to be 'fully funded' at all times. The UK Regulator's interpretation of this requirement is that a UK scheme that operates cross-border must meet the UK's statutory funding objective, which must be satisfied for the entire scheme. Separation or notional separation of the assets and liabilities relating to the qualifying persons into a special ring-fenced fund is not permitted. The initial requirement to become fully funded must be met within the following time limits:

- established scheme: at the time the application is made
- new scheme: within two years from the date the application for general authorisation is made.

Thereafter, UK cross-border schemes are required to obtain an actuarial valuation at intervals of not more than one year, and be fully funded within two years of the effective date of the valuation.

Rules that apply to pension schemes located in other EU states

A non-UK scheme will need to determine whether it is a cross-border scheme under the legislation of the other EU state where it is located, ie where it has its main administration and, if relevant, its registered office. The scheme then needs to follow the procedure for authorisation and approval from that other EU state. As part of the approval process, the authorities of that other state then contact the UK Regulator, who informs the other state of the relevant legal requirements in the UK with which the scheme must comply.

If the UK Regulator becomes aware that the scheme is contravening any of the UK's requirements, it notifies the authorities in the other EU state. The Regulator may also direct this employer to stop making contributions to the scheme.

COMING TO THE UK

Overseas Retirement Benefits Schemes

Individuals coming to the UK can join or remain in an Overseas Retirement Benefits Scheme, which is often a scheme in their home country or, sometimes, a special 'international' scheme set up for expatriate employees of an employer. The tax consequences are described below.

- **Employer contributions:** contributions by an employer to an Overseas Retirement Benefits Scheme will not create a taxable benefit in kind on the employee in the UK.
- **Employee contributions:** contributions by the employee to an Overseas Retirement Benefits Scheme can only be deducted when assessing UK taxable income if the individual claims Migrant Member Relief (MMR), treaty relief, or Grandfathered Corresponding Acceptance (see next section) and they claim the relief through their tax return.
- **Employer's corporate tax deduction:** contributions to an Overseas Retirement Benefits Scheme may be denied a UK corporate tax deduction until the benefits are paid out to the member. A current UK corporate tax deduction may be allowed if the individual's membership of the Overseas Retirement Benefits Scheme qualifies for Migrant Member Relief, Grandfathered Corresponding Acceptance, or relief under a double taxation treaty (see below).

UK tax relief and Overseas Retirement Benefits Schemes

There are three ways to get tax relief for an employee's own contributions to an overseas scheme or to get an immediate corporate tax deduction in the UK:

1. Migrant Member Relief
2. Grandfathered Corresponding Acceptance
3. treaty relief.

There are distinctions between an Overseas Retirement Benefits Scheme and an Overseas Pension Scheme; these determine the reliefs available.

Overseas Pension Scheme

'Overseas Pension Scheme' is a defined HMRC term and, in general, the scheme must be:

- established outside the UK
- regulated by the authority regulating pension schemes, if any, in the country where it is established
- open to residents of that country, ie the tax or regulatory status of the scheme does not prohibit residents from belonging to the scheme
- approved or recognised for tax purposes in the country where it is established.

If no pension regulatory authority exists, or if there is no tax approval of pension schemes in the relevant country, then the scheme must not pay benefits derived from funds contributed while in the UK (or contributed while subject to UK tax) earlier than the date a UK registered scheme could pay them. At least 70% of the UK-sourced funds must be applied to provide a lifetime pension for the individual. Not all Overseas Retirement Benefits Schemes meet the criteria for being an Overseas Pension Scheme.

Overseas Retirement Benefits Schemes that are not Overseas Pension Schemes

If an Overseas Retirement Benefits Scheme does not fall within the definition of an Overseas Pension Scheme (see definition above), it is not generally possible for the member to claim a deduction for personal contributions to such Overseas Retirement Benefits Schemes, nor for the employer to claim a UK corporate deduction (before benefits are paid out) for employer-financed contributions under Migrant Member Relief. In this case, unless the individual is eligible for Grandfathered Corresponding Acceptance or treaty relief (see overleaf), they are not subject to the Annual Allowance Charge, the Lifetime Allowance Charge or the Unauthorised Payments Charge.

If Corresponding Acceptance has been claimed on employer contributions to the scheme before A-day (see page 184) in the tax year ending 5 April 2006, the scheme is treated as though it is a Qualifying Overseas Pension Scheme and qualifies for Grandfathered Corresponding Acceptance. Where Grandfathered Corresponding Acceptance or treaty relief is claimed in respect of contributions, the rules regarding Annual Allowance, Lifetime Allowance and Unauthorised Payments Charges also apply as though the Overseas Retirement Benefits Scheme were an Overseas Pension Scheme.

Migrant Member Relief (MMR)

Under certain conditions, individuals can receive UK tax relief on their own contributions to Overseas Pension Schemes, and employers can seek a UK corporate tax deduction on their contributions to such schemes at the time of payment. The UK tax relief is called MMR, and in order to qualify for it:

- the scheme must be a Qualifying Overseas Pension Scheme:

    - it must be an Overseas Pension Scheme and not be excluded by HMRC from being a qualifying scheme
    - the scheme administrators must undertake in writing to notify HMRC of Benefit Crystallisation information in respect of members who enjoy MMR

- the member must:

    - be resident in the UK at the time for which MMR is claimed
    - have relevant UK earnings chargeable to UK income tax for that year
    - have joined the scheme before becoming resident in the UK
    - at any time in the 10 years before arriving in the UK have been entitled to tax

relief in respect of contributions to the scheme under the tax regime of the country in which he or she was then resident

☐ have notified the scheme manager that he or she intends to seek MMR and been told that the scheme manager will inform HMRC of Benefit Crystallisation information in respect of the scheme.

Most notably, under MMR an individual may be employed by a UK-resident employer and be domiciled in the UK. Members of some schemes that were previously unable to provide corresponding acceptance, such as Swiss or Australian pension schemes, are also able to claim MMR if they meet the conditions for it.

Grandfathered Corresponding Acceptance (GCA)

If, before 6 April 2006, an individual was granted Corresponding Acceptance in respect to membership of an Overseas Retirement Benefits Scheme, then it is possible to retain that status after 6 April 2006 subject to certain conditions.

- The individual must have Corresponding Acceptance for that Overseas Retirement Benefits Scheme before 6 April 2006.
- For future, immediate UK corporate tax deductions, the employer must have contributed to the scheme in 2005/06 and been allowed a UK corporate tax deduction by HMRC in respect of those contributions.
- For future tax deduction for employee contributions, the employee must have made a contribution to the scheme in 2005/06 and been allowed a UK income tax deduction by HMRC for this contribution.
- The scheme manager must have agreed in writing with HMRC to report Benefit Crystallisation information for members who have GCA after 5 April 2006.
- If any scheme rules change after 6 April 2006, the scheme must continue to correspond to a scheme that would be tax-favoured in the UK (ie a UK Registered Pension Scheme).

Where there is a claim for GCA on or after 6 April 2006, then the Annual Allowance Charge, Lifetime Allowance Charge and Unauthorised Payments Charge will apply to contributions (and benefits paid from those contributions) made after 6 April 2006.

GCA is not the same as MMR. For example, MMR requires the scheme to be an Overseas Pension Scheme, but GCA does not. Moreover, GCA does not require the member to have joined the scheme before coming to the UK, nor to have received tax relief on contributions to the scheme in a previous country. It is also worth noting that GCA for employer contributions is technically claimed separately from the GCA for employee contributions and that it is possible to be eligible for both, neither, or one but not the other. Eligibility for GCA depends on both having Corresponding Acceptance and having made a contribution to the scheme in 2005/06.

Treaty relief

Some of the UK's double tax treaties allow members of the other country's retirement benefits schemes to claim relief from UK tax for contributions to those schemes. The terms and conditions of the relief, and the schemes to which it relates, vary from treaty to treaty, and the exact wording of the relevant treaty should be consulted in each case. The type of Overseas Retirement Benefits Scheme covered is usually defined in the treaty, and often must be tax-approved in the other country. In the same way as for GCA, where there is a claim for treaty relief on or after 6 April 2006, then the Annual Allowance Charge, Lifetime Allowance Charge and Unauthorised Payments

Charge will apply to contributions (and benefits paid from those contributions) made after 6 April 2006.

It may be possible, subject to the terms of the relevant treaty, to claim a UK corporate tax deduction at the time of payment in respect of employer contributions to an Overseas Retirement Benefits Scheme covered by a double taxation treaty.

Annual Allowance, Lifetime Allowance and Unauthorised Payments Charges

So far as they derive from contributions made after A-day in respect of a member who is tax-resident in the UK (or has UK taxable earnings), the annual allowance and lifetime allowance apply to contributions to and benefits from:

- overseas pension schemes to which the employer has contributed while the employee was a UK tax-resident, whether or not UK tax relief is claimed
- overseas pension schemes where MMR is claimed
- overseas retirement benefits schemes where GCA is claimed
- overseas retirement benefits schemes where treaty relief is claimed.

Contributions on which UK tax relief has been given may also be subject to the Unauthorised Payments Charge. The Annual Allowance Charge is tested and applied to contributions to relevant Overseas Retirement Benefits Schemes (as detailed above) in a very similar way to UK Registered Pension Schemes. Where earnings include both those subject to UK tax and those not subject to UK tax, a pension contribution that covers both sorts of earnings is deemed to be split in the same proportion as the earnings, and only the UK portion is included in the annual allowance test. The liability for any Annual Allowance Charge lies with the scheme member and not the scheme.

The Lifetime Allowance Charge is only tested against the sum of contributions made to the relevant Overseas Retirement Benefits Scheme after 6 April 2006, at times when the individual's earnings from the relevant employment were generally subject to UK tax (ie the amounts tested for the annual allowance). Contributions before 6 April 2006 and all investment returns are excluded from the test, which is different from the way the test is applied to UK Registered Pension Schemes. Since the benefit accrued before A-day is not subject to the lifetime allowance, it is neither necessary nor possible to register benefits in a relevant Overseas Retirement Benefits Scheme for primary or enhanced protection.

With a relevant Overseas Retirement Benefits Scheme, the scheme member has the option to have the lifetime allowance tested at any point up to the time when benefits are taken. Like the Annual Allowance Charge, the Lifetime Allowance Charge is a liability of the scheme member and not the relevant Overseas Retirement Benefits Scheme. For some members and scheme administrators, it will be easier to report benefit accrual and test for the Lifetime Allowance Charge at the time of departure from the UK, when records of UK-assignment contributions are readily to hand. For other individuals, especially those with larger benefits from their time in the UK, there may be an advantage in delaying the time of testing for the lifetime allowance, since the latter is expected to rise as inflation rises.

The Unauthorised Payments Charge (and the Unauthorised Payments Surcharge) applies to any payment from a relevant Overseas Retirement Benefits Scheme. It applies if benefits are taken at a time or in a format that would not be allowed for a UK registered scheme and if, at the time of payment, the individual had been resident in the UK for tax purposes at any time in that UK tax year or any of the previous five UK tax years. The most common difficulties are likely to arise with benefits paid before age 55 (50 until April 2010), except in cases of serious ill health, and with lump sums of more than 25% of the benefits whether paid before or after age 55. Under UK law, benefits taken from UK tax-relieved contributions arising after A-day are deemed to have been taken first before other funds.

The individual is liable for the Unauthorised Payments Charge, not the foreign scheme's administrators. If an Unauthorised Payments Charge occurs, then the UK tax is 40% of the unauthorised payment. There is a further 15% surcharge, bringing the tax rate to 55% if the total of lump sums paid exceeds 25% of the benefit. Credit is given for foreign taxes paid on the same benefits.

UK REGISTERED PENSION SCHEMES

Joining a UK scheme and transferring benefits on leaving the UK

An alternative to remaining in or joining an Overseas Retirement Benefits Scheme is for an individual arriving in the UK to join a UK Registered Pension Scheme. Benefits can be accrued in the UK scheme in the normal way. The individual then has a choice of taking the benefits at retirement from the UK scheme or transferring them to a Qualifying Recognised Overseas Pension Scheme.

Transferring benefits from UK Registered Pension Schemes to overseas schemes

An option for an expatriate who comes to work temporarily in the UK is to join a UK Registered Pension Scheme and accrue benefits under the same terms as other members. On leaving the UK, the expatriate could then seek to transfer the accrued benefits to an Overseas Retirement Benefits Scheme.

It is possible to transfer benefits from UK Registered Pension Schemes to Overseas Pension Schemes if certain conditions are met. The receiving scheme must be a Qualifying Recognised Overseas Pension Scheme.

Unlike transfer payments between UK schemes, a transfer payment to an overseas scheme is a Benefit Crystallisation event, and the amount of the transfer is tested against and counts towards the lifetime allowance. If the transfer exceeds the individual's remaining lifetime allowance, the UK scheme administrator and the individual have both joint and several liability for a Lifetime Allowance Charge of 25% of the amount in excess of the lifetime allowance. Typically, the UK scheme would withhold this tax at the time of transfer.

It is not necessary to emigrate in order to transfer benefits from a UK Registered Pension Scheme to a Qualifying Recognised Overseas Pension Scheme. It is even possible to transfer benefits while remaining resident in the UK.

The funds transferred overseas remain subject to the UK Unauthorised Payments Charge and Surcharge, if benefits are taken at a time or in a format that would not be allowed for a UK Registered Pension Scheme, and if, at the time of payment, the individual had been tax-resident in the UK at any time in that UK tax year or any of the previous five UK tax years.

Liability depends on recent UK residence for tax purposes and not on the period elapsed since the transfer overseas. The most common difficulties are likely to arise with benefits paid before age 55 (50 until April 2010), except in cases of serious ill-health and with lump sums of more than 25% of the benefits, whether paid before or after age 55. Under UK law, benefits from UK tax-relieved funds are deemed by HMRC to have been taken first before other funds.

The individual, not the overseas scheme's administrator, is liable for any Unauthorised Payments Charge, but the administrators are responsible for complying with their undertaking to report benefit payments to HMRC. If an Unauthorised Payments Charge occurs, then the UK tax is 40% of the unauthorised payment. There is a further 15% surcharge, bringing the tax rate to 55%, if the total of lump sums paid exceeds 25% of the benefit. Credit is given for foreign taxes paid on the same benefits.

A possible difficulty is that a transfer from one overseas scheme to another could potentially be deemed an unauthorised payment under UK tax law, unless the second scheme can also meet the conditions for being a Qualifying Recognised Overseas Pension Scheme. A transfer to a second Overseas Retirement Benefits Scheme within six years of ceasing UK tax residence could create a UK tax liability for Unauthorised Payments Charge, even if the transfer was allowed under local laws.

There is no lifetime allowance test or charge when benefits funded by a transfer from a UK scheme are taken from the overseas scheme. This is because the lifetime allowance test is made at the point of transfer from the UK.

Qualifying Recognised Overseas Pension Scheme
'Qualifying Recognised Overseas Pension Scheme' is a defined HMRC term and, in general, the scheme must be:

- an Overseas Pension Scheme
- set up in an EU country, or in Norway, Iceland or Liechtenstein, or in a country with a suitable double taxation treaty with the UK. Alternatively, the benefits from the UK transfer must be paid no earlier than a UK registered scheme could pay them, and at least 70% of the transfer payment must be used to provide a life time pension
- a scheme whose administrators have given a written undertaking to report to HMRC the payment of benefits in respect of the relevant member(s)
- recognised by HMRC as meeting these requirements.

Transferring benefits from overseas schemes to UK Registered Pension Schemes
A UK Registered Pension Scheme may accept transfers from an Overseas Retirement Benefits Scheme. If the overseas scheme is a Recognised Overseas Pension Scheme, then the transfer may qualify for a lifetime allowance enhancement. This is measured as the amount of the transfer received relative to the standard lifetime allowance in the year in which it is received. If the individual registers the transfer with HMRC by 31 January of the fifth year following the tax year in which the transfer is made, then their personal lifetime allowance will be increased by this percentage.

HOW DOES THE TAX WORK?

Retiring in the UK with overseas benefits

The information provided below is based on an individual retiring in the UK and, as such, being a resident of the UK for tax purposes.

Pension

A pension from an Overseas Retirement Benefits Scheme paid to an individual resident in the UK for tax purposes is taxable in the UK.

■ If the pensioner is not domiciled in the UK, or is an Irish or Commonwealth citizen and is not ordinarily resident in the UK, then the pension is only taxed in the UK to the extent that it is remitted to the UK.

■ In other cases, 90% of the pension is taxable, whether or not the money is remitted to the UK. UK income tax is charged at the normal marginal rates of tax.

If the Overseas Retirement Benefits Scheme was funded by a UK entity and a UK corporate tax deduction was not given at the time the contributions were made, then it should be possible to seek a UK corporate tax deduction, provided the benefits paid are subject to UK income tax payable by the individual.

The pension may also be taxable in the source country. However, where the UK has a double taxation treaty, this often gives exemption from tax in the source country, provided the pension is taxed in the UK. There can be exceptions, and the treaty must be checked in each case. Some treaties will not give exemption from source country tax if UK tax is not charged because, for example, a non-domiciled individual does not remit the pension to the UK.

Lump sums

A lump sum from an Overseas Retirement Benefits Scheme is strictly taxable in the UK (minus all employee contributions and any employer contributions that have been treated as taxable income in the UK), whether or not the funds are remitted to the UK. Income tax is charged at normal marginal rates.

However, if foreign service has constituted a significant proportion of the employment to which a retirement benefit relates – ie 75% or more of total service is foreign, the whole of the last 10 years of service is foreign, or 10 of the last 20 years of service is foreign – then, by concession, the UK does not charge income tax on the lump sum. If the foreign service is not sufficient to procure a 100% reduction in UK tax, then part of the lump sum will be free from UK tax in the same proportion as the foreign service bears the total service. The above concession is further constricted in that it will not apply to any benefits derived from contributions which have received UK tax relief in cases where the benefits are received in such a manner as to generate an Unauthorised Payments Surcharge.

If the Overseas Retirement Benefits Scheme was funded by a UK entity and a UK corporate tax deduction was not given at the time the contributions were made, then it should be possible to seek a UK corporate tax deduction, provided the lump sum paid is subject to UK income tax payable by the individual. The lump sum may be taxable in the source country, too. Where the UK has a double taxation treaty, this often gives exemption from tax in the source country, provided the lump sum is taxable in the UK. However, there are exceptions – including the US – and the treaty must be checked in each case.

Retiring overseas with UK benefits

The information provided below is based on an individual retiring overseas and, as such, being non-resident of the UK for tax purposes.

Pension

In the absence of a double taxation treaty, a pension from a UK Registered Pension Scheme will have UK taxes withheld. If there is a double taxation treaty between the UK and the country of residence of the pensioner, then the treaty will often give sole taxing rights to the country where the pensioner is living, in which case a claim can be made to HMRC Centre for Non-Residents for authority for the pension scheme to pay the pension without deducting UK income tax. However, tax treaties vary and the exact terms of the relevant treaty need to be checked.

The Lifetime Allowance Charge at 25%, if relevant, applies to benefits from UK Registered Pension Schemes paid to pensioners resident overseas. This charge is not covered by double tax treaties and will usually be withheld by the UK scheme administrator, because the scheme administrator and the pensioner are jointly and severally liable for any Lifetime Allowance Charge.

The same principles apply to UK income tax on a pension from a UK Non-Registered Pension Scheme, including an unfunded pension from a UK company or entity. The Annual Allowance Charge, Lifetime Allowance Charge and Unauthorised Payments Charge do not apply to benefits from UK Non-Registered Pension Schemes. A UK corporate tax deduction for the employer's cost of benefits from a UK Non-Registered Pension Scheme would normally only be possible if, and to the extent that, the individual paid UK income tax on the benefit received, and would be available only at the time the individual was subject to UK income tax on the benefit.

Lump sums

A 'tax-free lump sum' from a UK Registered Pension Scheme is not subject to UK tax, although it might be subject to tax in the country of residence of the pensioner. However, a lump sum commutation of benefit above the lifetime allowance would be subject to the lump sum Lifetime Allowance Charge at 55%, which would usually be withheld by the UK scheme administrator. The charge is not covered by double tax treaties, and the scheme administrator and the pensioner are jointly and severally liable for any Lifetime Allowance Charge.

Lump sums from unapproved pension schemes are subject to UK income tax. Whether a double taxation treaty might prevent UK tax depends on the exact terms of the treaty. A UK corporate tax deduction would normally only be possible if, and to the extent that, the individual paid UK income tax on the benefit received and would be available only at the time the individual was subject to UK income tax.

Retiring overseas with UK tax-relieved overseas benefits

It is possible for an individual retiring overseas who is non-resident of the UK for tax purposes to take a pension or lump sum (having received tax relief in the UK) and not be liable to UK taxation under the terms of a double taxation treaty. The taxation treatment needs to be reviewed on an individual basis.

Even if the pension or lump sum is not subject to UK taxation, the individual may be subject to the Unauthorised Payments Charge (and the Unauthorised Payments

Surcharge). This applies if benefits are taken at a time or in a format that would not be allowed for a UK registered scheme and if, at the time of payment, the individual had been tax-resident in the UK at any time in that UK tax year or any of the previous five UK tax years. The most common difficulties are likely to arise with benefits paid before age 55 (50 until April 2010), except in cases of serious ill health and with lump sums of more than 25% of the total value of benefits, whether paid before or after age 55. Under UK law, benefits in respect of UK tax-relieved contributions arising after A-day are deemed by HMRC to have been taken before other benefits.

The individual, not the overseas scheme's administrators, is liable for the Unauthorised Payments Charge. If an Unauthorised Payments Charge occurs then the UK tax is 40% of the unauthorised payment. There is a further 15% surcharge, bringing the tax rate to 55%, if the total of lump sums paid exceeds 25% of the benefit. Credit is given for foreign taxes paid on the same benefits.

The benefits may also be subject to the Lifetime Allowance Charge.

NATIONAL INSURANCE
Social security contributions are generally not imposed on retirement income.

- Contributions to (registered) pension schemes should not be liable to National Insurance.
- A benefit payment that is within the terms of an authorised payment if made by a UK Registered Pension Scheme should not create a liability for National Insurance on payment.
- A benefit payment that falls outside the terms of an authorised payment from a UK Registered Pension Scheme could be liable for National Insurance. It is not clear whether the liability will be purely an employee liability or whether there will be a secondary (employer) liability and, if so, whether this secondary liability will fall on the employer or the pension scheme.

CHAPTER 10
PENSIONS AND DIRECTOR
LIABILITY

There are several 'laws' that make it clear that if it can go wrong, it will go wrong, or that if it does go wrong, there is little inkling in advance of how it will go wrong. These have different names: Murphy's Law, The Black Swan or 'No one expects the Spanish Inquisition', but, whatever the rule, there is an element of truth in them.

One solution is to do nothing. Fortunately, we all take risks in many areas of our work and life, and things get done – and mostly it works OK. This chapter explores how to manage the risks in relation to your pension arrangements, pay a reasonable price for managing the risks and put the risks into perspective. In most cases, most of the time, very little goes wrong; when it does go wrong, it can usually be fixed, and if it can't, it is not your fault. That is why this chapter is relatively short.

There are several risks to think about in pensions; they include:

- investment risks
- mortality risks
- inflation risks
- administrative risks
- liability risks
- fiduciary risks
- compliance and regulatory risks.

Most of the risks, in practice, can be managed reasonably simply, and some of them might be better ignored or managed in a simpler way than is often suggested. There has been something of a growth industry in creating new pension risk in recent years, often prompted by regulatory urging, and it might be sensible sometimes to step back and consider whether the management of the risk is necessary, appropriate and proportionate.

INVESTMENT RISKS
Most investment risks – that their capital value will reduce, disappear or not grow as anticipated – are inherent to the nature of investment. In the past such risks were simply managed by diversification, but at present a wide variety of options is on offer, including the following.

- **The purchase of derivatives,** ie gambling or insurance contracts against the possibility of failure. For example, you can buy a 'credit default swap', which is an insurance policy against the failure of a government bond. There is of course a cost to this, and the cover has a time limit. An alternative might be, for example, to invest in a variety of different government bonds, thus spreading the risk of failure.
- **The purchase of tracker or indexed funds,** which simply reflect the movement in the market. The management costs of such funds are low, but they will struggle to outperform the market – indeed they are not supposed to.

■ **The purchase of low risk investments** (or investments regarded as low risk) such as bonds. There is generally considered to be a close link between the riskiness of an investment and its expected return, the idea being that the lower the risk the lower the expected return. If there were such a thing as a risk-free investment, the return would be modest or very low indeed – and the cost of pension provision unaffordably high. Regulators and others such as accountants are very keen on pension fund trustees choosing what they think are low risk investments – and less concerned about the fact that they generally offer lower returns, higher costs and lower benefits.

There are many other investment risks, of course – for example, that inflation will wipe out the value of the investment (especially for bonds), that the tax rules will change or that the investments are not appropriate for the liabilities. Some observers, for example, think that LDI (liability driven investments) are the right strategy to use, since as members become older, it is necessary to have enough cash around to pay their benefits. They think, therefore, that the investments should be moved from equity-like investments to bond-like investments, which are less volatile and more secure. Others think that that strategy actually exposes members to other risks, such as inflation, and that the cost is too high. Each fund will take its own advice. In practice, diversification itself may often handle most of them, and 'de-risking', the buzz word of the moment, may be an expensive and sometimes pointless exercise.

MORTALITY RISKS

As mentioned before, for every hour that passes, our life expectancy increases by 15 minutes. Trying to work out how long all our employees will live is not easy, and in practice most of the actuarial projections over the last few decades have proved deeply inaccurate. It might seem sensible to take out protection against the funds running out before the last pensioner is dead.

Again, the cost is material and, in the case of some protection systems, such as longevity swaps, very time and resource intensive. You need people on your team who can manage such swaps on a day-to-day basis. For most pension schemes the alternative method of protection – the purchase of an annuity with an insurance company – is also an expensive option. The insurance company is required to invest in very low-risk investments, they have to reserve extra capital under their regulatory rules and they have expenses of their own – as well the need to make a profit. Pension schemes were invented to carry such risks at a reasonable cost, and it might take a very good reason to pass on that risk.

INFLATION RISKS

Inflation, even quite low inflation, can be a risk because the real value of investments – and benefits – can be badly affected by reductions in real value. The more pension funds invest in non-inflation-protected investments, the more exposed they are. Historically, pension funds invested in equities and then in index-linked gilts (the price of which are now very high indeed) to protect against inflation – and most pension funds did not give protection to members, so that over time benefits started to decline in real money.

The law now says that there must be at least limited protection for benefits both before retirement and once in payment, but it does not protect against serious inflation. The chances of inflation returning to serious levels (say 5% and above) is the subject of heavy debate at the moment, but even 3% a year halves the value of a pension after 10 years.

Inflation, however, can also be a saviour (for pension funds, if not the members); if benefits are reduced in real terms, while investments maintain their value in real terms, then any solvency problems are resolved after a few years. It may well be, for example, that sustained inflation would result in the Pension Protection Fund producing substantial surpluses in a few years, which will upset the pension funds that have had to pay high levies. It also emphasises that we should all work as long as we can, and retire as late as we can, to mitigate the effect of inflation on our future benefits.

It is possible to buy protection against inflation, again either by buying specialist bonds (index-linked gilts) or inflation-linked annuities or inflation-swaps. However, all these solutions are expensive and available usually only for the very largest funds. Few pension funds nowadays, for example, think it sensible to buy index-linked gilts at their present price, when buying equities or another investment might offer equivalent or even better value as a protection against inflation.

ADMINISTRATIVE RISKS

The administration of a pension scheme has never been easy and is now very complicated indeed. It has to cope with very complex regulatory provisions and a tax code which is a struggle for software writers to understand and manage. In practice, there is no such thing as a perfect administration system, and most administrators just try to do their best.

Accordingly, mistakes happen – and they usually happen to the benefits of your managing director. But even mistakes for the lower paid can, if not rectified soon, begin to build up costs – and trying to recover overpayments to a pensioner, for example, is not only difficult but can provoke severe ill-will.

There is a trend, which swings about every 10 years or so, on whether it is better to manage the administration in-house or outsource it to a specialist. The specialist may in turn have people in India or the Philippines doing most of the grunt work and offer considerable apparent savings. Very often, if things go wrong, the administrators will normally be insured and will pay up for overpayment of pensions, for example. In practice you should normally have mercy on them if things do go wrong; their margins are usually fairly tight, and you need to be pretty sure that another provider would be very much better, especially in the knowledge that changing administrators is probably more nerve-racking (and expensive) than getting divorced.

LIABILITY RISKS

Getting the numbers wrong can be expensive. Paying out the wrong sums, or failing to make proper reserves because the actuarial assumptions were incorrect, could prove very expensive. Actuarial consultancies have been all but ruined for putting a decimal point in the wrong place.

In practice the risk of an employer – or even trustees – being liable is very low, since they will invariably be acting on advice. However, it does no harm to have a reality check sometimes just to get a feel of whether the numbers look about right.

FIDUCIARY RISKS

Both employers and trustees are potentially liable for breach of trust – or, in the case of employers, for breach of a duty of good faith. Provided the paperwork looks reasonable and no money is stolen, in most cases even rather serious mistakes will not result in liability, despite warnings to the contrary. Control of liability is discussed below. There are now specialist 'fiduciary managers' who look after the investment management and, increasingly, executive trustees who look after the operation of the trust.

COMPLIANCE AND REGULATORY RISKS

Regulatory risks are more problematic. Firstly, regulators continually change the rules, and it is not always clear what the current regulations require. Secondly, there are some penalties against which the company or the trust cannot indemnify you; these are sometimes known as 'civil penalties', because they do not involve a criminal conviction, and the burden of proof against you is lower. On the other hand, most regulators are worried that some of these penalties are disproportionate and lack the protections needed under the Human Rights Act, and so are reluctant to bring cases against employers or trustees, except in the most egregious cases. In practice you can all but ignore the penalties, which look gruesome but are rarely, if ever, applied. The courts have been critical of high penalties imposed by regulators; a recent case saw a judge cut a regulator's order to a company to pay £5.2m down to £60,000. Regulatory risks in real life are low.

PROTECTION AGAINST RISKS

Things can and do go wrong. In practice few judges are keen to impose liabilities on employers or trustees for trying to do the right thing by their employees, and if there are good reasons, it is judicial practice to excuse liabilities, especially, for example, where the trustees are unpaid. There are, however, simple techniques for limiting the little liability that does exist, as shown below.

Insurance

Most directors' and officers' insurance carries modest protection for breach of contract and negligence involving pension schemes. Such policies are, however, usually restricted, and it is normally sensible to have dedicated insurance, which in particular carries on to protect you even after you have left the company and up to 12 years thereafter. If your business is owned by a foreign company, it is invariably very much better to have a UK insurance policy – if only because it is much easier to claim against in the remote event of you actually needing the cover. Whatever cover you have, you need protection against legal fees. Even if you are innocent of any breach of trust or negligence, simply defending yourself in court can prove expensive and ruinous.

Trustee exemption

Most pension fund deeds give exemption from liability to trustees – though not employers. The terms of the exemption clause can vary, and it is essential to ensure that it offers the most cover it can. Trustees should refuse to act unless the provisions are as wide as possible. Such clauses can protect you against all but actual fraud, and the courts are very supportive of them.

Trustee indemnity and employer indemnity

Even if you do something you should not have done, there can be clauses in the scheme documentation that allow or require the pension fund itself, and also the employer, to pay for any mistakes. Employer indemnity is very useful – but of course it is worthless if the employer goes bust. Of the two, trustee indemnity is more useful, but having both is best.

Corporate trustees
Again, unless you actually steal money from the pension fund, if you are a director of a company specially set up to be the trustee of the pension scheme, it is virtually impossible in practice for anyone to sue you. Being a personal trustee of the pension fund without a trustee company in the middle is riskier.

The judge
There is quite a lot of case law where the judges have made it clear that it is not the job of the courts to impose liabilities, unless they really have to. The Trustee Acts allow a judge to forgive you for a breach of trust where he or she thinks it appropriate to do so, and if a case ever gets that far (they don't) chances are that if you behave honestly and in good faith, they will let you off any liability.

CONCLUSION
Even though it entails risks, like anything else in life, the bottom line is that being involved in pensions is less risky than most of your existing activities in business and in your private life. Be aware, take advice – and don't worry about it.

If the decision is made to adopt insurance, however, it is important to have a policy specifically designed to respond to the needs of trustees and other individuals involved in the management of pensions. This is highlighted by the potential conflicts of interest which commonly exist when a trustee is also a director of the sponsoring employer company, with duties to the company and its shareholders. As a trustee, however, there is an overriding duty owed to the scheme beneficiaries, which is paramount. Accordingly, it is not recommended that reliance be placed upon a Directors & Officers (D&O) policy of insurance, as the cover will not be tailored to meet the specialised circumstances relating to pensions and there will potentially be competing calls on the policy. Furthermore, D&O policies will often contain an exclusion for any acts or omissions while acting as a trustee or administrator of the pension scheme.

Retired trustees

A trustee's personal exposure does not cease when they retire and their post-retirement situation may make them particularly vulnerable. Problems in pensions also often take a considerable time after the event to materialise. It is important, therefore, to check that the position of retired trustees and pension managers is properly protected. The solution is for retired trustees to have the guarantee of cover in the event that the scheme ceases to be insured. They can then rest assured that they have cover personal to them, irrespective of what the employer or trustees have or have not done about insurance since they retired. It is again important to check the extent of cover provided in this respect, as policies do vary.

OPDU Elite provides lifetime cover for retired trustees from the date of expiry of the main policy of insurance thus giving valuable peace of mind.

What should be covered?

The following is a guide to the main headings of cover which can be included:

- errors and omissions
- damages, judgements, settlements
- regulatory civil fines and penalties
- ombudsman awards
- defence costs
- full severability of cover
- individual representation
- maladministration
- public relation expenses
- extradition proceedings/bail bond costs
- prosecution costs
- employer indemnities
- exonerated losses
- litigation costs
- retirement cover – lifetime
- costs re: investigations by regulatory authorities
- media and arbitration
- court application costs
- third-party provider pursuit costs
- emergency costs
- discontinuance insurance for schemes in wind-up.

Court applications

Trustees and pension schemes can also incur significant legal expense in going to court to seek directions, or if they are joined by another party who is seeking the court's directions. Insurance can be obtained to cover those expenses which do not necessarily involve a legal liability upon the trustees, although the scheme will usually be responsible for the legal expenses of all the parties involved. There have been several high profile cases involving costs in excess of £1m which have had to be met from pension scheme funds.

OPDU Elite provides an extension to reimburse such costs – it is important to note that this type of legal expense would not usually fall within the scope of 'defence costs' as defined in many insurance policies.

Claims experience
OPDU's own claims experience has seen issues which have involved individual claim sums of up to £20m to date. One common feature, as one would anticipate, is the importance of the accuracy of data, and we therefore encourage trustees to ensure that regular data 'health checks' are undertaken. Other issues which have given rise to problems and potential liabilities include:

- incorrect formulas used for calculating benefits
- interpretation of Trust Deeds
- overpayment of benefits
- misapplication of scheme rules
- seeking court directions
- early retirement and ill-health disputes
- rectification proceedings
- accounting irregularities
- DC choices of investment funds
- Pension Sharing Orders
- general administration errors
- TUPE issues
- misrepresentations by trustees
- transfer values
- incorrect quotations
- discrepancies between scheme documentation and administration practice
- delays in transfer and payments of benefit assets
- PPF levy issues.

Cost
The cost of trustee liability insurance varies according to the size of the scheme, but is also dependent on several other factors. However, the cost starts at a few thousand pounds for a small scheme, and an approximate indication of cost should be able to be easily obtained for any size of scheme without having to complete a full application.

Conclusion
By taking out insurance, trustees can be confident that they are protected against liabilities that might arise in performing their duties, while also giving members comfort that their interests are being looked after properly in preserving the fund assets, which is particularly important today when deficits are common.

Jonathan Bull
Chairman & Executive Director
OPDU Limited

Jonathan.bull@opdu.com
www.opdu.com

OPDU is managed by THOMAS MILLER

CHAPTER 11
THE FUTURE

The one fact of life that applies in spades in pensions is that the system is continually changing. Part of the reason is that the world changing: the way we work, the length of time we are on average going to live, long-term interest rates, the economy and many other things ensure that the factors that give rise to a pension system never rest in stasis.

The two main factors described below, however, do not change.

1. For the foreseeable future, we have an ageing population that will need financial support in retirement – or at least in old age, when the ability to work diminishes.
2. Many of the changes are not driven by the forces of nature, but by anthropogenic forces. In other words, the legal, regulatory and tax rules seem to change almost daily, and it is often very hard to discern the policy drivers for these changes.

The problem that politicians and regulators face with pensions issues is that, as pensions are a long-term concern, changes to their system do not have an immediate political impact. For example, the tax changes in the late 1990s affecting the income of pension schemes did not really became apparent for around a decade (when the damage became all too apparent).

In addition to this, the UK policy is very hard to stabilise. For example, after 20 years of discussion, the government decided to simplify the pension's tax system, which had, since the 1950s, developed into around a dozen different tax regimes (different for occupational and personal pensions, for example). They also decided to go back to the first principles of pension's taxation (which are pretty simple), scrap the 1,300 pages of rules and develop a new unified, simplified system. In 2004 the Finance Act was passed to do just that (albeit it took around 200 pages of primary legislation). The intention was to scrap the hundred or so pages of HMRC guidance by making the system so easy to understand and administer that such guidance would be unnecessary. Within a year, however, HMRC thought it right to publish around 4,000 pages of guidance and, within the decade, the simplified system was amended by roughly another 400 pages of rules on anti-forestalling and, a little later, disguised remuneration. The purity of the system had hardly lasted a couple of years, and the UK seems alone in Europe in devising a system which lacks stability and promotes complexity.

There are similar concerns about the complexity of the regulation of pensions schemes. As defined benefit systems decline and defined contribution schemes (which in practice need little regulation because of their simplicity) become more common, regulation might be expected to decline. In fact it continues to expand almost daily to impose new obligations.

Unless there is a radical re-thinking of the regulatory framework, therefore, it is very likely that regulation and compliance requirements will continue to expand. The only hope is a slow growth of competition from Europe, where UK schemes can, if they wish, register with much simpler regulation. Several countries have made it clear they would welcome UK schemes coming to register with them, although few have yet done so.

The rest of this chapter explores what may be in the pipeline for pension provision in the UK over the next few years.

THE STATE SYSTEM

The state pension system is in a state of flux. It is, of course, difficult for the ordinary individual to understand, and the amounts of pension paid you can expect are variable in many cases. The Minster for Pensions in 2011 announced the government's intention, if it could, to simplify the system in due course so that the basic state pension would provide around £140 a week at age 66 – roughly the equivalent of £200 a week at age 70.

The advantages of the changes would include the fact that most people would have a financial target to beat, that means testing would mostly disappear, and that the basic pension would provide an amount that would be acceptable as a fallback position for most people. Some politicians object on the grounds that it might be non-contributory, ie paid to people who did not paid for it, but the relationship between benefits and contributions is today mostly symbolic. In due course, as the state system is currently unstable and complex,the indications are that over time it will be much simplified and made universal. Currently, the Treasury objects to the simplification because it fears it will cost the country more.

RETIREMENT AGES

Linked to state pensions are state pension ages. From October 2011 it became illegal to sack anyone without justifiable cause merely because they had reached a particular age (there might be exceptions for airline pilots, for example), but in future it looks as though expected ages of retirement will be linked to state pension ages, ie the earliest date at which the state will pay an old age pension. That age is scheduled to rise to 66 shortly (2020). It will then rise to 68 by 2046, but most commentators expect an age of 70 to come in well before then. In practice most of us will be expected to 'work until we drop' – a phrase used by the *Daily Mail* to damn the changes. Even at 70, many of those who reach that age might expect to have a pension for another 20 years – one of the longest holidays of most people's life.

COMPANIES AND PENSIONS

What is not predictable at this stage is whether companies will still be in the business of providing pensions. On the one hand, such provision has been made difficult and expensive for all the reasons set out in this book. Companies are also trying to reduce the scope of their involvement in employees' affairs, including the provision of pensions. On the other hand, provision through employers is very efficient, the government is encouraging it through auto-enrolment, and many employers see it as the decent thing to do, if they can. For the moment it looks as though employers will be involved in pension provision of one kind or another for many years to come, although it may be in different forms and different ways. It is very possible that unfunded pension systems will make a comeback, and that overseas schemes will become more popular.

What is virtually certain is that this book and whatever retirement policies you adopt in your company are unlikely to survive without a need for revision – perhaps major revision – in the next five years or so. The prayer must be that any further reforms are beneficial rather than not.

CONCLUSIONS

The provision of pensions through your company should be a good thing – but like any other good thing, such as a mansion or a yacht, it will need continual maintenance.

It is highly unlikely that the present pension's structure will last the decade, at least in its details, and you will need to spend just a little time in continual review. However, a decent pension system in your company can save a great deal of heartache, be highly cost-effective, and enable you and your colleagues to have a less financially stressful retirement than would otherwise be the case.

CHAPTER 12
CONCLUSIONS

Pensions are a long-term commitment for an employer, so it helps if you can get it right. However, what is right is not always clear – and what is right this year may not be right next year.

Here, therefore, are some guidelines that help in deciding what pension scheme to introduce, and how to manage it.

1. Bear in mind that even though a pension scheme is designed to operate for 60 years or more, and continual change is expensive and unsettling, external circumstances and the needs of the company suggest that things are bound to change, and the pension scheme structure needs to be able to cope with that.
2. Remember that any pension scheme will cost money and that it should deliver value for money – and that communication to members of the value it offers is worth every penny.
3. Pensions are complicated, and it does no harm to get in some expertise.
4. The sooner the scheme is started, the better it is for everyone in it.
5. For the lower paid, a pension scheme may be less sensible than an ISA.
6. For the higher paid, a non-UK pension scheme offers benefits for both the members and the company.
7. For the higher paid, an unfunded scheme may offer benefits for both the members and the company.
8. We are all going to live longer and work longer, and pensions are going to be more important rather than less important for all of us.
9. Relying on the state scheme alone is not going to be enough.
10. New kinds of (particularly defined contribution) schemes are going to emerge, and members and the company need to be ready for them.

APPENDIX I
OTHER SOURCES OF
INFORMATION

IFAS AND PERSONAL ADVISERS
Unbiased (formerly IFA Promotion)
Unbiased is an organisation that runs a website which helps you to find a local financial adviser (www.unbiased.co.uk).

Personal Finance Society
Personal Finance Society is a professional body for financial advisers in the UK. It has 29,000 members. (0208 530 0852; www.thepfs.org).

Institute of Financial Planning
Institute of Financial Planning is part of a US certifying body, which also helps to find local advisers (0117 945 2470; www.financialplanning.org.uk).

Money Advice Service
Money Advice Service (MAS) is an offshoot of the Financial Services Authority (or whatever replaces it – formerly the Consumer Financial Education Body). It is responsible for helping consumers understand financial matters and make informed choices by providing free, impartial financial information and advice. This is available online, in print, over the phone (0300 500 5000) or face-to-face. The website also has comparative tables, including one on annuities, where members of defined contribution schemes can enter their details and shop around for the best deal when choosing who pays them a pension when they retire. MAS offers a free financial education programme delivered free in the workplace. A list of printed guides from the MAS is available at www.moneyadviceservice.org.uk.

GOVERNMENT BODIES
Department of Work and Pensions
The DWP publishes a range of free pension guides in relation to state pensions on its Pension Service website. You can find information about pension arrangements on the DWP website at www.dwp.gov.uk/thepensionservice. For information on auto-enrolment, have a look at www.dwp.gov.uk/policy/pensions-reform and www.dwp.gov.uk/policy/pensions-reform/workplace-pension-reforms/#publications (they seem to be separate sites).

Gov.uk
Gov.uk has a useful search result if you type pensions into its search-box.

The Financial Services Authority (FSA)
The FSA is the financial services regulator set up by the government to regulate financial services and protect your rights. It sets standards that financial services firms have to meet, and can take action if they don't. The FSA regulates most types of financial services firms, such as banks, building societies, credit unions, insurance companies,

financial advisers, stockbrokers, and mortgage and insurance sellers. It has a register of firms it regulates (see www.fsa.gov.uk).

The Pensions Regulator (TPR)
The Pensions Regulator does what it says on the tin; unless you have a defined benefit scheme, in practice you should not need to look at it much, but it has useful guidance on auto-enrolment and NEST (see www.thepensionsregulator.gov.uk).

NEST (National Employment Savings Trust)
NEST is the fallback company pension scheme if you do not have your own. Their employer-dedicated helpline is 0300 303 1949 or you can contact employer.enquiries@ nestcorporation.org.uk (also see their website: www.nestpensions.org.uk).

TRADE BODIES
PENSIONSFORCE
PENSIONSFORCE (A National Association of Pension Funds' information service) offers presentations, normally free of charge, aimed at helping employees plan and save for their retirement (see www.pensionsforce.co.uk).

The Pensions Advisory Service (TPAS)
This is an independent voluntary organisation. Their website (www.pensionsadvisoryservice. org.uk) has a lot of guidance for members of pension schemes, including useful information on choosing an annuity at retirement. They also offer presentations on issues relating to pensions, normally free of charge.

WEBSITES
Set out below are some websites which may be useful for browsing; they include sources of information, regulatory websites, and news and information websites, all of which allow further exploration of issues raised in this book.

- www.asppa.org/main-menu/partners/cikr.aspx – Council of Independent 401(k) Recordkeepers (CIKR) (US) (see ASSPA)
- benefitslink.com/index.html – Benefits Link, information (US)
- ccactuaries.org – Conference of Consulting Actuaries (US)
- cerp.unito.it – Centre for Research on Pensions (CeRP), Turin, Italy
- crr.bc.edu – Boston University Center for Retirement Research
- dialspace.dial.pipex.com/town/road/xoq83 – local government pensions
- ec.europa.eu/social/main.jsp?catId=26&langId=en – EU coordination of social security schemes
- ec.europa.eu/internal_market/capital/docs/oxera_report_en.pdf – EU report on IORPS investments
- www.dol.gov/ebsa/ – Employee Benefits Security Administration (US)
- icpr.itam.mx/ – International Center for Pensions Research (Mexico)
- journals.cambridge.org/action/displayJournal?jid=PEF – CUP Journal of Pensions Economics and Finance
- www.asppa.org/TBD/NAIRPA.aspx – National Association of Independent Retirement Plan Advisors (NAIRPA) (US) (see ASSPA)
- professionalpensions.com – *Professional Pensions* (weekly)
- timeline.lge.gov.uk – time lined public local government pensions regulations
- www.northerntrust.com/tcharter – Transition managers code of practice

- web.worldbank.org/wbsite/external/topics/extsocialprotection/extpensions/0,,
  menupk:396259~pagepk:149018~pipk:149093~thesitepk:396253,00.html – World
  Bank pensions
- www.abcdboard.org – Actuarial Board for Counseling and Discipline (US)
- www.aca.org.uk – Association of Consulting Actuaries
- www.actuarialfoundation.org – The Actuarial Foundation (US)
- www.actuarialstandardsboard.org – Actuarial Standards Board (US)
- www.actuaries.asn.au – Institute of Actuaries of Australia
- www.actuaries.ca – Canadian Institute of Actuaries
- www.actuaries.org – International Actuarial Association
- www.actuaries.org.uk – Institute and Faculty of Actuaries
- www.actuaries.org/index.cfm?lang=EN&DSP=PBSS&ACT=INDEX – PBSS (International
  Actuaries Association
- www.actuary.org – American Academy of Actuaries (US)
- www.ageing.ox.ac.uk – Oxford Institute of Population Ageing
- www.aima.org – Alternative Investment Management Association
- www.apl.org.uk – Association of Pension Lawyers
- www.ariespensions.co.uk – Pensions information for techies
- www.artofpensions.com – pensions art
- www.asppa.org – American Society of Pension Professionals & Actuaries (ASPPA), (US)
- www.asppa.org/home-page/for-the-media/related-sites.aspx – ASPPA's list of
  related industry sites
- www.beanactuary.org – Be an actuary (US)
- www.cdc.retraites.fr/default.asp – French pensions research, in French
- www.insuranceeurope.eu – Insurance Europe
- www.pensionsarchive.org – Pensions Archive Trust
- www.civilservice-pensions.gov.uk – Civil Service Pension Scheme
- www.gov.uk/browse/working – government pensions advice
- www.dwp.gov.uk/pensionsreform – DWP
- www.efrp.org – European Federation for Retirement Provision
- www.frs17.com – private site explaining pension accounting principles
- www.gad.gov.uk – Government Actuary's Department
- www.gcactuaries.org – European Actuarial Consultative Group
- www.globalpensions.com – Global Pensions magazine
- www.gmb.org.uk/pensions – GMB Pension Guide
- www.ibisevisor.com – international benefits guide
- www.ici.org – Investment Company Institute
- www.ieba.org.uk – International Employee Benefits Association
- www.ifebp.org – International Foundation [of benefits] (US)
- www.ifsl.org.uk – International Financial Services London, research on pensions
  reform
- www.iipm.ie – Irish Institute of Pensions Managers
- www.institutionalinvestor.com – Watson Wyatt top 500 managers
- www.intelligencecentre.com – trustees investments
- www.investmentuk.org – Investment Management Association
- www.ipd.com – IPD pan-European property Index
- www.issa.int/engl/homef.htm – International Social Security Association
- www.johnralfe.com/ – idiosyncratic pensions commentary
- www.jscpa.or.jp – The Japanese Society of Certified Pension Actuaries
- www.lgps.org.uk – Local Government Pension Scheme
- www.life-academy.co.uk – Life Academy pre-retirement

- www.uss.co.uk/UssInvestments/Responsibleinvestment/marathonclub – Marathon Club on longer term investment
- www.fsa.gov.uk/consumerinformation/product_news/pensions – FSA consumer pensions
- www.napf.co.uk – National Association of Pension Funds
- www.nappa.org – National Association of Public Pension Attorneys (US)
- www.nhsbsa.nhs.uk/pensions – NHS pension scheme
- www.nikko-fi.co.jp – Japanese pensions information
- www.nipa.org – National Institute of Pension Administrators
- www.oecd.org/els/pensionsystems/ – OECD pensions
- www.opalliance.org.uk – Occupational Pensioners' Alliance
- www.opdu.co.uk – Occupational Pensions Defence Union
- www.pendragon.co.uk – Perspective pensions information service
- www.pensionprotectionfund.org.uk – Pension Protection Fund
- www.pensionreforms.com – international study group
- www.pensions.gold.org – World Gold Council
- www.pensionsadvisoryservice.org.uk – TPAS (The Pensions Advisory Service)
- www.pensionschampions.co.uk – TUC pensions training
- www.pensions-institute.org – Pensions Institute, City University
- journals.cambridge.org/action/displayJournal?jid=PEF – *Journal of Pension and Economics Finance*
- www.pensionsweek.com – *Pensions Week*
- www.pensions-ombudsman.org.uk – Pensions Ombudsman
- www.pensions-pmi.org.uk – Pensions Management Institute
- www.pensionspolicyinstitute.org.uk – Pensions Policy Institute
- www.pensions-research.org – IPRN website
- www.pensionstrategies.co.uk – adviser's research
- www.pensionsworld.co.uk – *Pensions World* magazine
- plainenglish.co.uk/news/protecting-your-pot-the-plain-english-guide-to-pensions. html – a plain English guide to pensions
- www.prag.org.uk – Pensions Research Accountants Group
- www.prg.org.uk – Independent Pensions Research Group
- www.qrops.net – QROPS advice
- www.rba.go.ke – Retirement Benefits Authority, Kenya
- www.pensionsage.com – *Pensions Age* magazine
- www.sias.org.uk – Staple Inn Actuarial Society
- www.soa.org – Society of Actuaries (US)
- www.spc.uk.com – Society of Pension Consultants
- www.sppa.gov.uk – Scottish Public Pensions Agency
- www.gov.uk/personal-pensions-your-rights – Stakeholder pensions, moribund
- www.teacherspensions.co.uk – Teachers Pension Scheme
- www.theactuary.com – *The Actuary* magazine
- www.thepensionsregulator.gov.uk – The Pensions Regulator
- www.trustees.org.uk – The Association of Corporate Trustees
- www.investmenttutor.com – Morley Fund Managers; investment education
- www.trusteeweb.co.uk – PMI trustees
- www.worksmart.org.uk/money/viewsection.php?sen=3 – Trades Union Congress (TUC)
- www.ubs.com – Pension Fund Indicators; International Pension Fund Indicators
- www.uksif.org/pension-funds – Social Investment Forum
- www.uksip.org – United Kingdom Society of Investment Professionals

- www.walker-gmg.co.uk – Walker Working Group Private Equity Working Group on Transparency and Disclosure
- policydialogue.org/programs/?ptid=2&prid=20 – Initiative for Policy Dialogue, Pensions (US)
- www.gcactuaries.org/publications.html – Groupe Consultatif Actuaries European

APPENDIX II
ABBREVIATIONS AND
INITIALISATIONS

NOTE

The alphabet soup of acronyms in the pension field can be confusing even for practitioners. The collection below is designed for non-technicians, and includes pensions industry and investment industry terms and abbreviations which the lay pensions trustee is likely to come across in practice. The selection has mostly been made on the grounds of practicality, but some of them are esoteric and will be stumbled across only by trustees of the very largest schemes.

Technical definitions designed for technicians can be found in Pensions Research Accountants Group/Pensions Management Institute, *Pensions Terminology*, 8th ed, 2011 and on the HMRC website (www.hmrc.gov.uk).

Obs (obsolete) signifies that a term is no longer current but is listed because it may apply to older arrangements

AA	Annual allowance
AADB	Accountancy and Actuarial Discipline Board
AAF	Audit and Assurance Faculty (of ICAEW)
ABI	Association of British Insurers (www.abi.org.uk)
ABO	Accrued Benefit Obligation
ABS	Admitted Body Status (public sector schemes)
ACA	Association of Consulting Actuaries (www.aca.org.uk)
ACCA	Association of Chartered Certified Accountants (www.accaglobal.com)
ACD	Authorised Corporate Director (in relation to OIECs)
ACT	(1) Advance Corporation Tax (obs) (2) Association of Corporate Treasurers
AEIP	European Association of Paritarian Institutions
AFIRE	Association of Foreign Investors in Real Estate (www.afire.org)
AGLS	Accrued GMP Liability Service (DWP)
AGM	Annual general meeting
AIC	Association of Investment Companies (www.theaic.co.uk)
AIFA	Association of Independent Financial Advisors
AILO	Association of International Life Offices (www.ailo.org)
AIM	Alternative Investment Market
AIMMI	Association for Institutional Multi Manager Investing
AIMR	Association for Investment and Research (obs, now CFAI)

AITC	Association of Investment Trust Companies (obs); see AIC
ALM	Asset Liability Modelling/Management
AMC	Annual management charge
AML	Additional maternity leave; no pension contributions need to be paid. See also OML and SML
AMNT	Association of Member Nominated Trustees
AMPS	Association of Member-directed Pension Schemes; club for managers of SASSs and SIPPs
AOP	Alliance of Occupational Pensioners (obs)
AP	Additional pension
APB	Auditing Practices Board (www.frc.org.uk/apb)
APC	Auditing Practices Committee (obs)
APCIMS	Association of Private Client Investment Managers and Stockbrokers
APL	Association of Pension Lawyers
APMI	Associate of the Pensions Management Institute
APP	Appropriate Personal Pension
APPGOP	All-Party Parliamentary Group on Occupational Pensions
APPS	Appropriate Personal Pension Scheme
APPSHP	Appropriate Personal Pension Stakeholder Pension
APREA	Asian Public Real Estate Association
APSS	Audit and Pension Scheme Services (HMRC, obs); formerly SFO, formerly PSO, now PSS
APT	(1) Association of Pensioneer Trustees (obs), see AMPS; (2) Awards in Pensions Trusteeship (PMI); (3) Arbitrage pricing theory
AREF	Association of Real Estate Funds (www.aref.org.uk)
ARP	Accrued Rights Premium
ARR	Age Related Rebate
ASB	Accounting Standards Board (www.frc.org.uk/asb)
ASCN/ASCON	Appropriate Scheme Contracted-Out Number
ASFA	Association of Superannuation Funds of Australia
ASFONZ	Association of Superannuation Funds of New Zealand
ASP	(1) Additional state pension; see S2P; SERPS; (2) Alternatively secured pension
ASPPA	American Society of Pension Professionals & Actuaries (www.asppa.org)
AUM	Assets under management
AUT	Apparent Unnotified Termination
AVC	Additional voluntary contributions (almost obs)
AVR	Actuarial Valuation Report
BA	Benefits Agency (obs), see Pension Service

BAS   Board for Actuarial Standards

BASPSC   Bulgarian Association of Supplementary Pension Security Companies (Bulgaria) (www.assoc.pension.bg/en)

BCE3   Benefit Crystallisation Event 3 (HMRC)

BIBA   British Insurance Brokers' Association (www.biba.org.uk)

BIIBA   obs; see BIBA

BOJ   Bank of Japan

bps   Basis points (one basis point is 1/100%)

BRIC   Brazil Russia India China

BSP   Basic state pension

BVCA   British Private Equity and Venture Capital Association

CA   (1) Certified Amount; (2) Companies Act; (3) Contributions Agency (obs)

CAIAA   Chartered Alternative Investment Analyst Association (US) (www.caia.org)

CalPERS California Public Employees Retirement System

CAPM   Capital Asset Pricing Model

CAPS   Combined Actuarial Performance Services (obs); see Russell Mellon CAPS

CAPSA   Canadian Association of Pension Supervisory Authorities (www.capsa-acor.org)

CAR   (1) Charity Assets and Residence (HMRC) division dealing with pensions policy; (2) Customer Agreed Remuneration (ie fees)

CARE   Career average revalued earnings (scheme)

CAT   Charges, Access and Terms

CBA   Cost Benefit Analysis

CBI   Confederation of British Industry (www.cbi.org.uk)

CCF   Common Contractual Fund (Ireland); see PFPV

CCP   Convertible cumulative preference

CCRPS   Cumulative convertible redeemable preference share

CDC   Collective defined contribution (Netherlands)

CDO   Collateralised Debt Obligation

CE   Cash equivalent

CEDR   Centre for Effective Dispute Resolution; operates pensions mediation

CEE   Central and Eastern Europe

CEEF   Central and Eastern European Forum; see EFRP

CEIOPS   Committee of European Insurance and Occupational Pensions Supervisors (obs); legal cartel of regulators; see now EIOPA

CEO   Chief Executive Officer

CEP   Contributions Equivalent Premium

CERES   Committee of Environmentally Responsible Investors (US) (www.ceres.org)

CESR	Committee of European Securities Regulators (www.cesr-eu.org)
CETV	Cash equivalent transfer value (obs); see CE
CFA	Chartered Financial Analyst
CFAI	Chartered Financial Analyst Institute (www.cfainstitute.org)
CFD	Contract For Differences
CFEB	Consumer Financial Education Body (obs); now Money Advice Service
CFP	Certified Financial Planner (www.financialplanning.org.uk)
CFXO	Collateralised Foreign Exchange Obligation
CGT	Capital gains tax
CIF	Common Investment Fund
CII	(1) Chartered Insurance Institute; (2) Council of Institutional Investors (www.cii.org) (US)
CIMPS	Contracted-In Money Purchase Scheme
CIP	Cumulative Irredeemable Preference Share
CLD	Consolidated Life Directive (EU)
CLO	Collateralised Loan Obligations
CMBS	Commercial Mortgage Backed Securities
CME	Chicago Mercantile Exchange
CMI	Continuous mortality investigation; actuarial study into longevity
CNV	Convertible bond
COCIS	Contracted-Out Contribution/Earnings Information Service
COD	Contracted-Out Deduction
COEG	Contracted-Out Employments Group (obs); see NISPI
COEL	Contracted-Out Early Leavers Section (HMRC/NISPI)
COMBS	Contracted-Out Mixed Benefit Scheme
COMMS	Contracted-Out data transaction using magnetic media service (HMRC/NISPI)
COMPS	CIMPS, COSRS, CISRS, etc Contracted-Out Money Purchase Schemes, Contracted-In Money Purchase Schemes, Contracted-Out Salary Related Schemes, Contracted-In Salary Related Schemes
COMPSHP	Stakeholder Contracted-Out Money Purchase Scheme
COPAS	Confederation of Occupational Pensioners' Associations (obs)
COPRP	Contracted-Out Protected Rights Premium
COSOP	Cabinet Office Statement of Practice
CP	Consultation paper
CPA	Compulsory purchase annuity
CPF	Combined Pension Forecast (DWP)
CPI	Consumer Price Index

CPPS	Convertible participating preference share
CR	Corporate responsibility
CRE	Commercial Real Estate
CREIF	National Council of Real Estate Investment Fiduciaries (US) (www.ncreif.com)
CREST	part of Euroclear's central securities depositary
CRSLS	Convertible redeemable secured loan stock
CSIPP	Corporate self-invested personal pension
CSR	Corporate social responsibility
CT	Corporation tax
CTA	Commodity Trading Advisor (US)
CULS	Convertible unsecured loan stock
D&B	Dun & Bradstreet; an (inappropriate) rating service used to determine pensions levy amounts
DB	Defined benefit
DBERR	Department for Business Enterprise and Regulatory Reform
DC	Defined contribution
DCC	Double Century Club
DEBRS	Diploma in Employee Benefits and Retirement Savings (PMI)
DGF	Diversified growth funds
DipIEB	Diploma in International Employee Benefits (see PMI)
DIS	Death in service
DMD	Direct Marketing Directive (EU)
DMO	Debt Management Office (of the Treasury) – (www.dmo.gov.uk) issues gilts
DPC	Diploma in Pension Calculations (see PMI)
DRA	Default Retirement Age; formerly 60 for women and 65 for men under UK employment law – has now been phased out
DRP	Dispute resolution procedure; see IDRP
DSS	Department of Social Security (obs); see DWP
DWP	The Department for Work and Pensions; governs contracting out, pensions policy and state pensions
EAT	Employment Appeal Tribunal
EBITDA	Earnings before interest, taxation, depreciation and amortisation
EBRI	Employee Benefits Research Institute (US)
EBT	Employee benefit trust
ECE	Employment Cessation Event
ECJ	European Court of Justice
ECON	Employer's Contracted-Out Number

ECR	Employer compliance regime; that bit of the Pensions Regulator that deals with employer compliance for auto-enrolment
ED	Exposure Draft
EDM	Emerging Domestic Markets
EEA	European Economic Area (ie EU + Norway, Iceland, Lichtenstein)
EEE	Exempt, Exempt, Exempt – only in Slovakia (tax); see also EET
EET	Exempt, Exempt, Taxed; formula for most EU pension systems on contributions, investments and benefits (tax)
EFAMA	European Fund and Asset Management Association (www.efama.org)
EFRB	Employer-financed retirement benefit
EFRBS	Employer-funded retirement benefits scheme (HMRC)
EFRP	European Federation for Retirement Provision (the club for NAPF equivalents around Europe)
EGM	Extraordinary general meeting
EHRC	Equality and Human Rights Commission (www.equalityhumanrights.com); formerly Commission for Equality and Human Rights, formerly Disability Rights Commission, Equal Opportunity Commission, etc
EIOPA	European Insurance and Occupational Pensions Authority; formerly CEIOPS
EIPC	European Investment Performance Committee; see IPC; GIPS
EIRS	Ethical Investment Research Service
EM	Emerging markets; places in which to invest that do not really have a stock market
EMEA	Europe Middle East Africa
EMPEA	Emerging Markets Private Equity Association (US)
EMTN	Euro medium term note
EOC	Equal Opportunities Commission (obs); see EHRC
EPB	Equivalent pension benefit
EPD	European Pensions Directive; see IORP
EPM	Efficient Portfolio Management
EPP	Executive Pension Plan (obs)
EPRA	European Public Real Estate Association (www.epra.com)
EPUT	Exempt property unit trusts; often bespoke, to deal with SIPP issues
ERF	Early Retirement Factor
ERI	Employer-related investment
ERISA	Employee Retirement Income Security Act 1974 (US)
ESG	Environmental, social and governance (UN); see SRI; SEE
ETF	Exchange traded funds
ETT	Exempt, Taxed, Taxed; see EET

ETV	Enhanced transfer value; somewhat disapproved of by TPR
EU	European Union
EVCA	European Private Equity and Venture Capital Association (www.evca.com)
FA	Finance Act
FAA	Flexible apportionment arrangement: an arrangement introduced in October 2011 by the DWP to ameliorate the impact of s75 employer debt obligations on plan sponsors
FAIF	Funds of Alternative Investment Funds (FSA)
FAS	Financial Assistance Scheme (www.dwp.gov.uk/fas)
FASB	Financial Accounting Standards Board
FATCA	Foreign Account Tax Compliance Act (US); it affects UK pension funds investing in the US
FBT	Family benefit trust
FCA	Financial Conduct Authority; it replaces in part the FSA and acts as consumer watchdog, sitting outside the bank of England but subject to its authority
FCF	Fraud Compensation Fund; replaced PCB, run by the PPF
FCP	*Fonds Commun de Placement* (Luxembourg); see PFPV
Fed	Federal Reserve (US)
FFA	Fellow of the Faculty of Actuaries (Scotland)
FGR	*Fonds voor Gemene Rekening* (Netherlands); see PFPV
FIA	Fellow of the Institute of Actuaries
FIAP	International Federation of Pension Funds Administrators (Chile) (www.fiap.cl)
FICO	Financial Intermediaries Claims Office; see APSS
FoA	Faculty of Actuaries (Scotland)
FOF	Fund of Funds
FOHF	Fund of Hedge Funds
FOMC	Federal Open Markets Committee (US); cf MPC
FOS	Financial Ombudsman Service
FPC	Financial Policy Committee; headed by the Bank of England governor, sits at the apex of financial regulatory architecture. It partly replaces the FSA; see also PRA and FCA
FPMI	Fellow of the Pensions Management Institute
FRAG	Financial Reporting and Accounting Group (obs); see ICAEW and AAF
FRC	Financial Reporting Council
FRED	Financial Reporting Exposure Draft
FRN	Floating rate note
FRS	Financial Reporting Standard

FSA	Financial Services Authority (obs, and quite right too); see now PRA (Prudential Regulation Authority), FCA (Financial Conduct Authority) and FPC (Financial Policy Committee)
FSAVC	Free-standing additional voluntary contributions (almost obs)
FSCS	Financial Services Compensation Scheme (FSA)
FSD	Financial support direction (TPR)
FSMA	Financial Services and Markets Act 2000
FSS	Funding strategy statement
FSSC	Financial Services Skills Council; certifies TKU NOS for TPR
FTSE100	Financial Times Stock Exchange top 100 quoted companies
FURBS	Funded unregistered [unapproved] retirement benefit scheme (obs); see EFRBS
FVD	Fair Value Difference (TPR)
GAAP	Generally Accepted Accounting Principles
GAD	Government Actuary's Department
GBP	£, pound sterling
GCA	Grandfathered Corresponding Acceptance; cross-border schemes
GDCV	Genuinely diverse commercial vehicle (HMRC)
GDP	Gross domestic product
GFA	Generic financial advice; cf Thoresen Report
GIP	Group Income Protection
GIPS	Global Investment Performance Standards (http://gipsstandards.org)
GMP	Guaranteed Minimum Pension; being the replacement (by the company scheme) for the state second tier pension. Nowadays, it may not be guaranteed or provide a minimum pension
GN	Guidance note; issued by the Board for Actuarial Standards
GP	General Partner
GPP	Group personal pension
GPPP	Group personal pension plan
GRI	Global Reporting Initiative; property investment measurement
GSAS	General Statement of Administration Standards; see PASA, RSPA
GShP	Group Stakeholder Pension
GSIPPS	Group self-invested personal pension scheme
GTAA	Global Tactical Asset Allocation
H1	First half of the year
HICP	Harmonised Index of Consumer Prices
HIERC	High income excess relief charge (HMRC)
HMRC	Her Majesty's Revenue & Customs; formerly the Inland Revenue
HMSO	Her Majesty's Stationery Office (obs)

HMT	Her Majesty's Treasury
HNW	High net worth (rich)
HNWI	High net worth (ie rich) individual
HRP	Home Responsibilities Protection
IAS	International Accounting Standard; IAS 19 is revised in 2013 so that companies in future have to disclose their pension liabilities by reference to the return on AA bonds, rather than actual scheme assets – not a good move
iBOXX	Index of cash bonds (US) (www.iboxx.com)
ICAEW	Institute of Chartered Accountants of England and Wales
ICAS	Institute of Chartered Accountants of Scotland
ICBP	International Consortium of British Pensioners (www.pension-parity-uk.com); it lost the *Carson* case which tried to get inflation-proofing for pensions paid overseas . . .
ICGN	International Corporate Governance Network (www.icgn.org)
ICTA	Income and Corporation Taxes Act
ICVC	Investment Company with Variable Capital; FSA definition of an OIEC
IDR	(1) Income drawdown; (2) Internal dispute resolution
IDRP	Internal Dispute Resolution Procedure
IEBA	International Employee Benefits Association
IFA	Independent financial adviser
IFP	Institute of Financial Planning
IFRIC	International Financial Reporting Interpretations Committee (IFRIC 14)
IFRS	International Financial Reporting Standard
IGG	Investment Governance Group (HM Treasury)
IHT	Inheritance tax
ILB	Index-Linked Bonds
IMA	(1) Investment Management Association; (2) Investment management agreement
INPRS	International Network of Pension Regulators and Supervisors (OECD)
INREV	European Association for Investors in Non-listed Real Estate Vehicles
IoA	Institute of Actuaries
IOPS	International Organisation of Pension Supervisors
IORP	Institutions for Occupational Retirement Provision [Directive]; ie European Pensions Directive 2003
IPA	Individual pension account (obs)
IPAC	Investment Professionals Advocacy Committee (UKSIP)
IPC	(1) International Pension Centre (DWP); (2) Investment Performance Council (see GIPS)

IPEBLA	International Pensions and Employee Benefits Lawyers Association
IPO	Initial public offering
IPPM	Institute of Payroll and Pensions Management
IPRN	International Pensions Research Network (OECD)
IPSPC	Independent Public Service Pensions Commission (Hutton Report, 2011)
IPTG	Independent Pension Trustees Group (PMI)
IR	Inland Revenue (obs); see HMRC
IRA	Individual retirement account (US)
IRNICO	Inland Revenue National Insurance Contributions Office (semi-obs); see NISPI
IRPS	Investment Regulated Pension Schemes (HMRC); see SASS, SIPP
IRR	Internal rate of return
IRSPSS	Inland Revenue Savings, Pensions, Share Schemes (obs) see PSS
ISA	Individual savings account
ISC	Institutional Shareholders Committee
ISDA	International Swaps and Derivatives Association (sets out standard contracts, eg swaps contracts)
ISIN	International Securities Identification Numbering
ISS	Institutional Shareholder Services
ITEPA	Income Tax (Earnings and Pensions) Act 2003
JOM	Joint Office Memorandum (obs)
JWG	Joint Working Group; occupational pension schemes; NAPF, ABI, etc
LA	Lifetime allowance (HMRC)
LAC	Lifetime Allowance Charge (HMRC)
LAEF	Lifetime allowance enhancement factor (HMRC)
LAPFF	Local Authority Pension Fund Forum
LBO	Leveraged buy-out
LDI	Liability driven investment
LEA	Late Earnings Addition; anti-franking
LEL	Lower earnings limit
LET	Low earnings threshold
LGPC	Local Government Pensions Committee
LGPS	Local Government Pension Scheme
LIBA	London Investment Banking Association
LLA	Later life adviser
LLP	Limited Liability Partnership
LOA	Leave of absence

LP	Limited partner; Limited Partnership
LPFA	London Pension Fund Authority
LPI	Limited price indexation
LPR	Legal Personal Representative
LRF	Late retirement factor
LRP	Limited Revaluation Premium
LSDB	Lump sum death benefit
LSE	London Stock Exchange
LTD	Long-term disability
M&A	Mergers and acquisitions
MAC	Multi-asset class
MAF	Market Adjustment Factor
MAS	Money Advice Service; formerly CFEB; part of FSA
MBO	Management buy-out
MCBPP	Multinational Cross-Border Pooling Products (US)
MDPSA	Member Directed Pensions Scheme Administration (PMI)
MEPP	Multi-Employer Pension Plan (Can)
MFR	Minimum Funding Requirement (obs) see statutory funding objective
MIFID	Markets In Financial Instruments Directive (EU)
MIG	Minimum Income Guarantee (obs) see State pension credit
MIR	Minimum Income Requirement
MLI	Market Level Indicator (obs)
MMR	Migrant Member Relief (HMRC) cross-border pension plans
MND	Member Nominated Director
MNT	Member nominated trustee
MPBR	More Principles-Based Regulation
MPC	Monetary Policy Committee (of the Bank of England)
MSCI	Morgan Stanley Capital International [Index]
MTF	Multilateral Trading Facility
MVA	(1) Market Value Adjustment; (2) Market Value of Assets (EU)
MVL	Market Value of Liabilities (EU)
MVR	Market Value Reduction
MWRR	Married women's reduced rate (HMRC/NISPI)
NAE	National average earnings
NAGDCA	National Association of Government Defined Contribution Administrators Inc (US)
NAO	National Audit Office; supervises TPR

NAPF	National Association of Pension Funds
NASRA	National Association of State Retirement Administrators (www.nasra. org) (US)
NAV	Net asset value
NBV	Net book value
NDPB	Non-departmental public body; ie quango
NEST	National Employment Savings Trust (formerly Personal Accounts, formerly NPSS); the fourth state pension
NI	National Insurance
NIC	National Insurance contributions
NICO	National Insurance Contributions Office (obs)
NINo	National Insurance number
NIRS	National Institute on Retirement Security (US); www.nirsonline.org
NIRS	National Insurance Recording System
NISPI	National Insurance Services to the Pensions Industry
NISPI COEL	Contracted-Out Early Leavers Section (HMRC/NISPI)
NISPI RPWB	Retirement Pension/Widows Benefit (HMRC/NISPI)
NMPA	Normal minimum pension age
NOSP	National Occupational Standards for Pensions [for trustees]; see FSSC
NPA	Normal pension age
NPC	National Pensioners Convention
NPD	Normal pension date
NPSS	National Pensions Savings Scheme (obs); see PA
NRA	Normal Retirement Age
NRD	Normal retirement date
NRE	Net relevant earnings (obs)
NURS	Non-UCITS Retail Scheme
OECD	Organisation for Economic Cooperation and Development (www.oecd. org)
OEIC	Open-Ended Investment Company
OFEX	Off Exchange (obs); now PLUS markets
OFP	*Organisations de Financement de Pensions* (Belgium); pan-European plan
OML	Ordinary maternity leave (26 weeks); pension contributions must be paid. See AML and SMP
OMO	Open Market Option
ONS	Office of National Statistics
OPA	Occupational Pensioners Alliance (www.opalliance.org.uk)
OPAS	Occupational Pensions Advisory Service (obs); see TPAS

OPB	Occupational Pensions Board (obs); see TPR
OPC	Occupational Pensions Committee (of CEIOPS) (EU)
OPDU	Occupational Pensions Defence Union (www.opdu.co.uk)
OPEB	Other Post-Employment Benefits (US accounting)
OPRA	Occupational Pensions Regulatory Authority (obs); see TPR
OPS	Occupational pension scheme
OPSG	Occupational Pensions Stakeholder Group (of EIOPA) (EU)
OPT	Occupational Pension Trusts (www.optrusts.com)
OTC	Over the counter; ie not quoted in a market
PA	(1) Pensions Act; (2) Personal Account (DWP)
PAB	Personal Accounts Board (DWP)
PADA	Personal Accounts Delivery Authority (DWP)
PAG	Pensions Action Group
PAIF	Property Authorised Investment Funds (Treasury)
PAYE	Pay as you earn
PAYG	Pay as you go
PBGC	Pension Benefit Guarantee Corporation (US)
PBO	Projected Benefit Obligation
PCAO	Pension Compensation Attachment Order (PPF) (MCA 1973 s25F/PA 2008)
PCB	Pensions Compensation Board (obs); see FCF
PCLS	Pension commencement lump sum
PCS	Professional Conduct Standards; actuarial
PCSO	Pension Compensation Sharing Order (PPF); MCA 1973 s21B/PA 2008
PCSPS	Principal Civil Service Pension Scheme
PEC	Private Equity Council
PEIA	Private Equity Investors Association
PEIGG	Private Equity Industry Guidelines Group
PEP	Personal Equity Plan (obs); see ISA
PFPS	Pension fund pooling scheme; same as PFPV
PFPV	Pension fund pooling vehicle; same as PFPS
PFS	Personal Finance Society; part of CII
PHI	Permanent Health Insurance
PIA	Pension Input Amount (HMRC)
PIE	Pension Increase Exchange; a way of reducing employer liabilities by offering cash in exchange for members agreeing to lose rights to pension increases
PIGS	see PIIGS

PIIGS	Portugal, Ireland, Italy, Greece, Spain
PIK	Payment-in-kind
PIL	Payment in lieu
PIP	Pension input period (HMRC)
PIPA	Pension and Investment Provider Awards; FT and *Pensions Week/ Pensions Management*
PIPE	Private Investment in Public Entities (US)
PIRC	Pensions Investment Research Consultants
PIV	Pooled investment vehicle; see PRAG, reporting on the economic shape of pension scheme investment portfolios, 2011
PIWG	Pensions Industry Working Group (HMRC)
PLA	(1) Personal lifetime allowance (HMRC); (2) Purchased life annuity
PLCUC	Pensions Litigation Court Users Committee
PLRC	Pensions Law Review Committee (the Goode Report)
PMI	Pensions Management Institute (www.pensions-pmi.org.uk)
PN	Practice Notes (HMRC, obs); see RPSM
PO	Pensions Ombudsman
POB	Professional Oversight Board (actuaries)
PPCC	Personal Pensions Contributions Certificate (obs)
PPEC	Pension Plan Executive Certificate (PMI)
PPF	Pension Protection Fund; the Fund uses your money to protect other people's pensions. How long it will survive in its present form is uncertain
PPFB	Pension Protection Fund Board
PPFO	Pension Protection Fund Ombudsman
PPI	(1) Pooled pension investment; (2) Payment protection insurance; (3) Pensions Policy Institute
PPIA	Protected Pension Input Amounts (HMRC)
PPP	Personal pension plan
PPPRP	Personal Pension Protected Rights Premium
PPS	Personal pension scheme
PQM	Pension Quality Mark (NAPF)
PR	(1) Pensions Registry; (2) Personal Representative; (3) Protected rights
PRA	(1) Pre-Retirement Association (obs); now Life Academy; (2) Prudential Regulatory Authority; a future agency, formed as one of the successors to the Financial Services Authority. The PRA will be part of the Bank of England and will carry out the prudential regulation of financial firms, including banks, investment banks, building societies and insurance companies
PRAG	Pensions Research Accountants Group (www.prag.org.uk)
PREA	Pension Real Estate Association (www.prea.org)

PRI	Principles for Responsible Investment (UN); see SRI
PRP	(1) Pensioner's Rights Premium; (2) Protected Rights Premium
PRT	Pensions Regulator Tribunal
PRTAC	Pension Risk Transfer Advisory Council
PSA	Pension Schemes Act
PSO	Pension Schemes Office (obs); see APSS
PSS	Pension savings statement (HMRC)
PSS	Pension Schemes Services (Forum) (HMRC)
PSTR	Pension Scheme Tax Reference (HMRC PSS)
PT	Primary Threshold
PTL	Pension Trustee Liability (insurance)
PTRAS	Pension Tax Relief At Source
PUCODI	Payable Uprated Contracted-Out Deduction Increments
PUP	Paid Up Pension
PURPLE	Pensions Universe Risk Profile (PPF/TPR), annual survey of registered pension schemes
PUT	Property unit trust
Q1	First quarter of the year
QDIA	Qualified default investment alternatives (US)
QEF	Qualifying earnings factor
QIF	Qualifying investment fund
QIS	(1) Qualified Investor Scheme (FSA); (2) Quantitative Impact Study (EU)
QNUPS	Qualifying Non-UK Pension Scheme (HMRC)
QOPS	Qualifying Overseas Pension Schemes (HMRC); cf QROPS, QNUPS
QPA	Qualification in Pensions Administration; see PMI
QPSIP	Qualifying pension scheme indemnity provision; Companies Act 2006 s235
QPSPA	Qualification in Public Sector Pensions Administration; see PMI
QROPS	Qualifying Recognised Overseas Pension Schemes (HMRC)
QSERP	Qualified Supplemental Executive Retirement Plans (US)
QWPS	Qualifying workplace pension scheme; cf NEST
RAC	Retirement Annuity Contract (obs)
RAP	(1) Retirement Annuity Policy (obs); (2) Retirement Annuity Premium (obs)
RAS	Relief at source (tax)
RDR	Retail Distribution Review (FSA)
REIS	Real Estate Information Standards
REIT	Real Estate Investment Trust

RIRC	Retirement Income Reform Campaign
RMBS	Residential Mortgage Backed Security
ROI	Return on investment
ROPP	Rebate Only Personal Pension (obs)
ROPS	Recognised Overseas Pension Scheme (HMRC); see QROPS
RP	Retirement Pension (state)
RPA	Responsible Paying Authority
RPC	Retirement Provision Certificate; see PMI
RPD	Retirement Provision Diploma
RPI	Retail Price Index
RPSM	Registered Pension Schemes Manual (HMRC)
RPWB	Retirement Pension/Widows Benefit (HMRC/NISPI)
RREV	Research Recommendations and Electronic Voting (NAPF); see ISS
RSPA	Raising Standards of Pensions Administration (obs); see now PASA (www.pasa-uk.com)
RST	Reference scheme test
RSTE	Raising Standards of Trustee Education (www.rste.co.uk)
RU64	(FSA) Conduct of Business Rule 5.3.16R(3) where a personal pension is recommended in preference to a stakeholder, the suitability letter must explain why (cf FSA CP 05/8, June2005); 2007.02.26 PSA PS 07/01
S&P	Standard Poor's
s179	Pensions Act 2004 s179
s226	Section 226 (ICTA 1988)
S2P	State second pension
s32	Section 32
s608	ICTA 1970
s67	Pensions Act 1995 s67; deals with modification of pension scheme rules
s75	Pensions Act 1995 s75; deals with debt on an employer
SAAC	Special Annual Allowance Charge (HMRC)
SAIMA	Specialist and Alternative Investment Manager Awards (*Professional Pensions* magazine)
SAPS	Self-administered pension scheme
SAS	(1) Statement of Auditing Standards; (2) Self-administered scheme
SCON	Scheme Contracted-Out Number
SDCS	Simplified Defined Contribution Scheme (obs)
SDRT	Stamp Duty Reserve Tax
SEE	Social Ethical and Environmental
SEPA	Single Euro Payments Area

SEPC	Self-Employed Premium Certificate (obs)
SERPS	State earnings-related pension schemes (obs)
SFO	(1) Statutory funding objective; (2) Superannuation Funds Office (obs); see APSS
SFP	Statement of funding principles
SFS	Summary funding statement
SHIP	Safe Home Income Plans
SHP	Stakeholder pension
SI	Statutory instrument
SIP	Statement of investment principles
SIPP	Self-invested personal pension
SLTA	Standard lifetime allowance
SMEP	Specified Multi Employer Plan (Canada)
SML	Statutory maternity leave (= 26 weeks ordinary maternity leave + 26 weeks additional maternity leave)
SMP	Statutory maternity pay (39 weeks)
SMPI	Statutory money purchase illustration
SoC	Schedule of contributions
SOLLA	Society of Later Life Advisers
SORP	Statement of Recommended Practice (accounting)
SPA	(1) State pension age; (2) Selected Pension Age; age chosen by personal pension plan members to draw retirement benefits
SPC	(1) Society of Pensions Consultants; (2) State pension credit
SPD	State Pension Date; earliest date that pension can be paid
SPEN	Scheme pension (HMRC)
SPG	SIPP Provider Group (obs); see AMPS
SRGL	Statement of Recognised Gains and Losses
SRI	Socially responsible investment
SSA	Social Security Act
SSAP	Statement of Standard Accounting Practice
SSAS	Small self-administered scheme
SSB	Short service benefit
SSF	Scheme specific funding
SSP	State Scheme Premium
SSP	Statutory sick pay
SSPA	Social Security Pensions Act
SUURBS	Secured unfunded unregistered [unapproved] retirement benefit scheme (obs); see EFRBS

SWF	Sovereign Wealth Fund
TA	Taxes Act 1988
TAA	Tactical Asset Allocation
TACT	The Association of Corporate Trustees
TAS	Technical actuarial standard
TCF	Treating Customers Fairly (FSA)
TCGA	Taxation of Chargeable Gains Act 1992
TCN	Third Country National
TCSP	Trust and Company Service Provider
TDF	Target Date Funds (US); also known as Life Cycle funds. See US Dept of Labor guidance, Investor Bulletin: Target Date Retirement Plans, www.dol.gov/ebsa
TEE	Taxed, Exempt, Exempt; see EET
TER	Total expense ratio
TESSA	Tax Exempt Special Savings Account (obs); see ISA
TFC	Tax-free cash
TFLS	Tax-free lump sum (obs); see PCLS
TKU	Trustee knowledge and understanding
TLP	Traded Life Policy
TM	Technical memorandum (Institute of Actuaries/Board for Actuarial Standards)
TOPIX	Tokyo Stock Exchange Index
TPA	Third Party Administrator
TPAS	The Pensions Advisory Service
TPD	Total and permanent disablement (Aus)
TPI	Taxes and Prices Index (obs)
TPR	the Pensions Regulator (sic), formerly the Occupational Pensions Regulatory Authority (OPRA), formerly the Occupational Pensions Board (OPB)
TPRT	The Pensions Regulator Tribunal
TUC	Trades Union Congress
TUPER	Transfer of Undertakings (Protection of Employment) Regulations 1981 and 2006
TV	Transfer value
TVAS	Transfer value analysis system
UAP	Upper accrual point (S2P)
UCITS	Undertakings for Collective Investments in Transferable Securities [EU Directive]
UEL	Upper earnings limit (HMRC)
UET	Upper earnings threshold (HMRC)

UKIPC	UK Investment Performance Committee; UK sponsors of GIPS
UKIPS	United Kingdom Investment Performance Standards
UKSC	United Kingdom Steering Committee (on Local Government Pensions)
UKSIF	United Kingdom Social Investment Forum
UKSIP	United Kingdom Society of Investment Professionals
UMP	Unauthorised member payment (HMRC)
UNEPFIPWG	United Nations Environment Programme Finance Initiative Property Working Group (Principles for Responsible Investment)
UPC	Unauthorised Payments Charge (HMRC)
USP	Unsecured pension rights; cf ASP
UURBS	Unfunded unregistered [unapproved] retirement benefit scheme (obs); see EFRBS
UUT	Unauthorised Unit Trust
VAn	Variable annuity
VAR	Value at risk
VAT	Value added tax
VCT	Venture Capital Trusts
VRQ	Vocationally Related Qualification
WB	Widows Benefit (state)
WGMP	Widow's Guaranteed Minimum Pension
WM	The WM Company; fund performance measurement
WRIC	Workplace Retirement Income Commission (NAPF, 2011)
WULS	Winding-up lump sum; OPS (Contracting-out) regulations 1996 Reg 60(2)(a) which seems to have the effect of preventing anyone under the age of 60 taking a WULS if they have GMPs

APPENDIX III
DEFINITIONS

These definitions have been garnered from a variety of sources, including Pinset Mason's Out-Law.com website, which includes an exhaustive glossary; where there is an HMRC in brackets, it indicates that it is an official definition. HMRC definitions are reproduced under © Crown Copyright (source: www.hmrc.gov.uk/manuals/rpsmmanual/rpsm20000000.htm).

Accelerated accrual
A rate of accrual that is higher than the typical 1/60 and 1/80 found in occupational pension schemes.

Accrual rate
Level at which benefits build up for each year of pensionable service in a defined benefit scheme. See accelerated accrual. The former HMRC restrictions on accrual rates no longer apply.

Accrued benefits
The benefits for service up to a given time, which may or may not be vested or preserved. They can be calculated in relation to current earnings or projected earnings, and might or might not be indexed.

Active member
An individual who has benefits currently accruing for or in respect of that person under one or more arrangements in the pension scheme (HMRC).
   A member of a scheme who is accruing benefits under that scheme in respect of current service. In other words, a pension scheme member who has not yet taken any retirement benefits (see also deferred member and pensioner member).

Actuarial assumptions
The set of assumptions used by the actuary in an actuarial valuation or other calculations (for example, rates of return, inflation, increase in remuneration, dividend increases and mortality).

Actuarial report
Written report – prepared and signed by the scheme actuary – on developments affecting the scheme's technical provisions since the last actuarial valuation.

Actuarial valuation
Written assessment, carried out by an actuary, to determine the ability of a defined benefit scheme to meet its future liabilities. It is usually done to assess the funding level and to recommend a contribution rate based on comparing the actuarial value of assets and liabilities of the scheme. Trustees must obtain an actuarial valuation at intervals of no more than one year or, if they obtain an actuarial report for the intervening years, at intervals of no more than three years. Following implementation of the statutory funding objective, the actuarial valuation will report on developments affecting the scheme's technical provisions since the last actuarial valuation was prepared.

Actuary

A professionally qualified person trained and specialising in risk, statistics and finance who gives advice on investment, life and general insurance, and pension business. Calculations made by actuaries include matters such as premium rates, profit testing bonus payments, life expectancy, establishment of mathematical reserves, etc. Each with-profits fund has a with-profits actuary advising the company on overall management of the fund. In addition, each life company has an 'Actuarial Function Holder', who is an approved person under the FSA rules. Actuaries that certify the reports of pension funds and insurance companies must be full members of the Institute of Actuaries and Faculty of Actuaries, and hold a practicing certificate from the Board for Actuarial Standards (BAS). The scheme actuary appointed by the trustees has a number of statutory responsibilities concerning scheme funding. There is more information on www.actuaries.org. uk; for actuarial reform, see also http://webarchive.nationalarchives.gov.uk and www. hm-treasury.gov.uk/morris_review_actuarial_profession.htm, where you can read the document which led to the current excessive control on actuaries (following the collapse of Equitable Life insurance company). An actuary is a mathematician who, by definition, always gets it wrong. They estimate what they think the funds will earn over the next 20 years or so, what your salary will be over the next 30 years and, on the basis of these and other assumptions, calculate backwards how much money needs to be put in the kitty now. Even though they can predict the future no better than an astrologer (according to one judge), they are worth every penny of their substantial fees.

A-day

6 April 2006, when the 'simplified' pensions tax regime came into force under the Finance Act 2004, as HMRC attempted to introduce a single tax regime for all UK pension schemes.

Additional state pension

The earnings-related state pension: from 1978 to 2002 the State Earnings Related Pension Scheme (SERPS) and, from 2002, the state second pension (S2P). It is a pension paid on top of your basic state pension. Self-employed people cannot build up an additional state pension.

Additional voluntary contribution (AVC)

A contribution paid by a member of an occupational pension scheme to secure additional benefits. Since A-day, occupational pension schemes are no longer obliged to (but may if they wish) offer members the option to add AVCs to their occupational pension scheme. AVCs enable members to buy additional or top-up benefits. Before A-day, member contributions of up to 15% of remuneration were generally eligible for tax relief to include ordinary contributions, AVCs and FSAVCs. Nowadays (2008), the 15% limit is replaced with a financial limit of annual earnings up to £50,000 (or £4,400 if higher). At one time members had a right to make such contributions, but compulsory provision for AVCs disappeared after April 2006 (see also annual allowance and lifetime allowance).

Administration

A statement of administration standards, with principles and checklist, is promoted by the 'Pensions Administration Standards Association' (www.pasa-uk.com).

Administrator

An HMRC technical term to describe the person with whom the buck stops, as far as they are concerned. It is your job to ensure that is not you and is someone like the pensions manager or insurance company. The administrator is a person or body responsible for the day-to-day management of the pension scheme. The administrator maintains members' records, calculates and pays benefits, and manages contributions; cf. scheme administrator, which is an HMRC obligation.

Age discrimination
By definition, pension schemes discriminate on the grounds of age, so although it is normally against the law, there are complex provisions allowing it most of the time in pension schemes. The rules came into force in December 2006. *Bloxham v Freshfields* allows age discrimination in pensions provision where justifiable. A similar case in the European Court of Justice suggests that governments can impose state retirement age limits in contracts of employment; see European Court of Justice Case, *Palacios de la Villa v Cortefiel Servicios SA; The impact of the age regulations on pension schemes: guidance on Employment Equality (Age) Regulations 2006 and their impact on occupational and personal pension schemes*, December 2006 (www.berr.gov.uk/files/file35877.pdf). Also see flexible retirement and discrimination.

Analyst
An individual who analyses investments such as companies to see if they are worth buying. They are astonishingly well paid. There are different kinds of analysts – equity analysts look at equities, quantitative analysts look at movement patterns in changes in investment values, and there are many others.

Annual allowance
The amount which an individual is permitted to gain tax relief on contributions to his pension arrangements each year. It is currently £50,000 pa; there is a formula for calculating the value of notional contributions involved where an employer promises defined benefits.

Annual Allowance Charge
If total pension inputs exceed an individual's available annual allowance, he is subject to an annual allowance tax charge. From 2011/12 onwards the charge is levied at an 'appropriate rate'. The appropriate rate is determined by adding the amount subject to the charge to the member's 'net income'. 'Net income' is total income subject to income tax, less any losses (mainly concerned with deductions for trade and property losses) less the individual's personal allowance. The appropriate rate is 20% on so much of the chargeable amount as, when added to net income, does not exceed the basic rate limit, 40% on the amount which exceeds the basic rate limit but does not exceed the higher rate limit, and 50% on any part of the excess which exceeds the higher rate limit.

Annuity
A policy (contract) from an insurance company that converts a pension fund or part of it into pension income. The latter is taxable. An annuity typically involves the a payment of a regular income by a life company to an annuitant (the individual receiving the annuity) in exchange for a lump sum, either for life or shorter periods. Annuities are typically used for pensions. In the UK they can broadly be classified into two types: a compulsory purchase annuity, which is bought from the proceeds of a pension fund and is taxable as earned income, or a purchased life annuity, which is bought with an individual's own capital and is taxed at a lower rate than a compulsory purchase annuity. There are three different types of pension annuities, commonly referred to as standard annuities, with-profits annuities and unit-linked annuities. Standard pension annuities are the most commonly purchased and account for over 90% of the UK market. The income from a standard pension annuity is guaranteed for the rest of the annuitant's life, whereas the income from a with-profits or unit-linked annuity fluctuates depending on the

investment performance of the underlying assets. There are various options which can be provided, including:

- annuity certain (where income is paid for a given period, whether or not the death of the individual occurs)
- deferred annuity (where income does not commence until some future specified date)
- escalating annuity (income which increases annually by a given amount – for example, 3%; the choosing of this option results in lower income compared with a level annuity over the initial years)
- immediate annuity (an annuity which starts to pay income soon after it has come into operation; for example, at the end of the month following the payment of the lump sum)
- joint life annuity (income usually relevant to two people, which continues until the death of the first person only)
- joint life and survivor annuity (income usually relevant to two people, which continues until the death of the second person)
- level annuity (income which is paid at a fixed rate throughout the life of the individual)
- temporary annuity (income is paid either for a fixed period or until earlier death)
- impaired life annuity (in return for the life company being convinced that an individual's health is such that their life expectancy is significantly shorter than a standard life, the life company is prepared to pay a higher amount of income on the expectation that this will be for a shorter period than a standard life)
- bulk annuities (the buy-out by a life company of the liabilities of a defined benefit – final salary – pension scheme; the pensions in payment are replaced by a series of annuities, and the benefits of the participants not yet retired are provided by deferred annuities).

At present the annuity in the EU is invariably provided by an insurance company, and the level depends on prevailing annuity rates, age when purchased and sex of the individual. An annuity may be subject to increases, and may be paid at stated intervals and either until death or the end of a specified period. Pension annuities in the UK under HMRC rules must commence by age 75. Most jurisdictions (though not all) require pension arrangements to include provision for payment of annuities, because the point of a pension system is to protect against living longer than expected. There is a pervasive campaign against compulsory purchase of annuities, which is deeply misplaced and benefits people who have over-provided for retirement. An annuity calculator is available on www.aspen-plc.co.uk. HMRC is determined to maintain the annuity requirement – a consultation document in February 2002 suggested as much – and the alternative to annuities (known as ASI – alternatively secured income – or ASP – alternatively secured pension) was severely weakened in the Finance Act 2007, which removes the facility to pass ASI funds on death (and quite rightly too).

Annuity rate
The rate at which a pension fund is converted into regular pension payments. For example, a £6,000 annuity from a pension fund of £100,000 has a 6% annuity rate.

Anti-avoidance
This is the term used to refer to Pensions Act 2004 provisions aimed at preventing employers from using corporate structures to avoid pension liabilities. If the Pensions Regulator believes an employer is attempting to avoid their pension obligations under a

defined benefit scheme, thus increasing the risk of a claim on the Pension Protection Fund, the following may be issued:

- a contribution notice, which can direct a person to pay a specified sum to the trustees of a pension scheme
- a restoration order, which can direct the restoration of the position applying immediately prior to the occurrence of a transaction at undervalue.

The Pensions Regulator may also issue a financial support direction requiring a person or persons to put financial support in place for a pension scheme.

Anti-forestalling (obs)
From 2011 HMRC attempted to impose additional limits on pension tax relief on incomes over £130,000, known as 'anti-forestalling'. The rules are astonishingly complicated (around 400 pages), breach all the principles of modern legislative drafting, breach the 2004/06 consensus on pensions tax simplification, are most likely unworkable – and, in any event, unnecessary, since pensions tax relief is fiscally neutral – and wealthier people do not gain (with the exception of the tax-free lump sum on retirement) any disproportionate tax relief.

Approval (obs)
Until A-day, occupational and personal pension plans required approval from HMRC to benefit from favourable tax treatment for contributions, benefits and investment return. Approval restricted the benefits that could be offered (for defined benefit schemes) and the contributions that could be paid (for defined contribution schemes or money purchase schemes). After A-day, favourable tax status was given to registered pension schemes, provided certain conditions are satisfied (see discretionary approval).

Arrangement
A contractual or trust-based arrangement made by or on behalf of a member of a pension scheme under that scheme. A member may have more than one arrangement under a scheme. (HMRC)

Asset
1. Any item of value.
2. The holdings of a fund, which may include stocks, shares, fixed-interest securities or cash.
3. The main types of investment available: bonds, equities, real estate, commodities, etc.

Auditor
An auditor is responsible for auditing pension fund accounts. In terms to pension schemes, the auditor helps the trustees obtain audited accounts and the auditor's statement regarding payment of contributions within seven months of the scheme year-end.

Authorised employer payment
In accordance with the Finance Act 2004, these are the only payments that an occupational registered pension scheme is authorised to make to a sponsoring employer.

Auto-enrolment
See automatic enrolment.

Automatic enrolment

The principle underlying the establishment of NEST, by which the 'nudge' theory of social engineering is adopted. The law (Pensions Act 2008) requires all employees to be automatically enrolled as members of a pension scheme chosen by the employer by 2012–16, but they have the right to opt out (with difficulty) if they wish; see Richard H Thaler and Cass R Sunstein, *Nudge: Improving Decisions About Health, Wealth and Happiness*, (Penguin, 2009). It is an arrangement whereby an employer automatically enrols an employee into a pension scheme and it has been compulsory since October 2012.

Average earnings

See career average.

Balance sheet

An account showing the assets of a company and its liabilities. Since the requirement for the inclusion of pension fund values and liabilities has been imposed, balance sheets can give a very misleading portrait of a company's value.

Bank

One of the following:

- a person within section 840A(1)(b) of the Income and Corporation Taxes Act 1988 (ICTA) (persons other than building societies etc permitted to accept deposits)
- a body corporate which is a subsidiary or holding company of a person falling within section 840A(1)(b) of ICTA or is a subsidiary of the holding company of such a person (subsidiary and holding company having the meanings in section 736 of the Companies Act 1985 or Article 4 of the Companies (Northern Ireland) Order 1986). (HMRC)

Bankruptcy

Under the Welfare Reform and Pensions Act 1999, in effect from 29 May 2000, pension rights are protected from a trustee in bankruptcy (see insolvency event).

Base rate

The rate of interest set by the central bank (Bank of England) which it charges commercial banks for loans. It is set on a monthly basis by the Monetary Policy Committee of the bank. It was formerly known as the Bank Rate.

Basic state pension

The benefit provided at state pension age to those with a sufficient National Insurance contribution record. The state pension is broadly based on the amount of National Insurance contributions a person has paid, has been treated as having paid or has been credited with during a working life. It is not related to earnings, unlike the state second pension.

Benefit crystallisation event

This is a defined event or occurrence that triggers a test of the benefits 'crystallising' at that point against on individual's available lifetime allowance. (HMRC)

There are nine such events. They are broadly something which triggers the payment of pension benefits where the pension provider will compare a member's benefits to the lifetime allowance. This usually happens when someone retires or dies. As since A-day tax legislation has permitted an individual to receive a pension whilst continuing to work for the same employer, a term had to be invented, since 'retirement' is not necessarily applicable. The nine benefit crystallisation events are as follows:

1. funds are designated to provide a member with an unsecured pension
2. a member becomes entitled to a scheme pension
3. a scheme pension already in payment to a member is increased beyond a permitted margin
4. a member becomes entitled to a lifetime annuity under a defined benefit scheme
5. a member reaches their 75th birthday under a defined benefit scheme without having drawn all or part of their entitlement to a scheme pension and/or relevant lump sum
6. a member reaches age 75 with an earlier designated unsecured pension fund which has not been secured by a lifetime annuity or scheme pension
7. a member becomes entitled to a relevant lump sum
8. a relevant lump sum death benefit is paid on the death of the member
9. a member's benefits or rights are transferred to a Qualifying Recognised Overseas Pension Scheme.

Intending simplification, the Finance Act 2004 invented many terms including this one, which is the term for either drawing benefits in the form of pension, alternatively secured pension, lump sum or transfer to an overseas scheme. When benefits are drawn in the form of a pension, alternatively secured pension, lump sum or a transfer to an overseas scheme, HMRC require a test to be done each year against pension increase to ensure their limits are not breached. It is an expensive and disproportionate way of controlling benefit levels (see also crystallisation event).

Bond
A form of loan. Typically, the investor should receive a regular coupon and the return of the principal originally lent when the bond matures. Note: not all bonds are interest bearing (see zero coupon bonds), and not all bonds are fixed rate (see indexation, and floating rate note). A bond is in fact a certificate of debt issued, for example, by a government or a company. Sovereign bonds are those bonds issued by a government.

Broker/dealer
An individual or firm acting as an intermediary between buyers and sellers, usually for payment of a commission. He/she may also buy securities to sell for a profit while fulfilling his/her role as dealer.

Capital gains/losses
The difference between an asset's buying price and the price it is sold at. In bond markets, investors can generate returns by making capital gains as well as through regular coupon (interest) payments.

Career average
This is a defined benefit basis used to calculate retirement benefits using earnings throughout an employee's career (rather than the more common approach of basing benefits on earnings near retirement). Also known as average earnings (see also defined benefit).

Category A
The part of the state pension based on the earner's own earnings record.

Category B
The part of the state pension based on the husband's earnings record. It is unfair to married men, ie a husband cannot use his wife's earnings record to gain benefits, while married women are able to do the reverse.

Category C (obs)
The third element to the basic state pension. It has been abolished.

Category E
A fifth element to the basic state pension. It rather generously (or pointlessly) pays 25p a week to all pensioners over the age of 80.

Collateral
Assets put up as security to protect a lender in case the borrower defaults.

Collateralised debt obligation (CDO)
A term for a piece of paper which says the pension fund has a share in the owning debts of other people which are collateralised, ie there is security (eg a house) for the debt. A collateralised mortgage obligation (CMO) is the same as a CDO, but secured usually on a dwelling.

Commodities
Raw materials such as crude oil, metals and agricultural products.

Company accounts
UK company accounts are required to cover pension expense. The accounting standard (known as FRS 17) is mandatory for accounting periods beginning on or after 1 January 2005. For listed companies' consolidated group accounts for periods beginning after 1 January 2005, a similar but different standard (known as IAS 19) must be used. An individual company or a consolidated group of unlisted companies can choose to use either FRS 17 or IAS 19.

Compliance
The current term for meeting the requirements of regulators.

Compound interest
A method of accumulating interest, where interest is paid on both the initial investment and the interest received during the period.

Consumer prices index (CPI)
The main measure of domestic UK inflation, which measures the prices of a fixed basket of goods and services bought by a typical consumer and is used as one measurement of retail price inflation. It is used by the Bank of England in its monetary policy. The other widely used index is the retail prices index. The general index of consumer prices published by the Office for National Statistics is now used as the benchmark for price growth for the purposes of uprating most state benefits since April 2011, and in some cases it is used in occupational and personal pension systems.

Contracting in
This is the opposite of contracting out – see below.

Contracting out
The ability to opt out of the state second pension (SP2) (formerly SERPS, and before that the graduated state pension scheme) and instead make additional contributions to a personal or occupational pension arrangement; it is normally the employer's decision whether or not to contract out, so that members lose rights to the state second pension and build equivalent rights in a private pension system. Major changes in contracting

out occurred at least half a dozen times during its operation. Some years ago, when it was introduced, the government offered an incentive to persuade people to contract out and anticipated the cost would be about £750m – it actually cost around £8bn, or 2p on the income tax. Contracting out is no longer possible for defined contribution pension arrangements and is expected to be phased out completely in due course, with considerable advantages to government finances.

Contributions – employer/member
Monies paid into a scheme by an employer and/or member.

Covenant

- legal safeguard put in place to protect bondholder's interests
- underlying promise of the employer to pay contributions to a pension scheme.

See also employer covenant.

Convertible
A debt instrument paying a fixed rate of interest which offers the holder the right to convert into the underlying shares of the company.

Corporate governance
Companies can get away with buying jets for the directors unless the shareholders (often pension funds) keep an eye on them; pension funds are under constant pressure to ensure companies are governed properly, but do not always have the tools or the time available, so they often delegate it to specialist organisations.

Credit
A corporate bond, ie money owed by a company. It is sometimes also called debt.

Crystallisation event
An event where pension benefits become payable – ie annuity purchase, death, starting an unsecured pension, etc – and at which time a test against the lifetime allowance is carried out.

D&B (Dun & Bradstreet)
The agency that has been given the job by the Pension Protection Fund of rating the financial strength of employer sponsors of pension funds. It is possible to bend their rules, so as to reduce the amount of levy payable.

Death benefit
The death benefit is the amount payable under the policy in the event of a death claim. This can be simply the sum assured; the greater value of either the sum assured and the value of accumulated investments; or for a with-profits policy, the aggregate of the sum assured plus bonuses declared to date.

Death-in-service benefits
Benefits paid to a scheme member (or their estate or dependants) upon death while working in the company which is the sponsor of the plan.

Decumulation
Selling assets to pay benefits; an annuity is one form of decumulation.

Default

- The failure to pay interest or principal of a debt promptly when due.
- The failure to meet payments on a futures contract as required by an exchange.

Deferred member

An individual who has rights under a pension scheme and who is neither an active member nor a pensioner member (HMRC).

Member who is no longer an active member of the scheme (usually as a result of leaving the employment to which the scheme relates) but who is entitled to preserved benefits when he or she retires at some future date. Also known as a deferred pensioner.

Deficit

Not enough money in a pension scheme – based on certain assumptions.

Defined benefit

Benefits calculated by reference to a fixed formula, irrespective of the contributions paid or investment performance. The most common type of defined benefits are:

- final salary
- career average or career average revalued earnings (CARE).

There is sometimes a debate amongst policymakers and lawyers about whether hybrid schemes (such as cash balance plans) are defined benefit or defined contribution. For regulators they are defined benefit; for accounts purposes they are considered defined contribution.

Defined benefit scheme

A private pension scheme where the pension is related to the member's salary or some other value fixed in advance. It is sometimes called a salary-related scheme.

Defined contribution

A scheme that provides retirement benefits based on the build-up of a 'pot' of money, accumulated through the investment of contributions paid by both the employee and the employer. It is a more contemporary term for what used to be called money purchase arrangements, and defined contribution arrangements are (usually) a form of employer-sponsored pension plan, which makes no promises as to benefit levels but simply provides for whatever contributions are made, together with any gains over the years, to be used eventually to buy retirement benefits. Depending on the accumulated values, and the costs of annuities at the time of purchase, the eventual benefits will vary. There are innumerable surveys of DC plans; they include, for example, Mercer UK Defined Contribution Survey (annual), Mercer (www.mercer.com). Mercer disclosed that, by 2007, 63% of all DC plans had been established since 2000. Benefits are calculated by reference to contributions made by the member and/or the employer, together with any interest/investment returns. When the member retires, the resulting sum of money is used to buy an annuity.

Defined contribution scheme

A private pension scheme where the individual receives a pension based on the contributions made and the investment return that they have produced. It is sometimes referred to as a money purchase scheme.

Department for Work and Pensions (DWP)
The government department with overall responsibility for the rules governing pension schemes and the administration of the state pension.

Dependant
A person who was married to, or a civil partner of, the member at the date of the member's death is a dependant of the member. Additionally, if the rules of the pension scheme so provide, the above test can be extended to apply not only at the date of the member's death, but to extend to the point in time when the member first became actually entitled to a pension under the pension scheme. A child of the member is a dependant of the member if the child has:

- not reached the age of 23, or
- has reached age 23 and, in the opinion of the scheme administrator, was at the date of the member's death dependent on the member because of physical or mental impairment, or
- is covered by any of the transitional provisions described in HMRC guidance notes.

A person who was not married to the member or was not in a civil partnership with the member at the date of the member's death and is not a child of the member is a dependant of the member if, in the opinion of the scheme administrator, at the date of the member's death the person was:

- financially dependent on the member
- the person's financial relationship with the member was one of mutual dependence, or
- the person was dependant on the member because of physical or mental impairment.

Further information on the concepts used in this definition can be found on page www. hmrc.gov.uk/manuals/rpsmmanual/RPSM10104040.htm.

Derivatives
Financial instruments, such as futures and options, the value of which is derived from that of underlying securities. Some say they are so-called investments which are one stage removed from reality. For example, instead of buying a share in Marks & Spencer, you might buy the right to buy a share in Marks & Spencer in three months' time at a price fixed now and hope that the price will rise in the meantime. If the price falls you will still have to buy the share at a loss, with money you might not have at the time. For most pension funds they are not suitable, unless used in conjunction with some other strategy, such as the intention to buy an investment overseas. Take great care and special advice. Derivatives include swaps, futures and options – they are not explained because you should normally keep away from them.

Determination (Pensions Ombudsman)
A decision by the Pensions Ombudsman is known as a determination and is final and binding on all parties. A determination can only be appealed on a point of law to the High Court in England and Wales, the Court of Session in Scotland and the Court of Appeal in Northern Ireland.

Discount rate
The rate of interest used to find the present value of a future cash flow. If the discount rate used in a pension fund is a high one (ie the actuary thinks the pension fund will perform well in the future) the amount of money needed today is less. A discount rate

reduces the current value of a future liability amount by recognising that investment returns or interest over time will help repay the liability. The discount rate used is often related to the assumed rate of return on bond yields.

Discretionary approval (obs)
Discretionary approval involved a system of HMRC approval of pension arrangements without which tax relief was not available; HMRC was not obliged to recognise such arrangements. HMRC general approval has been replaced by HMRC registration.

Discrimination
It is unlawful to discriminate on the grounds of sex, marital status, civil partner status, race, colour, nationality, ethnic or national origin, religion or belief, sexual orientation, disability and age. See also age discrimination treatment and equal treatment.

Dispute resolution
Pension scheme disputes between the member and the trustees can be resolved using a range of different methods, including internal dispute resolution, TPAS (which operates a network of volunteer advisers), the Pensions Ombudsman, the courts and alternative dispute resolution by way of arbitration or mediation.

Dispute resolution procedure (DRP)
DRP or IDRP (internal dispute resolution procedure) was simplified and reformed by the Pensions Act 2007, which allows trustees to adopt a one-stage procedure (instead of the former two-stage procedure) if they wish. Regulations in 2008 set out the details, and if you really have to have extra help, there is a TPR Code of Practice (October 2007).

Diversification
Holding a range of assets to reduce risk. Legally required for pension funds (Pensions Act 1995), despite anything to the contrary in the deed.

Diversified growth funds (DGF)
A DGF invests in a variety of different assets classes within a single fund.

Dividend
The proportion of company net profits paid out to equity investors.

Divorce
There are three main ways in which pensions are taken into account in divorce proceedings.

1. Offsetting: this ensures that the distribution of other assets held by both parties takes into account the value of the pension held by one of the parties.
2. Attachment order: (formerly called earmarking) requires the payment to the former spouse of part or all of a member's pension (and/or lump sum) as and when they fall due.
3. Pension sharing orders: share the value of the member's pension between the member and the former spouse, dividing it at the date of divorce and putting part or all of it in the former spouse's name.

Double taxation
This refers to the payment of tax twice, both at the point of payment and at the point of receipt, where the payment is received in a country that is not the country in which it was paid. Countries may voluntarily enter into double taxation agreements to prevent tax being levied twice.

Drawdown
Known also as income drawdown/withdrawal or unsecured pension, it allows members under the age of 75 to continue investing in their funds, whilst drawing a limited proportion as income.

Early leaver
Person who ceases to be an active member of a pension scheme before their normal pension age and does not receive their pension immediately.

Early retirement
This occurs when a member retires before their normal pension age and takes a pension before their normal pension age, which may be reduced to reflect early payment. Retirement before age 50 is not permitted by HMRC except in the case of certain high risk jobs or in cases of ill health. This rose to age 55 in 2010 (see also ill health early retirement).

Earnings
For a company, the net profits available for distribution to shareholders.

Earnings before interest, tax, depreciation and amortisation (EBITDA)
A crude measure of the success or otherwise of a company, to be used only in conjunction with a range of other measures.

Effective date
The effective date, in scheme funding, is the date at which the scheme's assets and liabilities are assessed, using information on the membership and economic conditions at the time. The choice of effective date may affect the valuation significantly.

EFRBS
See employer-funded retirement benefits scheme.

EFRP
See European Federation for Retirement Provision.

Emerging markets
The investment markets of developing economies; they usually have crude or non-existent stock markets which makes investments harder to value, and harder to buy and sell.

Employer covenant
A concept invented by the Pensions Act 2004 relating to the ability of the employer to discharge any deficits in its sponsored plan and their willingness to continue to sponsor.

When agreeing the schedule of contributions to the scheme from the sponsor, trustees take the strength of the covenant into account (the paradox being that if the covenant is weak, and the employer finds it difficult to pay contributions, that is just when such payments are critical). The strength of a covenant depends on future profits and cashflows, as well as the available funds if the employer ceased trading. Such covenants are rated very crudely by Dun & Bradstreet for the PPF and by, for example, Standard & Poor's as part of a charged-for service to which few subscribe (see Standard & Poor's, 'The Pensions Covenant', quarterly).

Employer-funded retirement benefits scheme (EFRBS)
The current term for an unregistered (formerly unapproved) scheme, formerly known as FURBS, UURBS, etc. Registered schemes are not currently attractive for high earners, since there is 30% tax on contributions, plus 40%/50% tax on the benefits received. EFRBS are more tax efficient than registered schemes. It needs to be notionally open to all employees (to avoid a 20% inheritance tax charge) but offers the advantage of no income tax or National Insurance contributions on employer's contributions, benefits taxed at the employee's marginal rate, corporation tax relief when the benefits are paid and may pay other benefits (in some cases) than normally permitted to registered pension schemes.

Engagement
The way in which sensible investment managers discuss issues (ie problems) with the companies in which they invest, ie they talk to them.

Enhanced protection
If a member had exceeded or were likely to exceed their pension rights at 5 April 2006, they could safeguard them against a future tax charge. Enhanced protection is a transitional arrangement available to members of registered pension schemes to protect the benefits they accrued before A-day from the 'recovery charge' (ie one of the taxes on pensions over the lifetime allowance). An individual may register with HMRC for enhanced protection, whether or not the value of their pension savings exceeds the standard lifetime allowance at A-day. This ensures that the lifetime allowance does not affect pension accrual prior to A-day. A member with enhanced protection may lose it in certain circumstances, eg if a relevant benefit accrual occurs. A member must have registered with HMRC by 5 April 2009 to obtain enhanced protection. Enhanced protection allows the value of pre-A-day benefits to be linked to indexation or movements in future earnings or investment growth. Enhanced protection removes the Lifetime Allowance Charge, subject to several important conditions.

Enhanced transfer value (ETV)
Exercises have been carried out to persuade members and former members to take their accrued rights away somewhere else. There are advantages in administrative savings for pension funds – but the cost in advisory fees (each member should really receive individual financial advice) and cash incentives may be too high. There is mixed feedback on the success of such exercises, and TPR has issued guidance on the practice. There was for a brief period a substantial tax advantage in surrendering pension in exchange for cash, but this no longer applies.

Enterprise value/earnings before interest, depreciation, tax (EV/EBITDA)
A method of valuing companies calculated by dividing a company's enterprise value (market value of equity plus net debt of the company) by its earnings before interest, tax, depreciation and amortisation. This measure relates short-term cash flow generation to market valuation.

Environmental, social and governance (ESG)
See socially responsible investments (SRI).

Equal treatment
Principle requiring sexual equality with respect to contributions and benefits (sections 62 to 66 of the Pensions Act 1995).

Equities
Stocks and shares quoted on a stock market (see also equity).

Equity
The shares in a company. Investors in equities are a company's owners who are entitled to its profits after other claims on the company have been met.

Equivalent pension benefit (EPB)
Benefit that an employer must provide for an employee whose employment was contracted out of the State Graduated Pension Scheme (between 1961 and 1975) – see the National Insurance Act 1965 and the Social Security (Graduated Retirement Benefit) (No 2) Regulations 1978.

ERISA
The Employee Retirement Income Security Act [1974]: US pension legislation, now sometimes used as a generic term to cover the whole US pension market.

Estate
The inherited estate is the expression used to describe surplus assets in a with-profits fund. The estate has often built up over many years as a direct result of a long-term policy of declaring less in bonuses than has been earned in surpluses (smoothing) and forms part of the capital supporting the business.

European Economic Area (EEA)
This refers to an institution which:

■ is an EEA firm of the kind mentioned in paragraph 5(a), (b) or (c) of Schedule 3 to the Financial Services and Markets Act 2000 (certain credit and financial institutions), or
■ qualifies for authorisation under paragraph 12(1) or 12(2) of that Schedule, or
■ has permission under the Financial Services and Markets Act 2000 to manage portfolios of investments. (HMRC)

European Federation for Retirement Provision (EFRP)
A club of country-based associations of pension funds designed to be more effective in EU lobbying. The UK's NAPF is a leading member. It operates out of Brussels with a small secretariat and budget, and has so far focused its efforts on representing the special interests of funded second-tier pension plans, as most commonly found in the UK, Ireland and the Netherlands, although it has wider ambitions (see www.efrp.org).

European Pensions Directive
Directive 2003/41/EC of the European Parliament and of the Council of the European Union of 3 June 2003 on the activities and supervision of Institutions for Occupational Retirement Provision (also known as the IORP Directive). It imposes funding requirements on DB schemes and provides for cross-border recognition of occupational schemes. It does not provide for cross-border tax relief, without which a cross-border scheme is impractical, but EU case law does require that. UK HMRC rules and TPR rules are almost certainly in breach of the Directive and EU tax requirements.

Exchange traded fund (ETF)
A vehicle that is traded on a stock exchange and whose performance is designed to track a given market index. Exchange traded funds represent a low cost, highly liquid 'form' of index investing.

Executive pension plan (EPP)
Scheme sold by insurance companies and used to provide benefits for senior employees. Each insurance policy is earmarked to provide benefits for a single member.

Exoneration clause
A clause in a pension scheme deed that exonerates trustees from almost all liability; despite criticism from the Pensions Ombudsman, such clauses are looked on favourably by the courts.

Expected return
The anticipated average future return; the actual return will generally differ.

Fiduciary
A person or entity who acts for the benefit and on behalf of another person or group of persons. A fiduciary holds a legally enforceable position of trust.

Final salary scheme
Benefits calculated by reference to salary at date of leaving, irrespective of the contributions paid or investment performance. An occupational pension scheme that provides benefits based on accrual rate, pensionable service and pensionable salary. It is the most common type of defined benefit scheme, in which benefits are based on a fraction (commonly 1/60th) of the member's final pensionable salary at retirement for each year of pensionable service.

Financial Assistance Scheme (FAS)
The FAS was established in May 2004 and is intended to provide financial assistance to people whose defined benefit scheme wound up with insufficient assets to satisfy in full the scheme liabilities but who are not protected by the PPF. It applies only where the wind-up of the scheme took place between 1 January 1997 and 5 April 2005, and where the employer became insolvent before 28 February 2007 (see www.dwp. gov.uk).

Financial Conduct Authority (FCA)
Previously known as the Consumer Protection and Markets Authority (CPMA), this is a future (2013) agency formed as one of the three successors to the unlamented Financial Services Authority. The agency will regulate financial firms providing services to consumers and maintain the integrity of the UK's financial markets. It will focus on the regulation of conduct by both retail and wholesale financial services firms. The head of the FCA will be Martin Wheatley, formerly chairman of Hong Kong's Securities and Futures Commission. The original name of Consumer Protection and Markets Authority (CPMA) was changed after the Treasury Select Committee pointed out that it could mislead consumers. (See also Financial Policy Committee (FPC).)

Financial Ombudsman Service (FOS)
An independent, levy-funded body that considers complaints between consumers and financial firms.

Financial Policy Committee (FPC)
The FPC is an official committee of the Bank of England, parallel to the existing Monetary Policy Committee, responsible for monitoring the economy of the United Kingdom. It focuses on the macro-economic and financial issues that may threaten long-term growth prospects. It will replace (together with the Financial Conduct Authority and the

Prudential Regulation Authority) the FSA in 2013. The committee, to be headed by the Governor of the Bank, addresses any risks it identifies by passing on its concerns to the Prudential Regulation Authority.

Financial Services Authority (FSA)
The body which regulates the financial industry in the UK and which is paid for by the industry; it is fortunately being abolished in 2013 and replaced by the Financial Policy Committee (FPC), the Prudential Regulation Authority (PRA) and the Financial Conduct Authority (FCA), which may or may not be better. The new bodies will probably preserve the mindset of the FSA, which will be a shame.

Financial support direction
The Pensions Regulator has the power to direct an employer or a person 'connected' or 'associated' with it (such as a holding company) to put financial support in place for a scheme providing defined benefits within a specified time (section 43 of the Pensions Act 2004).

Financial Times Stock Exchange (FTSE)
An index of stocks and shares.

Flexible apportionment arrangements (FAA)
Introduced in October 2011, amendments to the Employer Debt Regulations attempted (again) to make the legislation more flexible for corporate groups engaged in restructuring exercises and corporate transactions. The amendments made only relatively minor improvements to the legislation. The Occupational Pension Scheme (Employer Debt) Regulations 2005 were designed (amongst other things) to ensure that members' benefits are properly funded when their employer ceases to participate in a defined benefit pension scheme. Since their introduction, various attempts have been made to make the legislation more flexible for corporate groups. In April 2010 'general' and *de minimis* easements were introduced, which ensured that no employer debt arises when two employers merge in a corporate restructuring, provided certain conditions are met. In practice, these easements are rarely used. The October 2011 changes introduced a new 'flexible apportionment arrangement' giving greater flexibility over the timescale within which employers can take advantage of a 'grace period' (during which no employer debt is treated as having arisen). A flexible apportionment arrangement (in theory at least) offers corporate groups another mechanism for apportioning pension liabilities between group companies, where a company within the group is due to exit a defined benefit pension scheme. The system is similar to a scheme apportionment arrangement (SAA) (one of the existing options for apportioning liabilities between group companies). In particular, an FAA normally requires trustees to be satisfied when an exiting employer ceases to participate that the 'funding test' has been met (to ensure that the security of members' benefits is not reduced); the liabilities of the exiting employer can only be apportioned to another group employer that participates in the scheme. The key additional flexibility under a FAA (when compared to a SAA) is stated below.

■ When the employer ceases to participate, there is no need to certify the amount of the debt which is being apportioned (because the 'receiving employer' assumes all the exiting employer's scheme liabilities).
■ If two FAAs were entered into shortly after each other, the trustees have the flexibility to agree that the 'funding test' need not be carried out again (on the basis that they understand the financial strength of the 'receiving employer' from the first FAA).

The changes are relatively trivial but highlight the damage to corporate restructuring that the complex and inflexible s75 structure involves. Employers now have up to two months (as opposed to one month) to notify their scheme's trustees that they wish to benefit from a 'grace period' where they cease to employ any active members in the scheme, but plan to do so again within the next 12 months; and trustees have the discretion to extend an employer's 'grace period' from 12 months to 36 months.

Flexible lifetime annuities
See drawdown.

Flexible retirement
The ability to continue working for an employer but simultaneously draw some or all of the pension benefits from that employer's scheme. From A-day, previous HMRC restrictions were removed, thus enabling this facility to be offered. To take advantage of flexible retirement, scheme rules must allow it. A DWP consultation paper was published in October 2007. (See also age discrimination.)

Floating rate note (FRN)
A bond whose coupon varies with (short-term) interest rates. Floating rate bonds are generally issued by banks or companies whose earnings are closely tied to interest rate fluctuations as a way of matching interest payments to earnings more closely.

Foreign Accounts Tax Compliance Act (FATCA)
The Foreign Accounts Tax Compliance Act is a US law that requires UK pension funds to certify that none of their members is a US resident – and if they are, who they are and how much their pension rights are. In due course it is possible that they will be exempt, but in the meantime trustees and others may be subject to a draconian tax on their US investments and be in breach of EU data protection law if they divulge this information. The hope is that the US will eventually repeal the law; in the meantime, it is a severe impediment to holding US investments.

Forestalling
See anti-forestalling.

Franking
Practice of using occupational pension scheme rights (which were not indexed) to pay for the index-linking of GMPs. This meant that any inflation-linked improvement to the GMP led to the corresponding reduction of any non-GMP benefits. The legislation to prevent this is known as anti-franking legislation. New rules applied from 2000 to members leaving a scheme after 1 July 2000 so that they receive at least the greater of the pre-6 April 1997 accrual or GMP plus post-5 April 1997 benefits.

Fraud Compensation Fund (FCF)
A fund designed to compensate members of pension schemes where loss arises as a result of an offence (such as theft or fraud) committed after 6 April 1997. It is managed by the board of the PPF and financed by a fraud compensation levy payable by all schemes eligible for this compensation (not just PPF eligible schemes). There are therefore three pension compensation funds: the FAS, the PPF and the FCF.

Free-standing additional voluntary contribution (FSAVC)
These are AVCs made to arrangements sitting alongside an approved scheme or, since A-day, to registered pension schemes. Historically, FSAVC schemes were used by trustees

to meet the pre A-day obligation to give members access to an AVC facility where the approved scheme does not offer an AVC facility.

FTSE/NAPF Pensions Index
An index of pension values which never grew beyond its embryonic stage.

Funded unapproved retirement benefits scheme (FURBS)
Prior to A-day, these were mainly top-up pension schemes created to provide retirement benefits for executives in excess of those permitted from an approved scheme. They were granted limited tax relief by HMRC. Post A-day, they were largely replaced by employer-financed retirement benefit schemes.

Funding level
Comparison of a scheme's assets and liabilities. It is determined as part of an actuarial valuation and is usually expressed as a percentage. The funding level will vary depending on the actuarial's assumptions, so that a scheme could be 100% funded on the statutory funding objective basis, but at a lower level on a discontinuance basis.

Funds
A collection of assets managed in accordance with an objective for the mutual benefit of all of the investors. The investors' share in a unit-linked life or pensions fund is represented by the number of units within the fund that they have been allocated by the life company.

FURBS (obs)
See funded unapproved retirement benefits scheme.

GAAP
Generally Accepted Accounting Principles.

GAD
See Government Actuary's Department.

Genuine Diverse Commercial Vehicle (GDCV)
Indirect investments held through a GDCV will not be subject to tax charges when held as a scheme investment by an investment regulated pension scheme.

Gilts
A UK government issued and guaranteed bond. They are marketable sterling government bonds issued by the DMO on behalf of the UK government as part of its debt management responsibilities. They are issued to finance the borrowing requirement, to refinance maturing debt and, incidentally, to help pension funds manage their liabilities (www.dmo.gov.uk).

Global Investment Performance Standards (GIPS)
This is an American system of measuring investment performance that is gaining credence in the UK, especially as multinationals seek to compare the performance of their pension funds. GIPS were introduced by a US organisation, the Association for Investment Management and Research, and modified versions are now being adopted by the UK and other countries (especially Germany, Australia and Switzerland). GIPS allow measurement in one country to be recognised for accounting purposes in another country (see also United Kingdom Investment Performance Standards).

Global Tactical Asset Allocation (GTAA)
A multi-asset class strategy that makes high-frequency allocation shifts between asset classes and regions using only a fraction of the total portfolio.

GMP
See Guaranteed Minimum Pension.

Goode Report
The report of the Pensions Law Review Committee, chaired by Professor Sir Roy Goode and published in September 1993; the implementation of its recommendations led almost directly to the destruction of DB pension schemes in a prime example of the law of unintended consequences.

Governance
The organisational structure and approach to exercising control over an occupational pensions scheme by its trustee board (see also corporate governance).

Government Actuary's Department (GAD)
A government department that provides actuarial advice and guidance to the government and public sector schemes. (HMRC)

Government bond
A bond issued by a government.

Graduated pension scheme
A state earnings-related scheme that started on 3 April 1961 and terminated on 5 April 1975. It was possible for members to be contracted-out of this, they were provided, instead, with benefits known as equivalent pension benefits (EPBs). It was replaced by the state earnings-related pension scheme (SERPS). (See also state second pension.)

Graduated Retirement Benefit
An increase in state pension based on graduated National Insurance contributions paid between 1961 and 1975.

Grandfathered Corresponding Acceptance (GCA)
Ability to claim tax relief after 5 April 2006 on terms similar to MMR where the individual and company claim relief in the 2005/06 tax year.

Group personal pension scheme
Collection of personal pension plans with the same provider in which employees of an employer participate. Each member has a separate policy with the provider but contributions from employer and/or employees are collected together by the employer and paid directly to the provider. Often GPPs will be branded and packaged to resemble an occupational pension scheme provided by an employer. However, unlike trust-based occupational pension schemes, GPPs are contract-based schemes like any personal pension plan, set up between the provider and the individual. GPPs are commonly regarded as vehicles that avoid much of the regulatory burden of trust-based schemes.

HMRC defines the Scheme as: Arrangements administered on a group basis under a personal pension scheme which are available to some or all of the employees of the same employer or some or all of the employees of employers which are in the same group of companies. For this purpose a 'group' is formed by a company and all of its '75% subsidiaries'. If any of those '75% subsidiaries' have '75% subsidiaries' the group includes them and their '75% subsidiaries' and so on. '75% subsidiary' is defined in section 838 of the Income and Corporation Taxes Act 1988. This is intended to be an objective test according to the facts. The key to the test is simply as to whether in operating the arrangements the personal pension provider has decided that administration on a group basis is appropriate. If there is any doubt, the individual should be able to obtain confirmation from the personal pension provider that the arrangements involved are 'arrangements administered on a group basis'. (HMRC)

Guarantee credit
An element of pension credit available to men and women who have reached the qualifying age (which is linked to women's state pension age). It tops up income to a 'standard minimum guarantee'. This level may be increased for people with caring responsibilities, severe disabilities or certain housing costs, such as mortgage interest.

Guaranteed Minimum Pension (GMP)
GMPs stands for Guaranteed Minimum Pensions and has the same meaning as in the Pension Schemes Act 1993. (HMRC)

Guidance from the Pensions Regulator
The Pensions Regulator produces guidance to help improve understanding of work-based pension schemes and to promote good practice. In some cases it can be treated as quasi-law or at least influential in helping judges come to their decisions.

Hedge fund
A fund that seeks to generate investment return by using non-traditional investment strategies, utilising mechanisms such as short selling, gearing, programme trading and arbitrage, and tools such as options, futures, swaps and forwards (derivatives in general).

Hedging
An operation to secure an investor against a potential loss or to minimise a potential risk by offsetting the exposure to a specific risk, by entering a position in an investment with an opposite pay-off pattern. The term is often applied to the currency markets (currency hedging). It involves reducing the risk of unfavourable movements in commodity or security prices, or exchange or interest rates, by engaging in offsetting transactions.

Her Majesty's Revenue and Customs (HMRC)
The merged departments of Inland Revenue, National Insurance and Customs and Excise, struggling to overcome its opposing culture streams of Customs (which has historically been confrontational) and Revenue (which was supposed to treat taxpayers as customers). Its misery is accentuated because it is now responsible for tax credits and Personal Accounts which pay money to people, rather than take it off them – arrangements which need different systems and cultures. It used to handle the tax approval of pension schemes and taxation of contributions and benefits, and it is still involved with the registration of schemes. As part of its tax simplification drive it has produced around 4,000 pages of tax code.

Housing benefit
Income-related benefit to assist with the costs of rent (to a private landlord or in respect of a council dwelling).

Hybrid arrangement
An arrangement where only one type of benefit will ultimately be provided, but the type of benefit that will be provided is not known in advance because it will depend on certain given circumstances at the point benefits are drawn. For example, a hybrid arrangement may provide the member with other money purchase benefits based on a

pot derived from the contributions that have accrued over time, but subject to a defined benefit minimum or underpin. If the benefits provided by the money purchase pot at the point benefits are drawn fall below a certain defined level, for example 1/60ths of final remuneration for every year worked, that higher defined benefit will be provided. The benefits will therefore be either other money purchase benefits, or defined benefits. When benefits are drawn, if the benefits actually provided are other money purchase or cash balance benefits then the arrangement will become a money purchase arrangement. If the benefits provided are defined benefits then the arrangement will become a defined benefits arrangement. (HMRC)

Hybrid scheme
Occupational pension scheme offering both defined benefit and money purchase benefits.

IAS 19
See International Accounting Standard 19.

IDR
See internal dispute resolution.

IFRIC 14
A former International Accounting Standard, IAS 19, set a limit on the amount of pension surplus that could be included on a company's balance sheet to that amount that could be reasonably returned (eg by way of actual return, or future contribution holidays). This was usually less than the full value (unlike any deficit, which always kept its full value). In practice accountants found it hard to value the amount. From January 2008, the IFRIC 14 standard applied (covering quoted companies), which allows a higher amount to be shown where there is an unconditional right to return of surplus. Lawyers now need to be involved to work out what the rules are on return of surplus (www.iasb.org).

Ill health early retirement
Ill health early retirement takes place where a member retires on medical grounds before his or her normal pension date. The benefit payable to the member in such circumstances may or may not exceed that payable on early retirement in other circumstances.

Illiquid/Non-liquid asset
An asset which cannot be readily converted to cash, such as property.

Income drawdown
Also known as an unsecured pension. It allows a pension scheme member to continue to invest in a fund whilst drawing a limited income. It is available only to those under the age of 75 and is also known as income withdrawal.

Income withdrawal
See income drawdown

Indemnity clause
An indemnity clause provides that any liability a trustee may incur is reimbursed by the pension scheme or the employer. They are only effective if the scheme or the employer is able to pay. They provide less protection for trustees than an exoneration clause, which prevents any trustee liability arising (see also exoneration clause).

Indemnity insurance

This is insurance specifically to cover liabilities that trustees may incur for breach of trust, legal expenses and other exposures. It is usually in effect with a provider where the premium is paid either by the employer or from the scheme assets (the latter would require a specific provision in the rules to allow this).

Independent financial adviser (IFA)

The independent financial adviser channel represents the largest distribution channel available to a life company. To meet the need of clients, an independent financial adviser is able to select products from the whole of the market. This choice might be influenced by many factors including price, flexibility, service, brand, financial strength, range of funds, etc. IFAs are remunerated either by charging their clients fees or, more usually by being paid initial and renewal commission by the life company.

Independent trustees

Individual or corporate trustee, independent of the employer and members. They are trustees who are not connected with the employer or the fund's advisers. They are increasingly common these days to help other trustees avoid any pressures arising from conflicts of interest.

Index

A market containing all the stocks of a particular asset. For example, the FTSE All-Share Index contains all the public limited companies listed on the UK equity market issuing shares.

Index fund

A passively managed fund.

Indexation

Defined benefit pension arrangements for the moment have to have both their value and their benefits indexed – originally to the retail prices index, but more recently mostly to the consumer prices index. Indexation is likely to prove a contentious issue as the government tries to remove indexation obligations just at a time when inflation is likely to increase.

Index-linked gilt (ILG)

A bond issued by the UK government (gilt) whose interest (coupon) and capital (principal) payments are linked to the UK retail prices index (RPI). Note: many pension fund liabilities are wage inflation linked and/or consumer prices index-linked. Earnings have historically grown faster than prices, and the CPI normally rises slower than RPI, so the asset is not a perfect match for such liabilities.

Index-linking

See indexation.

Individual pension account (IPA)

This is a pooled investment vehicle designed as a tax wrapper for groups of smaller investment vehicles, such as unit trusts and OEICs. They are a means of investing pension assets in unit and investment trusts in accordance with the member's choice, and can be changed according to the individual's preferences over a working lifetime. IPAs are not pension schemes, but can be used by occupational pension schemes or personal pension plans for investment purposes.

Inducement offers
See enhanced transfer values.

Inflation
A measure of the rate of increase in general prices, eg the movement over time in the consumer prices index (CPI).

Inheritance tax
A tax on property arising upon death; most pension benefits are immune.

Initial public offering (IPO)
The first public sale of a company's equity (shares) resulting in a quoted stock price on a securities exchange.

Insolvency
This can be defined by two alternative tests (section 123 of the Insolvency Act 1986).

1. Cash flow test: a company is solvent if it can pay its debts as they fall due, no matter what the state of its balance sheet (Re Patrick & Lyon Ltd [1933] Ch 786).
2. Balance sheet test: a company which can pay its debts as they fall due may be insolvent if, according to its balance sheet, liabilities (including contingent liabilities) exceed assets.

Insolvency event
An event which is regarded as an act of insolvency; without it a scheme is not eligible for entry into the Pension Protection Fund.

Institutional investor
An investor such as a pension fund, insurance company or charity.

Institutions for Occupational Retirement Provision
See European Pensions Directive.

Insurance company
Either:

- a person who has permission under Part 4 of the Financial Services and Markets Act 2000 to effect or carry out contracts of long-term insurance, or
- a European Economic Area (EEA) firm of the kind mentioned in paragraph 5(d) of Schedule 3 to the Financial Services and Markets Act 2000 (certain direct insurance undertakings) which has permission under paragraph 15 of that Schedule (as a result of qualifying for authorisation under paragraph 12 of that Schedule) to effect or carry out contracts of long-term insurance. (HMRC)

Insured scheme
A scheme in which the trustees take out an insurance policy for each member, which guarantees that each member will receive all the benefits that the scheme rules provide.

Interest
The return earned on funds which have been loaned or invested (ie the amount a borrower pays to a lender for the use of his/her money).

Internal dispute resolution (IDR)

IDR is a means of dealing with member grievances in connection with their pension scheme, with the objective of avoiding external interference. It was introduced as a legal requirement for occupational pension schemes by the Pensions Act 1995 in April 1997. Scheme trustees are required to operate a (at one time two-stage) system to allow members and others to complain: firstly (usually) to the scheme manager or administrator and secondly, if dissatisfied, to the trustees (or perhaps the chairman). Following IDR, a member may submit his claim to TPAS or the Pensions Ombudsman. The 2007 Pensions Act amended the provisions of the Pensions Act 1995 to allow schemes to adopt a single-stage dispute arrangement. It is up to trustees to determine whether they wish to opt for this type of arrangement (see also dispute resolution).

Internal rate of return (IRR)

The average return on an investment over its life, based on its current price and its future cash flows.

International Accounting Standard 19 (IAS 19)

This specifies the calculation basis of pension cost that should be recorded in the company profit and loss account, and what pension liabilities should be shown in the company balance sheet. Generally, it requires assets and liabilities to be valued regularly so that values in the accounts are not materially different from an up-to-date scheme valuation. Like FRS 17, assets must be measured at fair value and liabilities are measured using the projected unit method.

International Financial Reporting Standards (IFRS)

International Financial Reporting Standards accounts represent a standard way in which pensions and life company accounts have to be presented. In life funds, some amount of value is ascribed to future margins deemed to arise within the in-force book of business and a certain amount of expenses is deferred each year. Ordinarily, the results are more positive than the statutory results used in the FSA returns, but not as positive as the embedded value results favoured by the actuarial community. In pension funds, the rules are more complicated.

Investment consultant

An adviser on investment strategy and/or the selection of investment managers.

Investment Governance Group (IGG)

A group established by HM Treasury and chaired by the Pensions Regulator to oversee the development of best practice and guidance in investment governance, and the application of the Myners principles.

Investment management agreement

Agreement between an investment manager and the trustees of a scheme that sets out the basis on which the manager will manage a portfolio of investments for the trustees. A standard agreement, which has been agreed with the NAPF, is published by the Investment Management Association; this should save pension funds from having to pay substantial legal costs to check every agreement, but it is not yet in general use – partly because the IMA, for unfathomable reasons of their own, make it difficult to get copies.

Investment only

This refers to the provision of DC pension services where the investment manager only offers investment management services, as opposed to bundled, where the investment manager also manages the administration and member communication aspects.

Investment trust
A closed-end, incorporated fund established to produce income through investing in other companies. They have a fixed number of shares, trade like stocks or exchanges, and are regulated by the UK Investment Company Act of 1940.

Investments
Assets of a pension fund; cash is not (in law) normally regarded as an investment.

IPA
See individual pension account.

IPO
See initial public offering.

IRA
Individual retirement account – a US version of a personal pension.

ISA/PEP
Individual savings account – a tax-favoured savings account introduced on 6 April 1999 which replaced personal equity plans (PEPs) and TESSAs. ISAs are not an investment in their own right; they are a tax-free 'wrapper' in which an individual can shelter investments. People over the age of 18 living in the UK can invest a maximum of £7,200 in each tax year. Until 5 April 2004 ISAs benefited from a 10% tax credit on UK equities. Stock and share investments which can be held in an ISA include unit trusts, open ended investment companies (OEICs), investment trusts, ordinary shares, preference shares and fixed interest corporate bonds. PEPs in existence at 6 April 1999 may continue to be held outside an ISA with the same tax advantages. Income from ISA investments is tax-free and does not need to be reported on tax returns. ISAs are also exempt from CGT. ISAs are a sensible alternative to pension provision for the lower paid, because they offer the same tax neutrality as pensions – but with the advantage that they can be spent at any time.

LDI
See liability-driven investing.

LEL
See lower earnings limit.

Leverage

- When an investor has more than a 100% exposure to a market, or part of a market, typically resulting from the use of debt or derivatives (futures and options).
- The US term for gearing.

Levy
Various annual levies must be paid on pension schemes. The main ones are the Pension Protection Fund levy and the Fraud Compensation Fund levy.

Liabilities
A scheme's liabilities are its future benefit payments and expenses. The scheme is in deficit if the current value of its liabilities is more than the assets – or in surplus if the liabilities are less.

Liability-driven investing (LDI)
LDI is an investment philosophy which aims to help defined benefit pension schemes to establish a risk framework from which they can measure investment risk and set

investment strategy. Some consider that pension scheme trustees always tried to reflect the nature of their liabilities with the assets they bought, and that LDI is nothing new. There also some who believe that most LDI is flawed, since it attempts to match assets and liabilities perfectly, whereas such assets are not usually available; in any event, there is poor understanding of whether, for example, the practice of matching the liabilities of pensioners with bonds (rather than equities) is sensible when such payments may now have to be made for 30 years or more.

Life Academy
Formerly the Pre-Retirement Association and now publisher of an annual lecture.

Life expectancy
At a given age, life expectancy is the average number of years that a male or female aged X will live thereafter, and it is calculated using age- and gender-specific mortality rates at ages X, X+1, X+2, etc. Life expectancy is calculated by a number of bodies, including the Office for National Statistics (ONS) and the Institute of Actuaries. There is a death clock at www.deathclock.com for personal use, and some insurers produce scary statistics showing we are all going to live longer than we think. The GAD (2007) calculated in December 2007 that the average life expectancy of men reaching 65 in 2007 was 12 months greater (at 20.7 years) than had been calculated two years prior. A man born in 1942 who reaches the age of 65 could, on average, expect to live 30.6 of his adult life in receipt of the state pension – and for a man born in 1991 this rises to 31%, even though he will not receive his pension until age 68. There are also local life expectancies published by ONS. Some suggest that some of us may live to 1,000 years (www.mfoundation.org). See also longevity/longevity risks and mortality assumptions.

Lifestyle
A structured approach to investment, designed to take account of investment risk over a working life and to remove the need for members to make investment choices.

Lifestyling
An investment strategy where a member's investments are switched automatically as they get older to more secure holdings, such as cash.

Lifetime allowance (LA)
The maximum value of funds a pension scheme member can accumulate without incurring a tax charge. It is the overall maximum amount of pension savings that any one individual can accumulate in a Registered Pension Scheme without being subject to the Lifetime Allowance Charge. The exact figure will be whatever the 'standard lifetime allowance' for the tax year concerned is, or a multiple of this figure if protection has been granted. Post A-day there are no limits on the benefits payable from registered pension schemes. However, if an individual's total benefits from all the registered pension schemes in which they have accrued rights exceed a given amount, known as the lifetime allowance, then a tax charge will be levied on any payments in excess of it. The 2011/12 lifetime allowance is £1.5m, reduced from £1.8m. It has been poorly devised under a Treasury misapprehension that pension contributions are tax-privileged.

HMRC states that: The exact figure is whatever the 'standard lifetime allowance' for the tax year concerned is or a multiple of this figure where certain circumstances apply. (HMRC).

Lifetime Allowance Charge
A charge to income tax that arises on any chargeable amount generated at a 'benefit crystallisation event'. The rate of charge is either 25% or 55%, depending on whether

the 'event' giving rise to the charge was the payment of a lump sum or not. The scheme administrator and member are jointly liable to the charge, except where the chargeable amount arises following the death of the member. Here, the recipient of the payment giving rise to the charge is solely liable (HMRC).

On the occurrence of a benefit crystallisation event, if benefits valued at that time exceed the lifetime allowance, then a Lifetime Allowance Charge is imposed: 25% of any amounts taken as pension and 55% of any excess which is taken as a lump sum. Scheme administrators and members are jointly liable for this tax except where the chargeable amount arises following a member's death. In such a case, the recipient of the payment giving rise to the charge is solely liable. It is therefore a tax charge that is levied on any excess funds for any individual who has pension value more than the lifetime allowance.

Limited price indexation (LPI)
The requirement under the Pensions Act 1995 to grant annual increases to pensions in payment under an occupational pension scheme. Increases had to be at least in line with increases in the RPI, subject to a 5% limit, ie limited price indexation (LPI). LPI did not affect AVCs and FSAVCs. LPI only applied to accrued benefits in respect of service (for defined benefit schemes) and contributions paid (for defined contribution) after 5 April 1997. The Pensions Act 2004 changed this. For benefits accruing after 6 April 2005, defined benefit schemes only need to provide increases to pensions in payment at the lower of the increase in the RPI and 2.5% per annum. There is no legal requirement for pensions from occupational defined contribution schemes and personal pension plans to increase in payment where contributions were paid on or after 6 April 2005. However, these provisions are not overriding, and scheme rules may require amending if they provide differently.

Liquidity
The ease with which a particular bond can be traded, related to the size of the market for that bond.

Loan stock
Another name for a bond normally used in connection with those issued by non-government bodies such as companies.

Loans
Occupational pension scheme resources may not at any time be invested in an employer-related loan. In accordance with section 40 of the Pensions Act 1995, employer-related loans are:

■ loans to the employer or any such person
■ shares or other securities issued by the employer or by any person who is connected with, or an associate of, the employer
■ employer-related investments, eg a guarantee or security for obligations of the employer. This does not apply to small self-administered schemes (SSASs) and self-invested pension plans (SIPPs).

Local Government Pensions Committee (LGPC)
A committee of councillors constituted by the Local Government Association (LGA), the Welsh Local Government Association (WLGA) and the Convention Of Scottish Local Authorities (COSLA).

Longevity/longevity risk

The fact that people increasingly live longer. While a good thing, it unfortunately also means increased pension liabilities. The potential for further increases in life expectancy present a non-quantifiable risk for pension schemes, as the pension is paid until death.

Long-term

- In the Eurobond market, this refers to initial maturities longer than seven years.
- Under standard accounting practice, this refers to long-term debt with a remaining maturity greater than one year.

Low earnings threshold

This is an annually revised amount used to determine if employees on low earnings should be deemed to be earning at least the low earnings threshold, thus earning state second pension credits. In the case of low earners, individuals earning less than the low earnings threshold, but more than the lower earnings limit, will be treated for state pension purposes as if they had earnings equal to the low earnings threshold.

Lower earnings limit (LEL)

This is an annually revised amount which represents the minimum level of earnings that an employee needs to qualify for benefits, such as state pension and 'jobseekers allowance'. If an employee's earnings reach, or exceed, this level but do not exceed the low earnings threshold, they will not pay National Insurance contributions (primary Class 1) but will be treated as having paid them when claiming these benefits. The limit is below that of the Primary Threshold, the start point for employees to pay National Insurance contributions. It is the minimum level of weekly earnings on which a person is treated as paying National Insurance contributions for benefits purposes. A person receiving contribution credits or paying flat rate voluntary or self-employed contributions is treated as having earnings at the LEL for each weekly credit or contribution. The LEL is linked to the standard rate of basic pension; once the Pensions Act 2007 reforms apply, the link is broken as the basic pension starts to be increased in line with average earnings.

Lower earnings threshold

In relation only to the state second pension is:

- the level of earnings up to which the state second pension accrues at a 40% rate and, once simplification operates under the Pensions Act 2007, the S2P accrues at a flat rate
- the amount of earnings a person is deemed to have if they earn above the qualifying earnings factor but below the LET – or they are accruing state second pension because they are a carer or are sick or disabled.

Lump sum

The percentage of accumulated pension benefits a member can take as a tax-free lump sum upon retirement; the tax-free lump sum paid to a member of a pension scheme when their benefits come into payment.

Marathon Club

A group of pension funds and others interested in managing pension funds as if the long-term really did matter (www.uss.co.uk/UssInvestments/Responsibleinvestment/marathonclub).

Market value

The market value of an asset held for the purposes of a pension scheme is to be determined in accordance with section 272 of the Taxation of Chargeable Gains Act 1992 and section 278(2) to (4) Finance Act 2004 (where dealing with a right or interest in respect of money lent directly or indirectly to certain parties). (HMRC)

It is the price at which an asset might reasonably be expected to be sold in an open market.

Markets In Financial Instruments Directive (MIFID) (EU)

The Markets In Financial Instruments Directive is an EU directive that incorporates a revised set of investment regulations within the EU from 1 November 2007. Occupational pension schemes, as 'a client who possesses the experience, knowledge and expertise to make its own decisions and properly assess the risks it incurs' are designated as professional clients of investment managers and enjoy a slightly lower standard of care than retail investors.

Maturity

- For a bond, the time at which the principal of the bond is repayable and it ceases to exist.
- For a pension fund, broadly the average age of the membership and the time until benefits are payable.
- The event of a life policy reaching the end of its term. For an investment policy this will result in the accrued value of the plan being payable, whereas for a protection policy such as a term policy it will result in the policy lapsing without value.

Maxwell, Robert

A businessman and politician who died in 1991 after falling off his yacht. His death exposed large losses in the pension funds of his businesses and the government commissioned a report (the Goode Report, 1993) into a reform of pension law. It is largely due to that episode that pension law is now so grotesquely over-regulated.

Median

The result found by arranging the values in order of size and picking the middle-ranking value. In a symmetric distraction, the mean and median are identical.

Member

Person who has joined a pension scheme and is entitled to benefit under the scheme.

MIFID

See Markets In Financial Instruments Directive.

Migrant Member Relief (MMR)

Ability to claim UK income tax and corporate tax relief for employee and employer contributions to Overseas Pension Schemes.

Minimum Funding Requirement (MFR)

Before it was repealed by the statutory funding objective, section 56 of the Pensions Act 1995 specified that the funding level of a defined benefit scheme should not be less than its actuarial liability. A prescribed set of actuarial assumptions were used to calculate the MFR. Schemes could be fully funded on the MFR basis but hugely in deficit on other bases, such as buy-out. MFR was replaced with effect from 30 December 2005 by the statutory funding objective, but transitional provisions apply until schemes have had their first actuarial valuation under the new regime.

Minimum pension age
From minimum pension age, members can enjoy their pension scheme benefits. They must take these benefits between the ages of 50 and 75. From 6 April 2010, this minimum age increased to 55. It is the earliest date at which a member can take retirement benefits, other than on grounds of ill health.

Money purchase
See defined contribution.

Morgan Stanley Capital International (MSCI)
It issues, amongst other things, certain investment performance indexes.

Mortality assumptions
Mortality assumptions predict the rate at which scheme members die before or after retirement. They are usually based on information from UK pensioners and assured lives; in cases involving larger schemes, the actuary may adopt assumptions more appropriate to its own membership (for example, an employee working in manufacturing may have a lower life expectancy than a white-collar employee).

Multinational Cross-Border Pooling Products (MCBPPs)
An MCBPP is a US construct that allows the pension plans of a multinational, which may be located in different international jurisdictions, to pool their investments into a single entity for investment purposes (see US Department of Labor, Employee Benefits Security Administration, Advisory Opinion 2008-04A, 10 April 2008; www.dol.gov/ebsa/regs/aos/ao2008-04a.html).

Myners Review
The Myners Review was a Treasury investigation into UK institutional investment (chaired by Paul Myners, later Chairman of PADA) in October 2001 – especially into why it provided so little private equity funding. The review concluded that trustees were too risk averse. In February 2002 the Treasury issued consultation papers on trustees' familiarity with investment issues, on independent custody and on shareholder activism, and the Pensions Act 2004 introduced a new standard for trustees' knowledge and understanding, especially of investment matters. The NAPF now monitors trustees' compliance with these guidelines and in October 2007 said they should be revised.

National Association of Pension Funds (NAPF)
The club of pension funds, representing trustees, sponsors and members (www.napf.co.uk). Amazing value for money.

National Employment Savings Trust (NEST)
The current name for the former Personal Accounts, and the even more former National Pension Savings System (NPSS), which is intended to provide a workplace pension arrangement for that half of the population who is not a member of such a scheme. It was proposed by a Pensions Commission under the chairmanship of Adair Turner. It is intended to be a default pension scheme available to members and employers who cannot find a suitable private provider. Auto-enrolment into NEST comes into effect from 2012–16. It is designed to help those lower down the income scale but may fail (see www.nestpensions.org.uk).

National Institute on Retirement Security
The US equivalent of the NAPF.

National Insurance contributions (NIC)
Payments deducted from pay or declared through self-assessment, used by the DWP to fund the state pension and other state benefits, ie paid or credited contributions to the National Insurance Fund. Class 1 National Insurance contributions are compulsory for employees and employers. Class 2 and 4 National Insurance contributions are compulsory for self-employed earners. Class 3 National Insurance contributions are voluntary. National Insurance contributions provide entitlement to specific benefits, including pensions from the state.

National Insurance Services to the Pensions Industry (NISPI)
A directorate within National Insurance Contributions Office and part of HMRC (qv). It deals with workplace and personal pensions that are contracted out of the state additional pensions (SERPS and S2P).

Net
After allowing for deductions of, for example, tax or investment fees.

Net asset value (NAV)
The company's assets minus all liabilities; also known as shareholder funds. It can be applied in the context of investment trusts or property companies where shares can trade at a premium/discount relative to the NAV.

Net relevant earnings (NRE)
The total earnings for an individual (including salary, bonuses and value of many benefits in kind for employees and trading profits of the self-employed) for the tax year. This figure is used to calculate the amount of contributions an individual can make to pension arrangements without incurring a tax charge. From A-day, an individual can contribute the lower of either 100% of net relevant earnings or the annual allowance (2007/08 £225,000 rising to £255,000 in 2010/11).

Nominal

■ This often means 'before allowing for inflation'. If inflation is positive the nominal return on an asset is greater than its real return.
■ For a bond, the value on the face of the bond.

Nominal amount/value
The value stated on the face of a security.

Normal minimum pension age
From A-day, this is the earliest age at which a member is allowed to draw benefits from a registered pension scheme, other than in the case of ill health. This used to be age 50. Scheme trustees must have implemented the new normal minimum pension age of 55 by 6 April 2010. Transitional regulations allow members to protect existing rights which were in place at A-day to receive their benefits at an earlier age.

Occupational pension scheme
A pension scheme established by an employer or employers and having (or is capable of having) effect so as to provide benefits to or in respect of any or all of the employees of that employer or employers, or any other employer (whether or not it also has effect so as to provide benefits to or in respect of other persons, or is capable of having such effect). (HMRC)

Now known as a 'workplace pension scheme'. There are legal issues relating to which schemes fall within the definition, and hence they are subject to specialised regulation.

Occupational pensions
A pension provided by an employer, where the pension scheme takes the form of a trust arrangement and is legally separate from the employer.

Occupational Pensions Regulatory Authority (OPRA) (obs)
The now disbanded UK regulator of occupational pension schemes for the period 1997–2005. Following a number of government inquiries in April 2005, which considered it was a disproportionate and risk-avoiding regulator, it was replaced by the Pensions Regulator.

Open Market Option (OMO)
The right to choose an annuity from an insurance company offering the best deal in the market using the fund in a pension scheme. It may not necessarily be the insurer with the best or highest annuity; good administration and solvency are also important.

Open-Ended Investment Company (OEIC)
A collective investment scheme structured as a limited company in which investors can buy and sell shares on an ongoing basis.

Opting out (of a pension scheme)
Describes situations in which an employee decides to leave an occupational pension scheme or chooses not to join one.

Options
The right, but not the obligation, to buy or sell a fixed quantity of a commodity, currency or security at a fixed price, on or until a particular date.

Ordinary shares
Securities which represent an ownership interest in a company. If the company has also issued preference shares, both have ownership rights. They are called common stock in the US.

Overseas Pension Scheme
A pension scheme is an Overseas Pension Scheme if it is not a registered pension scheme but is established in a country or territory outside the UK and satisfies the requirements in the Pension Schemes (Categories of Country and Requirements for Overseas Pension Schemes and Recognised Overseas Schemes) Regulations 2006 – SI 2006/206. (HMRC)

Overseas Retirement Benefits Scheme
An overseas employer-financed retirement benefits scheme, but not necessarily within HMRC's definition of Overseas Pension Scheme.

Over the counter (OTC)
A transaction between two counterparties who engage in a transaction directly, rather than through a recognised exchange.

Past service
It refers to service by a member before the current date.

Payable Uprated Contracted-Out Deduction Increments (PUCODI) (Pensions Act 2011)
A PUCODI is the annual increase which is paid with an individual's state pension where the individual has deferred receipt of their Guaranteed Minimum Pension and earned increments. New awards of PUCODI were abolished by the Pensions Act 2011 from April 2012. Where individuals contracted out of the additional state pension between 1978 and

1997 and delayed taking their contracted-out benefits, they earned increments on those benefits. The benefits are payable by the pension scheme, but since the increments are not fully indexed by that pension scheme, the government added small amounts to the scheme member's underlying state additional pension. The original policy intention was to ensure parity between those who were contracted out and those who were not. However, past policy changes to the state pension and contracted benefits eroded the policy intention. The Pensions Act 2011 removed the provision from the state for new awards of small top-up amounts to a person's state pension from April 2012 where that person is a member of a defined benefit contracted-out scheme who delayed taking their pension or was the survivor of such a member. Awards which were made and in payment before that date were not affected (see the House of Commons Library, Pensions Bill, Research Paper 11/52, 16 June 2011). Around 120,000 people receive the increment in their own right, with 80% receiving less than £1 a week (the maximum was £14).PUCODI would have been unable to have been paid after 2012 since contracting out for defined benefit schemes was abolished and there would have been no records able to track the rights (DWP, Pensions Bill 2011, Summary of impacts, 17 May 2011).

Payment schedule
A document setting out the contributions required to be paid by the sponsoring employer of a defined contribution scheme. It also provides for the due dates of these contributions.

Payment-in-kind (PIK)
An investment term, payment-in-kind notes are a junior form of debt with equity-like characteristics since borrowers do not need to pay back interest charges until the term of the loan has expired. Other forms of PIK arrangements are also found, such as paying (transferring to) the bondholder an amount of stock (in the company issuing the bond or in another, typically related, company) with value equal to the current interest due.

Pension credit
Term used:

■ to refer to the tax credit for those unable to claim the MIG
■ in relation to pension sharing on divorce, where it is the amount of benefit rights that the ex-spouse or ex-civil partner of a scheme member becomes entitled to following a pension sharing order.

HMRC defines this as: The pension sharing provisions in the Welfare Reform and Pensions Act 1999 (WRPA) introduced the 'pension debit' and 'pension credit'. The 'pension debit' is the amount by which the value of the original member's pension rights are reduced and the 'pension credit' the corresponding amount by which the ex-spouse's or ex-civil partner's pension rights are increased. Section 29 WRPA determines the value of the pension credit to be transferred to the ex-spouse or ex-civil partner. (HMRC)

Pension fund pooling scheme
See pension fund pooling vehicle.

Pension fund pooling vehicle
A tax exempt unit trust. These were designed by HMRC as a response to competition from European investment managers and to ensure tax transparency for pension fund investors. They have been operating since June 1996.

Pension guarantee
Incorporated into an annuity, a guarantee ensures that pension instalments for a specified period are paid, even if the member dies before the period expires. It also

describes a pension scheme paying a balance of money to meet a guaranteed total – usually to the pensioner's dependants on the early death of a pensioner. This amount is often established in relation to a multiple of the annual rate of pension or the accumulated contributions of the deceased member.

Pension Input Amount (PIA)

The annual increase in an individual's pension provision (which should not exceed the annual allowance) which is calculated over the pension input period. Although the annual allowance applies on a tax year basis, the PIA is a measure which is not specified as having to be calculated over the tax year – it can cover a different period and is defined by the trustees of a plan. For DC members the PIA is the total of tax relievable contributions paid by the member and any contributions paid by the employer on behalf of the member. For DB members the PIA is calculated as the increase in the value of final salary during the pension input period. In order to calculate the increase, the accrued annual pension is valued using a factor of 10:1. There is no PIA in an arrangement for the tax year in which the individual crystallises all benefits under that arrangement, known as 'last year PIA exemption'.

Pension input period (PIP)

Before pensions' tax simplification (Finance Act 2004), HMRC limited pension contributions in relation to each tax year. Simplification meant that there are now only two main limits: the lifetime and the annual. The annual limit is £225,000 (2008) or £235,000 (2009). The simple system has now been complicated by the PIP: a rolling window of up to a year in which contributions can be made up to the annual limit. Each PIP starts with the first pension contribution and lasts for a maximum of 12 months. The pension input period has a start and end date. For DB arrangements, the start date of the first PIP is the date on which benefit accrual starts. For active members on 6 April 2006 (A-day) the start date of the PIP was set as 6 April 2006. For DC members the start date of the first PIP is the date of the payment of the first contribution (which, for members active on 6 April 2006, is the first date on or after 6 April 2006). In DC arrangements either the trustees or the members can set the PIP end date. A pension input period is generally a 12-month period (with the exception of the first one) and is usually set by the trustees by nominating the PIP and notifying members. When no action is taken to make this nomination, a default position applies, though it is complicated and difficult to administer. The period will always commence when an individual's rights begin to accrue under a scheme, but thereafter pension input periods may end on a convenient annual date. The first pension input period will, unless otherwise changed, end at the anniversary of the start date, so a period starting on 1 June 2006 will end on 1 June 2007. It can come to an end earlier than the anniversary if the scheme administrator, or in a money purchase scheme, the trustees or the member opt to end it sooner. This earlier date is referred to as a nominated date. A nominated date allows a change to be made to the fixed period relating solely to the anniversary of the member entering into the arrangement. Why they just couldn't use tax years is a mystery.

In short, HMRC states that it means: The period beginning with the relevant commencement date and ending with the earlier of a nominated date or the anniversary of the relevant commencement date and, secondly, each subsequent period beginning immediately after the end of a period which is a pension input period (under either this or the earlier paragraph) and ending with the appropriate date. (HMRC)

Pension Protection Fund (PPF)

The PPF is a discontinuance fund which takes assets from the underfunded schemes of insolvent employers and provides a reduced level of benefits (www.pensionprotectionfund. org.uk). It imposes a levy on solvent funds and employers to pay for its deficits (around

£750m pa) and because of increased buy-outs by solvent schemes, the universe of such schemes able to pay levies is diminishing, while the call by such schemes is increasing; the long-term viability (or at least the benefits indicated) of the PPF is very much in doubt. Conditions and restrictions apply for PPF eligibility and compensation.

Pension Protection Fund levy
PPF compensation is funded through a levy on defined benefit schemes and defined benefit elements of hybrid schemes.

Pension Quality Mark
An award scheme operated by the National Association of Pension Funds open to employer-sponsored defined contribution schemes (including occupational, workplace personal pension and personal accounts) evaluating contribution levels, governance and communications. It requires a minimum total of 10% (6% from the employer) contribution rate.

Pension Risk Transfer Advisory Council (PRTAC)
A trade body representing buy-out providers, managed by the Tax Incentivised Savings Association ((TISA) Cleveland Business Centre, Middlesbrough TS1 2RQ; 01642 207200; www.tisa.uk.com).

Pension savings statement (PSS)
A statement which must by law be given by a pension scheme to a member whose benefits exceed the annual allowance or any other member on request within three months; the reason is that members need to know if their pension accrual from all sources will exceed their annual allowance.

Pension scheme
A pension scheme is a scheme or other arrangements which is comprised in one or more instruments or agreements, having or capable of having effect so as to provide benefits to or in respect of persons on retirement, on death, on having reached a particular age, on the onset of serious ill-health or incapacity or in similar circumstances. (HMRC)

Pension Scheme Tax Reference (PSTR)
Provided by HMRC to the scheme administrator, it is a number needed to help complete the Pension Scheme Return for HMRC.

Pensionable earnings
The earnings used to calculate benefits and/or contributions. Full details are usually set out in the schemes rules. This may include/exclude:

■ overtime
■ annual bonus
■ car allowance
■ earnings pensioned through the state.

Pensioner
Person who is currently receiving a pension from a scheme.

Pensioner member
A person receiving benefits from a scheme who remains a member of the scheme; sometimes a pension member is awarded a right to vote in the appointment of member-nominated trustees.

Pensions Ombudsman
Independent person appointed under section 145 of the Pension Schemes Act 1993 to investigate complaints and disputes from scheme members beneficiaries about the way a pension scheme is run. They also investigate complaints and disputes between trustees of schemes and employers, and between trustees of the same or different schemes. The Pensions Ombudsman has the power of enforcement and awards penalties for distress and inconvenience. See determination and dispute resolution.

Pensions Policy Institute (PPI)
A charitable academic organisation funded by the industry and well-wishers to provide independent research on pensions and pensions policy. It is a wonderful source of basic materials and research (www.pensionspolicyinstitute.org.uk).

Pensions reform
Pensions reform from the government has been in continual process since around 1983, with a new act virtually every couple of years. Indeed, almost alone in government, pensions reform has its own minister and has done for over a decade; there is no health reform or transport reform minister, for example. The name of the minister is not given, as it changes on average every nine months and would make this book outdated before it was published. The list of previous ministers includes Frank Field, Ian McCartney, Steven Timms (twice), Mike O'Brien, James Purnell, Malcolm Wicks, John Denham, and so on. In addition, there have many White Papers and other reports, including the Goode Report, the Turner Report, the Thoresen Report, the Pickering Report, the Lilley proposals, the Hague Bill, the Keith Joseph proposals, the Barbara Castle reforms and the Norman Fowler's White Paper.

Pensions Regulator (TPR)
The Pensions Regulator was established under the Pensions Act 2004 to replace the dysfunctional OPRA in April 2005. Its main purposes are to:

■ protect the benefits of members of company pension arrangements (whether trust or contract based)
■ keep claims on the Pension Protection Fund to a minimum
■ facilitate good pension administration.

In order to achieve these purposes, it has extensive powers, including:

■ provider of information, education and assistance to pension schemes and their advisers
■ power to serve: improvement notice, third party notice, freezing order, prohibition order, contribution notice, financial support direction and restoration order.

In the longer term its role will diminish as the number of defined benefit schemes diminishes – but it is trying to find a role for itself in defined contribution schemes. The statutory regulator, in the meantime, is required to be proportionate, sensible and balanced rather than simply procedural.

PENSIONSFORCE
An NAPF/DWP initiative to help employers explain how their pension plans work to their workforce, for free. (www.pensionsforce.co.uk).

Personal Accounts
A new system of personal pension savings accounts (similar to the National Pension Savings Scheme) proposed by Lord Turner's Pensions Commission and to be introduced

in 2012, and now known as NEST. All employers will be required to offer auto-enrolment in the scheme to their employees unless they have a more generous occupational pension scheme which already enrols employees automatically. Employers will be required to contribute 3% of salary (between proposed limits of £5,000 and £33,000) to the scheme, with employees paying 4% and the government 1%.

Personal Accounts Board (obs)
The governing board of Personal Accounts Delivery Authority (PADA), now NEST.

Personal Accounts Delivery Authority (PADA) (obs)
Now replaced by NEST, it was a quango charged with exploring whether Personal Accounts can be delivered at the administrative price that government policy suggested it might (ie 0.03% of contributions). The figure was suggested by Lord Turner in the Pensions Commission Report which led to the introduction of the Personal Account, but despite the suggestion it has never been shown that lower costs are more important than higher performance. The drive to lower costs may be a distraction, and meanwhile no one is really sure whether the system will cope. For an equivalent horror story, see the collapse of the Japanese personal accounts, which lost the pension account records of 50 million people (Hiroshi Yumoto, *Pension holder hunt could be 'endless'*, Daily Yomiuri, online, 13 December 2007). The Chief Executive was Tim Jones, former Chief Executive of retail banking at NatWest, and the Chairman was Paul Myners.

Personal Equity Plans (PEP) (obs)
Personal Equity Plans are not an investment in their own right. They are a tax-free wrapper used to hold investments. PEPs were discontinued on 6 April 1999 and replaced by individual savings accounts (ISAs). PEPs in existence were allowed to continue to grow with similar tax privileges and are now treated as stocks and shares ISAs. Stock and share investments which could be held in a PEP include unit trusts, open ended investment companies (OEICs), investment trusts, ordinary shares, preference shares and fixed interest corporate bonds. Income from PEP investments is tax-free and you don't have to report it on your tax return. Capital gains are also exempt from CGT.

Personal lifetime allowance (PLA)
This is the amount of an individual's pre-A-day rights registered with HMRC for protection from the imposition of a Lifetime Allowance Charge.

Personal pension
A personal pension is a pension which operates like a money box for an individual. They save money each month and hope that when retirement is reached, there will be enough to buy a reasonable pension after the investment management charges, dealing fees, commission expenses, marketing overheads and administration costs have been paid – and that the Stock Market will not have collapsed three days before retirement. It can be useful, however, for young, mobile employees.

Personal pension plan (PPP)
A scheme provided by an insurance company to enable individuals to save for a private retirement income. A personal pension plan can be registered with the Pensions Regulator as a stakeholder pension scheme if certain conditions are met (see group personal pension scheme and self-invested personal pension).

Personal pension scheme
A pension scheme previously approved by the Board of Inland Revenue under section 631 Income and Corporation Taxes Act 1988. (HMRC)

PFPV
See pension fund pooling vehicle.

Pillar
First, second and third elements of a holistic pension system. The first pillar is the state pension, the second pillar is workplace pensions and the third is private savings.

PIP
See pension input period.

Pooled pension investment (PPI)
System of investing a pension fund in a range of stocks, shares and other investments (see individual pension account).

Premium

- For securities selling above par, the difference between the price of a security and par.
- An amount that must sometimes be paid above par in order to call an issue, ie a call premium.
- Occasionally used as interchangeable with margin or spread when the latter two refer to a percentage above a given amount or rate.
- The price paid for an asset.
- The additional price an investor is prepared to pay for an asset with attractive characteristics.
- The cost of life cover; usually paid monthly but can be paid annually and sometimes quarterly. For most policies the plan will come to an end if the premium is not paid for one month.

Preservation
Preservation is a law which states that you do not forfeit your pension rights just because you leave your employer sometime before retirement. It is not a perfect law, but it is very much better than it used to be, and it is getting better all the time. The principle of UK pensions law protects pension rights built up in the past.

Primary Threshold
The minimum level of weekly earnings on which an employed person pays National Insurance contributions. It is the weekly equivalent of the standard personal allowance for income tax.

Principal employer
The employer with prime responsibility for the management and funding of the pension arrangement in a multi-employer scheme, eg in a scheme which caters for other members of the group (see also sponsoring employer).

Private equity
Equity-related capital used to finance change in an unquoted (ie non-public) company; see www.bvca.co.uk. Private equity is an investment in shares which are not quoted on the stock exchange, and are therefore less marketable (and liquid) than public equity (ie quoted shares). Because of the perceived lack of transparency (corporate governance rules do not apply to private companies) and because the investments are often highly geared (ie they use the company's own money or borrowings to carry out the deal) there has been heavy criticism in the press – and employers that are funded with private equity may be less financially stable than publicly quoted companies, because of the level of borrowings.

This means they may be less likely to be able to fund the pension scheme (see TUC, *Private equity – a guide for pension fund trustees,* October 2007; www.tuc.org.uk).

Protected Pension Input Amounts
The amounts that were paid before the impact of the Finance Act 2009 on pension contributions in relations to earnings over £150,000.

Protected rights
The name given to the fund built up by contracting out of the state second pension; they are the rights which, in a Contracted-Out Money Purchase scheme, replace the rights an individual would have earned under SERPS. Since they are money purchase, you have no idea what they are until retirement, so that they are not in fact protected at all. 'Protected rights' is the collective term for the National Insurance rebate, associated tax relief and investment return. As protected rights no longer exist after April 2012, this may help to simplify administration in terms of record-keeping, member communications and benefit processing.

Proxy
A written authorisation given by a shareholder to someone else to vote on their behalf at a company's annual general meeting (AGM) or extraordinary general meeting (EGM).

Public service pension scheme
A pension scheme:

- established by or under any enactment
- approved by a relevant governmental or Parliamentary person or body, or
- specified as being a public service pension scheme by a Treasury order. (HMRC)

Qualifying earnings factor
The minimum level of earnings on which a person must have paid, been treated as having paid or been credited with National Insurance contributions in a tax year in order to make it a qualifying year for basic state pension.

Qualifying Non-UK Pension Scheme (QNUPS)
From April 2010, UK residents can transfer non-UK pension assets into a QNUPS; a QNUPS is available for UK residents and UK domiciled and expatriates. There is no limit on the amount that can be paid into a QNUPS, and they can accept property, unquoted shares and art as assets. The fund has a tax-free roll-up and there is up to 30% available as a tax-free lump sum; there is also no requirement to have earned income, and there is no age restriction on investing and no age-75 drawdown or annuity requirement. Funds can be used as security for a loan of up to 25%, and the fund is free of IHT both before and after benefits start.

Qualifying Overseas Pension Scheme (QOPS)
An Overseas Pension Scheme is a Qualifying Overseas Pension Scheme if it satisfies certain HMRC requirements. The scheme manager must notify HMRC that the scheme is an Overseas Pension Scheme and provide evidence to HMRC where required. The scheme manager must also sign an undertaking to inform HMRC if the scheme ceases to be an Overseas Pension Scheme, and comply with any prescribed benefit crystallisation information requirements imposed on the scheme manager by HMRC. The Overseas Pension Scheme must not be excluded by HMRC from being a Qualifying Overseas Pension Scheme. (HMRC)

See also Recognised Overseas Pension Scheme, Qualifying Recognised Overseas Pension Scheme and Qualifying Non-UK Pension Scheme.

Qualifying Recognised Overseas Pension Scheme (QROPS)

A QROPS is a foreign pension scheme that HMRC recognise as being capable of accepting a transfer value from a UK registered pension scheme. HMRC impose rules on QROPS before they are regarded as acceptable, and these include that it is recognised for tax purposes by the local jurisdiction, is open to membership by locals and reflects either EET or TTE tax systems. The maximum lump sum is restricted to 30% of the fund value and the minimum retirement age is not lower than the UK HMRC ages (55 from 2010). It has so far been used by expatriates to export their pension arrangements, so as to avoid the Lifetime Allowance Charge, and there is no obligation to buy a lifetime annuity; it also provides the ability to leave money to heirs, no liability to UK tax on pension income and investment freedom. HMRC publish a list of their rules and recognised schemes on www.hmrc.gov.uk/pensionschemes/qrops.pdf. It is almost certain that HMRC requirements breach EU freedoms and are not enforceable on transfers within the EU, but as yet there have been no challenges.

HMRC defines this as: A Recognised Overseas Pension Scheme is only a Qualifying Recognised Overseas Pension Scheme if it satisfies certain HMRC requirements. The scheme manager must notify HMRC that the scheme is a Recognised Overseas Pension Scheme and provide evidence to HMRC where required. The scheme manager must also sign an undertaking to inform HMRC if the scheme ceases to be a Recognised Overseas Pension Scheme and comply with any prescribed information requirements imposed on the scheme manager by HMRC. The Recognised Overseas Pension Scheme must not be excluded by HMRC from being a Qualifying Recognised Overseas Pension Scheme. (HMRC)

Contrary to popular belief, a QROPS is available for use by UK residents.

Raising Standards of Pensions Administration (RSPA)

RSPA is a campaign group and registered charity designed to do just what their name says (www.pasa-uk.com). It issues a statement of standards of service that pension schemes should provide to members.

Raising Standards of Trustee Education (RSTE)

RSTE is a campaign group and registered charity designed to do just that (www.rste.co.uk). Although its title refers to trusteeship in general, its activities are confined to pension trustees.

Rating

If as a result of the underwriting process, the life company is not prepared to accept the risk at standard rates, it may offer to provide the cover for a higher premium by 'rating the life'. This is often expressed as a percentage of the standard rates (eg +100% would indicate that a life is assessed as being twice as likely to die as a standard one). In exceptional cases, a life may be postponed, meaning that the life company will wait for, say, 12 months before being prepared to offer any kind of terms, or alternatively a life may be declined, meaning that the life company is simply not prepared to offer any terms to the applicant.

Real estate

Buildings or land.

Real Estate Investment Trust (REIT)

A company that owns and usually operates income-generating real estate. REITs are normally quoted on a stock exchange.

Real value
The value of an asset after allowing for inflation. If the value of an asset and the level of consumer prices both double, the asset's real value is unchanged.

Recognised Overseas Pension Scheme (ROPS)
A Recognised Overseas Pension Scheme is an Overseas Pension Scheme which is established in a country or territory mentioned in regulation 3(2) of the Pension Schemes (Categories of Country and Requirements for Recognised Overseas Schemes) Regulations 2006 – SI 2006/206. An Overseas Pension Scheme which is not established in such a country is a Recognised Overseas Pension Scheme if it satisfies the requirements prescribed in regulation 3(4) of those regulations. (HMRC)

See Overseas Pension Scheme, Qualifying Recognised Overseas Pension Scheme (QROPS) and Qualifying Non-UK Pension Scheme (QNUPS).

Reference scheme test
Test carried out to compare the benefits provided by a COSR scheme with those under the reference scheme to ensure that they are at least equal. The scheme actuary of a COSR scheme must certify that the scheme complies with the reference scheme test.

Registered pension scheme
The current term for a UK tax-approved pension scheme, a pension scheme is a registered pension scheme at any time when, either through having applied for registration and been registered by the Inland Revenue, or through acquiring registered status by virtue of being an approved pension scheme on 5 April 2006, it is registered under Chapter 2 of Part 4 of the Finance Act 2004. (HMRC)

Since A-day, a pension scheme must be registered with HMRC to receive favourable tax treatment. Some schemes are deemed to be registered where they were an approved scheme prior to A-day and have not notified HMRC that they do not wish to be a registered pension scheme. Schemes set up before 6 April 2006 were normally automatically registered.

Registered Pension Schemes Manual (RPSM)
When pension tax simplification was introduced in 2005, this manual was said to be unnecessary; it is around 3,600 pages long, very complicated and exemplary of everything that is wrong with the pensions fiscal system (www.hmrc.gov.uk/pensionschemes).

Registration
The process of obtaining registered pension scheme status from HMRC.

Relevant UK earnings
This means:

- employment income
- income which is chargeable under Schedule D and is immediately derived from the carrying on or exercise of a trade, profession or vocation (whether individually or as a partner acting personally in a partnership)
- income to which section 529 of Income and Corporation Taxes Act 1988 (ICTA) (patent income of an individual in respect of inventions) applies.

Relevant UK earnings are to be treated as not being chargeable to income tax if, in accordance with arrangements having effect by virtue of section 788 of ICTA (double taxation agreements), they are not taxable in the United Kingdom. (HMRC)

Remuneration
In a defined benefit scheme, the amount of pension earned is invariably related to the amount of salary; HMRC calls this remuneration. So far as scheme rules or an

employer's policy is concerned, it can include or exclude bonuses, commission and other fluctuating emoluments.

Reporting
This involves providing members with annual or quarterly updates on the performance of their chosen investment funds, as well as an obligatory annual forecast on the value in today's terms of their accumulated benefits at present and at retirement.

Retail prices index (RPI)
[This] is the general index of retail prices (for all items) published by the Statistics Board. Where that index is not published for a relevant month any substitute index or index figures published by the Office for National Statistics may be used. (See section 989 Income Tax Act 2007.) (HMRC)

It is increasingly being supplanted for pension increase purposes by the CPI (Consumer Prices Index).

Retirement
Retirement is a relatively new concept (not more than 100 years old). The Prudential issues an annual *Class of XXXX Retirement Report* which outlines some of the figures and issues posed by retirement.

Return
The income on an asset together with its capital appreciation, expressed as a proportion of the asset's initial price.

Revalued earnings
For the purpose of calculating benefits, these are earnings that have been subject to indexation.

Revalued earnings scheme
Scheme in which the benefits are based on revalued earnings for a given period (SERPS is a notable example).

Risk management
A system which identifies, assesses and prioritises risk and identifies resources to minimise, monitor and control it.

s179
The valuation to determine scheme underfunding for the purposes of enabling risk-based Pension Protection Fund levies to be calculated is provided for in section 179 of the Pensions Act 2004. The section sets out the method of valuation for calculating liabilities for Pension Protection Fund purposes. The results of the valuation are combined with the results of the s179 valuations for all other schemes that are eligible for the PPF to assess the general level of scheme underfunding, and they are used to set the levy quantum and scaling factor. The s179 results for an individual scheme are also used to calculate the pension protection levy for that scheme.

Salary sacrifice
Salary sacrifice is an agreement between the employer and employee by which the employee foregoes future remuneration in exchange for the employer paying the equivalent amount as a contribution to a pension scheme. HMRC are often suspicious of salary sacrifice arrangements, but it is perfectly legal if properly documented. By foregoing remuneration, an employer and employee may reduce their obligations to pay National Insurance contributions. Salary sacrifice may offer significant advantages to employers, with opportunities to millions in National Insurance payments, and often with

union support. From April 2008 the ceiling for paying the standard 11% rate of National Insurance contributions rose and applies to income up to £40,040 a year. Pension salary sacrifice can be offered as a stand-alone option or alongside other salary sacrifice arrangements, such as childcare vouchers. Alternatively, it can operate under the umbrella of, or perhaps as a precursor to, a broader flexible benefits scheme offering the potential for further National Insurance savings and greatly enhanced employee appreciation of their benefits package (see, for example, www.mercer.com/referencecontent. jhtml?idContent=1304490). Salary sacrifice may not be appropriate for everyone, but where employees are contributing to a contracted-out, trust-based pension scheme, salary sacrifice may be beneficial for most employees since there can be a positive effect on state benefits. For members of contracted-in trust or contract-based group personal pension and stakeholder pension schemes, and taking account of factors such as age, sex and salary, the impact of salary sacrifice on some state benefits can be less attractive.

Savings credit
A component of pension credit which provides additional support for those aged 65 and over with income above the savings credit threshold.

Scheme administrator
Before A-day, this term referred to the person or body responsible for the day to day management of the pension scheme, including maintaining members' records, calculating and paying benefits, and managing contributions. Under the Finance Act 2004, this is the person who is appointed in accordance with the scheme rules for tax purposes and will generally be one of the trustees, the scheme managers (if contract-based) or any authorised delegate. They must make a declaration to HMRC that they understands their responsibilities, which include making quarterly returns to HMRC in respect of any income tax due from the registered pension scheme, and that they intend to discharge them. Penalties for non-compliance apply.

HMRC defines this as: The person(s) appointed in accordance with the pension scheme rules to be responsible for the discharge of the functions conferred or imposed on the scheme administrator of the pension scheme by and under Part 4 of Finance Act 2004. This person must be resident in an EU member state or in Norway, Liechtenstein or Iceland (EEA states which are not EU states). The person must have made the declarations to HMRC required by section 270(3) Finance Act 2004. (HMRC)

Scheme auditor
An auditor of a pension scheme is not permitted to be also a trustee of it.

Scheme pension
A pension entitlement provided to a member of a registered pension scheme, the entitlement to which is an absolute entitlement to a lifetime pension under the scheme that cannot be reduced year on year (except in narrowly defined circumstances) and meets the conditions laid down in paragraph 2 of Schedule 28 to Finance Act 2004. (HMRC)

It is a pension paid from a scheme either directly or by way of an annuity. Scheme pension is a broad term covering all types of pensions being paid from a fund that is not an unsecured pension or alternatively secured pension (ie income drawdown) and is not an annuity. It is invariably a set amount rather than a fluctuating amount, and has become important in recent years as the government introduced inheritance tax on any redistribution of funds to other family members from 6 April 2008. There is an additional tax charge of an 'Unauthorised Payments Charge' (40%), a scheme sanction charge (15%) and Unauthorised Payments Surcharge (15%, where the amount distributed is more than 25% of the total fund value). If death occurs after 75, the remaining fund is then assessed for IHT – a total tax rate of 82%. The rules do not apply to schemes with 20 or more members. Oddly, scheme pension may suffer higher rates of tax (as above) than unsecured pensions on relation to death before age 75, where there is a stand-alone tax of 35%. This is part of pensions tax simplification.

Scheme return
All registered schemes (ie registered with HMRC to gain fiscal neutrality) must file a return with the Pensions Regulator on an annual basis. The return is also used by the PPF to help calculate the levy.

Sector
Stock markets are divided into sectors, which are comprised of companies from the same industries (eg telecommunications sector, oil sector, media sector, etc).

Securities
Assets tradable in standardised units on secondary markets, particularly equities and bonds.

Selected Pension Age (SPA)
The age chosen by a personal pension plan member to draw retirement benefits.

Self-invested personal pension (SIPP)
This is a personal pension plan that allows a member to select the scheme's investments. SIPPs are particularly attractive to the higher paid. They give the opportunity to invest in a wide range of investments other than (and as well as) insurance products, including property. Contributions to a SIPP count towards an individual's annual allowance, and benefits from a SIPP count towards an individual's lifetime allowance. They are personal (as opposed to workplace) pensions placed through an institution (an insurance company or bank) where the contributor decides on the investments. They are also known as member-directed plans.

Self-investment
This is where a scheme's assets are invested in connection with the employer's business. In most cases, as a result of section 40 of the Pensions Act 1995, up to a maximum of 5% of a scheme's assets can be invested in this way, although different rules apply to a small self-administered scheme.

Sexual discrimination
There are many kinds of possible discriminations in pension schemes; the one that causes most angst is sexual discrimination, because it can in many cases be actuarially justified (women, for example, live longer than men, and their pensions are more expensive). A decision in 2011 by the European Court of Justice outlawed different annuity rates by 2013.

Share
A stake in a company which confers ownership rights on the holder. Shares are also known as equities.

Short service benefit (SSB)
Under the preservation legislation, this is a pension benefit which must be provided for a member who leaves the scheme before retirement and does not receive an immediate pension.

Small self-administered scheme (SSAS)
This is an occupational pension scheme. HMRC requires these schemes to meet special conditions, such as:

■ maximum of 12 members
■ assets must not be insurance policies.

Following A-day, HMRC relaxed some of the rules applying to SSASs (for example, they no longer require a pensioneer trustee). An SSAS is usually for small businesses, and it gives members more investment control and flexible retirement options.

Socially responsible investments (SRI)
Since July 2000, all occupational pension schemes must state in their statement of investment principles how, if at all, they have considered social, environmental and ethical matters in their investment strategies.

Specialist (mandate, portfolio)
A specialist investment mandate or portfolio is usually one involving a single asset class, region or investment style (as opposed to 'balanced').

Sponsoring employer
In relation to an occupational pension scheme [it] means the employer, or any of the employers, to or in respect of any or all of whose employees the pension scheme has, or is capable of having, effect as to provide benefits. (HMRC)
   See also principal employer.

Spread
The difference in yield between two different bonds. It is typically used to describe the extra yield offered by corporate bonds over gilts.

SRI
See socially responsible investments.

SSAS
See small self-administered scheme.

Stakeholder
A requirement that employers with five or more employees must set up a payroll deduction facility to allow employees (if they wish) to make pension contributions to a provider chosen by the employer. It is one of a range of failed pensions policy initiatives; the DWP website dedicated to stakeholder has been removed, but the legislation continues.

Stakeholder pension scheme (obs)
A type of personal pension plan offering a low-cost and flexible alternative, and which must comply with requirements laid down in legislation. Since October 2001, employers had to offer employees access to a designated scheme (or an acceptable pension alternative by way of an occupational pension scheme or a group personal pension). A stakeholder pension scheme is very similar to a personal pension plan but must meet minimum statutory criteria as to lower and capped fees. An employer does not have to contribute to this scheme on its employees' behalf. It must be registered with HMRC, satisfy the CAT standards and be registered with the Pensions Regulator as a stakeholder scheme. It is being phased out as auto-enrolment applies.

Standard lifetime allowance
The standard lifetime allowance creates a ceiling on the tax-advantaged benefits value that can be built up by an individual in all schemes: it is the overall ceiling on the amount of tax-privileged savings that any one individual can accumulate over the course of their lifetime without taking any special factors into account that may increase or decrease the tax-privileged ceiling. For the year 2006/07, this amount is £1,500,000. The standard lifetime allowance for following tax years will be specified by an annual order made by the Treasury, and will never be less than the amount for the immediately preceding tax year. It is the lifetime allowance to which neither primary protection nor enhanced protection applies (see lifetime allowance).

State earnings-related pension scheme (SERPS) (obs)
The state earnings-related pension was an extra state pension that employed people could earn up to 5 April 2002 by paying extra National Insurance contributions once their earnings reached the lower earnings limit. Earners could choose to contract out of SERPS by joining an appropriate occupational or personal pension plan which provided alternative and equivalent benefits. SERPS was replaced by the state second pension from 6 April 2002. Not to be confused with a United States SERP, which is a senior executive retirement plan.

State pension
This is a pension payable by the State on reaching state pension age. It is calculated by reference to an earner's National Insurance contribution payment history. It is composed of the basic state pension and the state second pension.

State pension age/State pensionable age
The earliest age at which the state pension is normally payable. Currently, it is 65 for men and 60 for women. From 2010 to 2020, state pension age for women (and men) will be gradually increased to age 66, and by 2026 to 67. A claim is required to get a state pension.

State pension credit
The third pillar of state pensions; it comprises both the guarantee credit and the savings credit.

State second pension (S2P)
Additional state pension that replaced SERPS and is paid in addition to the basic state pension. It is the alternate name given to the state additional pension since April 2002. It is based on contributions paid as an employee or credits for caring or ill health.

Statement of funding principles
A statement of funding principles is a written statement that trustees must prepare (in consultation with the employer) and maintain, setting out their policy to ensure that the statutory funding objective is met. It sets out the actuarial methods and assumptions to be used for the scheme's actuarial valuation as well as the approach to be adopted to rectify any shortfalls; it was first introduced by the Pensions Act 2004.

Statement of investment principles (SIP)
A statement of investment principles prepared under Pensions Act 1995 s35 or under the Local Government Pension Scheme (Management and Investment of Funds) Regulations 1998 SI 1998 No 1831 (as amended by SI 1999 No 3259) reg 9A. It is a written statement that trustees are required to prepare and maintain, setting out the principle governing decisions about investments in relation to an occupational pension scheme. Trustees are required to obtain advice from a suitably qualified person and must consult with the sponsoring employer.

Statutory funding objective (SFO)
Also known as scheme specific funding, the SFO requires all defined benefit schemes (unless exempt) to hold sufficient assets to cover their technical provisions. The assets which may be taken into account in the calculation, along with the actuarial assumptions and methods to be used when calculating technical provisions, are set out in regulations. A defined benefit scheme that does not meet the SFO will be required to submit a recovery plan aimed at rectifying the shortfall position to the Pensions Regulator.

Stock market
A place for dealing in stocks and shares [equities] such as the London Stock Exchange.

Stocks
Equities (shares) and (in the UK) bonds (loan stocks).

Superannuation
Used by some schemes, particularly those in the public service, to describe a member's contributions.

Surplus
The financial result at the end of a financial accounting period expressing the excess funds available after accounting for movement of the liabilities within a fund and, therefore, potentially available for distribution by way of a bonus declaration or withheld via the process of smoothing to bolster the estate of a with-profits fund. It occurs where the actuarial value of a scheme's assets is greater than the actuarial value of its liabilities. The surplus is the difference between the two and is known as an actuarial surplus.

Survivors
This is the modern term for 'widows and widowers'; it is shorter and discrimination-free.

Switching
The name given to the process of changing the choice of funds in which a policy is invested. Ordinarily, the units of one fund are redeemed and units are purchased in another fund. It can also be that many funds are redeemed for purchase into one new fund or, alternatively, that one fund is redeemed and invested in a selection of other funds. The purchase of units as part of a switch is done at the bid price, thus preventing another bid/offer spread being incurred by the policyholder. A charge is sometimes levied for this service.

Tactical Asset Allocation (TAA)
The adoption by an investment manager of an asset allocation different from the benchmark in order to enhance return. Tactical Asset Allocation is used to reflect the portfolio manager's short-term market views.

Target date
An approach whereby investments are structured in line with a pre-set date, thus meaning that risk is gradually eliminated as the target date approaches. The target date aims to cater for members who are unwilling to take investment decisions.

Tax privilege
Phrase used in Treasury documents as part of a propaganda campaign to suggest that pensions are 'fiscally privileged'. In fact, UK pension arrangements in theory follow the 'EET' system, ie tax exemption on contributions into the scheme, tax exemption on the build-up and then taxation on the benefits. Apart from the tax-free lump sums, pension funds are

broadly fiscally neutral and they are not particularly advantageous to the higher paid (and nor do the higher paid receive disproportionately higher tax reliefs).

Tax relief
Alleged 'incentive' given to those contributing to pension schemes. The government pays 20% (non-earners and basic rate tax payers) or 40% (higher rate tax payers) of a member's gross contribution. In fact, pension schemes are designed to be fiscally neutral (ie although the government loses tax on the contributions, it recovers it on the benefits). Tax relief does not excessively benefit the higher paid, since they pay higher tax on their benefits in due course.

Term (of a bond)
The time remaining until the final payment on the bond.

The Pensions Advisory Service (TPAS)
This is an independent and non-profit organisation that provides free information and guidance to any individual who has a complaint or dispute with their occupational or personal pension arrangement.

TKU
See trustee knowledge and understanding.

Top-up pension scheme
Scheme that provides a member with benefits in addition to those provided under another scheme.

Transfer payment
Payment of a capital sum from a pension scheme when a member leaves a scheme. It is paid to another pension scheme or to an insurance company if a buy-out policy is purchased for the member, or it can be used to purchase a buy-out policy for the member in lieu of benefits that have accrued to the member. A transfer payment may either be made in accordance with the scheme rules or in exercise of a member's statutory rights.

Transfer value
Amount paid as a transfer payment. There are rules about how members' transfer values are calculated to ensure that there is a balance of interests between the leaving member and the staying members, and which take into account any scheme deficit and possible future employer default.

Transfers
All members of workplace pension schemes have the right to move their rights to another arrangement. It may not, given the way in which transfer values are calculated, be a good idea in most cases.

Transitional arrangements
As part of the tax simplification regime, transitional arrangements designed to protect the benefits that members accrued before A-day will operate as of A-day. There are two types of transitional protection: primary protection and enhanced protection. Members have three years from A-day in which to register for transitional protection.

Trust
This is established when a person gives another cash or assets which are then used for the benefit of a third person. The person who establishes the trust is called the settlor because they 'settle' property on another: the trustee. The trustee takes care of the

trust property and uses it for the benefit of the beneficiary in whose favour the trust was established. Most occupational pension schemes are set up under trust for three reasons: security, tax relief and enforceability. Trusts are used in many ways and are often used with life assurance policies, particularly where the policy is taken out to provide family protection, inheritance tax funding, partnership and shareholder protection, etc. If the life assurance policy is set up under a trust, the proceeds are paid to the trustees, who then pass them on to the beneficiaries in accordance with the terms of the trust deed. There are advantages in setting up the policy under a trust. Firstly, the proceeds are, subject to certain conditions, paid outside of the deceased's estate and therefore avoid any potential inheritance tax charge. Secondly, the trust funds can be paid to the trustees without the need for grant of representation (outside probate). This means that the proceeds can be paid by the insurance company within a matter of days after production of the death certificate. The most commonly used trust for life assurance policies is a flexible power of appointment trust. This gives the settlor power to change beneficial interest and appoint new trustees during their lifetime.

Trust-based scheme
A scheme that is set up by the employer as an independent trust and run by a trustee board in line with the rules set out in the trust deed.

Trustee
Individual or company appointed to carry out the purposes of a trust in accordance with the provisions of the trust instrument and general principles of trust law.

Trustee knowledge and understanding (TKU)
The knowledge and understanding as required by Pensions Act 2004 ss247–249. Extensive guidance from the Pensions Regulator sets out the level and extent of such TKU as it expects. Trustees of occupational pension schemes must have knowledge and understanding of their scheme. This includes being conversant with key documents including the scheme rules, statement of investment principles, statement of funding principles and administration-related documents. It also includes having knowledge and understanding of the law relating to pensions and trusts, the principles relating to the funding of occupational pension schemes and the principles relating to the investment of assets. This is a requirement of sections 247–249 of the Pensions Act 2004.

UK Corporate Governance Code
This is the current version of what used to be called the Combined Code, agreed by the investing institutions such as the NAPF and published by the Financial Reporting Council (www.frc.org.uk/Our-Work/Codes-Standards/Accounting-and-Reporting-Policy.aspx).

UKIPS
See United Kingdom Investment Performance Standards.

Unauthorised employer payment
An unauthorised employer payment is:

■ a payment by a registered pension scheme that is an occupational pension scheme to or in respect of a sponsoring employer or a former sponsoring employer which is not an authorised employer payment
■ anything which is treated as being an unauthorised payment to a sponsoring employer or former sponsoring employer under Part 4 of Finance Act 2004. (HMRC)

Unauthorised member payment (UMP)
An unauthorised member payment is:

- a payment by a registered pension scheme to or in respect of a member or a former member of that pension scheme that is not an authorised member payment
- anything which is treated as being an unauthorised payment to or in respect of a member or former member under Part 4 of Finance Act 2004 (HMRC).

Unauthorised payment
A payment made to a member or employer by a pension scheme that is not authorised by HMRC. This is subject to a tax charge. Any payment made to a member that does not fall within the definition of an authorised member payment is considered to be an unauthorised member payment. Examples of unauthorised payments include paying a pension commencement lump sum of more than 25% of the value of the benefits (where protection does not apply) or paying a child's pension beyond age 23 (though this is acceptable in some circumstances). Unauthorised payments automatically attract a tax charge known as an Unauthorised Payments Charge and in some circumstances an additional surcharge.

Unauthorised Payments Charge (UPC)
A charge in respect of an unauthorised member payment from a UK Registered Pension Scheme, or an Overseas Retirement Benefits Scheme in respect of which UK tax relief has occurred after 5 April 2006. It can be up to 82% of the amount, which some expert observers consider to be illegal under human rights legislation, which requires certain penalties to be treated as criminal penalties and subject to necessary checks and balances (such as a right to appeal) which do not exist with UPC.

The rate of charge is 40% of the unauthorised payment. An unauthorised payment can also be subject to an Unauthorised Payments Surcharge and a scheme sanction charge.

Unauthorised Payments Surcharge
Tax due under section 209 of the Finance Act that is paid in addition to the Unauthorised Payments Charge. The tax will be due where total unauthorised payments go over a set limit in a set period of time of no more than 12 months. The rate of tax is 15% of the unauthorised payments. (HMRC)

Unauthorised unit trust (UUT)
A unit trust that is suited to the needs of institutional investors but cannot be marketed to the general public.

Underfunding
This term describes the situation in which a scheme's assets are insufficient to meet its liabilities.

Unfunded unregistered retirement benefits scheme (UURBS)
Prior to A-day, these schemes operated in a similar manner to FURBS but held no funds to back the promise. If the employer became insolvent, the pension could not be paid. Since A-day, UURBS have been treated as employer-financed retirement benefit schemes, receiving similar treatment to other pension schemes that provide taxable benefits to employees.

Unit
The way in which holdings in a unit-linked fund are described to facilitate the understanding of what share of a fund is owned by each individual investor. Units do not exist other than as the notional, mathematical representations of a share in the fund.

Unit trust
Trust set up as a pooled fund in which investors purchase units. It is supervised by the FSA. The fund/investment manager determines the price of the units based on the net asset value of the fund.

United Kingdom Investment Performance Standards (UKIPS)
This is a localised adoption of the US code known as the Global Investment Performance Standards (GIPS). UKIPS shares GIPS' objectives:

- to conform to a global standard for the calculation and presentation of investment performance
- to ensure accurate and consistent investment performance data for reporting, record-keeping, etc
- to promote fair competition between investment firms without barriers to entry for international firms
- to foster a notion of self-regulation within the investment management industry.

The UKIPS replaced the Pension Fund Investment Performance Codes (PFIPC) in April 2000. The National Association of Pension Funds (NAPF), which produced the UK edition, also approves the GIPS for globalised funds, thus enabling performance measurers to compare like with like. It assists trustees and others to ensure that asset managers do not manipulate their performance statistics and that their advisers select well performing fund managers.

Unsecured pension
Before 6 April 2011, payment of income withdrawals direct from a money purchase arrangement, or income paid from a short-term annuity contract purchased from such an arrangement, to the member of the arrangement (aged under 75) and which met the conditions laid down in paragraph 6 and 8 to 10 of Schedule 28 to the Finance Act 2004. (HMRC)

Upper accruals point (UAP)
Initially, this is the same as the upper earnings limit; it took effect from 6 April 2009. At that date the UEL jumped from £34,840 to £40,040 – an increase of £5,200 which involved an additional £500 in National Insurance contributions. The change involves a change of policy, since the contributions link to benefits changes and the contributions become more of a tax than a related-contributions benefit. It is the upper limit for state pension accruals.

Upper earnings limit (UEL)
Earnings limit above which employees (but not employers) pay reduced rate (1%) National Insurance contributions.

Upper earnings threshold
In relation only to the state second pension, this is the top band of earnings over the lower earnings threshold (qv) on which the state second pension accrues at the 10% rate. The UET is set at three times the LET minus twice the qualifying earnings factor.

Valuation

- A summary of an investment portfolio showing the holdings and their value as at a certain date.
- A valuation predicts future scheme payments then compares these with assets. The result determines whether the scheme has a funding surplus or deficit.

Valuation assumptions
In practice it is not possible to forecast accurately future benefits, investment growth and benefit payment dates in a pension scheme. Scheme actuaries, therefore, make valuation assumptions, including financial assumptions and demographic assumptions when they prepare valuations, but they are only assumptions.

HMRC defines this as: The valuation assumptions in relation to a person, benefits and a date are assumptions:

1. if the person has not reached such age (if any) as must have been reached to avoid any reduction in the benefits on account of age, that the person reached that age on the date, and
2. that the person's right to receive the benefits had not been occasioned by physical or mental impairment (HMRC).

Value added tax (VAT)
VAT is an issue for UK pension funds since, in the past, they have had to pay it on the services they receive, and it is recoverable if they are part of their employer's group. There have been two big issues: one is that if they become part of the group, HMRC then say they put the assets of the scheme at risk if the employer fails to pay VAT. This is highly improbable. The second is that even employers cannot set off the VAT on the investment management expenses. The latter is the subject of a challenge (2008) managed by the NAPF in the European Court of Justice and HMRC will almost certainly lose. The key case is *JP Morgan Claverhouse v HMRC 2007*; pension schemes should put in protective claims to guard against being out of time.

Vesting
See preservation.

Volatility
The fluctuations in an asset's return.

Widower's/Widow's Guaranteed Minimum Pension (WGMP)
Minimum pension that an occupational pension scheme is required to provide for the surviving spouse of a member as one of the conditions of contracting out (unless it is contracted out through the provision of protected rights) for pensionable service before 6 April 1997.

Widows/widowers
Now generally referred to as survivors. A widow/er is a person married to a member at the time of the member's death.

Winding up
The process of terminating an occupational pension scheme, usually by transferring members' benefits to individual arrangements. There is a three-module learning kit on the Pensions Regulator's website on winding up: one for winding up a DB scheme with a solvent employer, one for winding up a DB scheme with an insolvent employer and one for winding up a DC scheme (www.trusteetoolkit.com). Winding up refers to the process of terminating a scheme. The scheme's assets are realised and used to meet the scheme's liabilities. This is generally done by purchasing annuities for pensioners and deferred annuities for active and deferred members, or by transferring the assets and liabilities to another pension scheme, in accordance with the statute (see section 75 of the Pensions Act 1995) and the scheme documentation. Employers sponsoring defined benefit schemes are no longer able to wind them up, thus leaving non-pensioner

members with only rights to cash equivalent transfer values (CETVs). Regulations set out that, generally, employers must now ensure that the rights accrued by members will be met in full where schemes commence winding up on or after 11 June 2003.

Yield

A measure of the income return earned on an investment. In the case of a share, the yield expresses the annual dividend payment as the percentage of the market price of the share. In the case of a property, it is the rental income as a percentage of the capital value. In the case of a bond, the running yield (or flat or current yield) is the annual interest payable as a percentage of the current market price. The redemption yield (or yield to maturity) allows for any gain or loss of capital which will be realised at the maturity date.

APPENDIX IV
SOURCES

The Pensions Regulator, Detailed guidance: a quick reference, May 2011
The Pensions Regulator, An introduction to workplace pension changes, April 2011
The Pensions Regulator, Workplace pensions law is changing, May 2011
The Pensions Regulator, Employer duties and defining the workforce, May 2011
The Pensions Regulator, Assessing the workforce, May 2011
The Pensions Regulator, Pension schemes, May 2011
The Pensions Regulator, Automatic enrolment, May 2011
The Pensions Regulator, Opting in and joining, May 2011
The Pensions Regulator, Opting out, May 2011
The Pensions Regulator, Safeguarding individuals, May 2011
The Pensions Regulator, Keeping records, May 2011
The Pensions Regulator, Getting ready, May 2011
The Pensions Regulator, The different types of worker, Resource, May 2011
The Pensions Regulator, Employer duties and safeguards, Resource, May 2011
The Pensions Regulator, Information to members, Resource, May 2011
The Pensions Regulator, Workplace pensions reform for software developers, 14 April 2011
DWP, Pensions Bill 2011: MP's information pack, 19 May 2011
DWP, Government response to consultation: the application of pension legislation to the National Employment Savings Trust Corporation regulations 2011, March 2011
DWP, Automatic enrolment and workplace pension reform: the facts, May 2011
DWP, Guidance on certifying money purchase pension schemes and the money purchase element of certain hybrid pension schemes, July 2011
DWP, Workplace pension reform: completing the legislative framework for automatic enrolment, consultation on draft regulations, July 2011
DWP, Automatic enrolment and workplace pension reform: the facts, May 2011
DWP, Workplace Reform Secondary Legislation, Impact assessment, 1 July 2011
DWP, Automatic enrolment and pensions language guide, July 2011
NEST, Employer Terms and Conditions, undated
NEST, Order and rules of the National Employment Savings Trust, The National Employment Savings Trust Order 2010 SI 2010 No 917
The Occupational and Personal Pension Schemes (Automatic Enrolment) Regulations 2010 SI 2010 No 0772
The Automatic Enrolment (Miscellaneous Amendments) Regulations 2011 SI 2011 No 0000
The Automatic Enrolment (Miscellaneous Amendments) (No 2) Regulations 2011 SI 2011 No 0000
The Automatic Enrolment (Offshore Employment) Order 2011 SI 2011 No 0000
The Compromise Agreements (Pensions Act 2008) (Description of Person) Order 2011 No 0000

ENDNOTES

INTRODUCTION

1. Aubrey de Grey, *The Mitochondrial Free Radical Theory of Aging*, 1999.
2. A long time ago. The Code of Hermopolis in Egypt set out a code of law for annuities, around 500BC.
3. Very roughly, the UK birthrate is about 1.6 per woman of child-bearing age, whereas the replacement ratio is 2.1. Although the population is increasing slightly at present, the fact remains that the workforce is reducing just as the pensioner population is increasing. There were roughly five workers to every pensioner after the Second World War; there are now about two.
4. The Turner Report; see http://www.webarchive.org.uk/wayback/archive/20070802120000/http://www.pensionscommission.org.uk/index.html
5. See, for example, Toko Sekiguchi and Sachiko Sakamaki, *Japan Pension Stabbings Revive Lost Records Scandal* (Update1) 20 November 2008, (Bloomberg). ('This week's fatal stabbings of former Japanese pension officials and their families threaten to reignite public outrage at missing data on 50 million people, which helped drive two prime ministers from office in a year'.) Tata, a major Indian software company, was the only company to tender for the NEST computer system.
6. For details of UK pensions systems see, for example, Pensions Policy Institute, *The Pensions Primer*, 12 May 2011, available online at www.pensionspolicyinstitute.org.uk/uploadeddocuments/Primer/2011/PPI_Pensions_Primer_Update_May_2011.pdf. See also Pension Facts, May 2011, www.pensionspolicyinstitute.org.uk/default.asp?p=67.
7. Category A is based on the individual's contributions; Category B is based on a spouse's or civil partner's qualifying years; Category C is non-contributory and is payable to widows of men who were over 65 on 5 July 1948; Category D is non-contributory and is payable to people over age 80 who satisfy certain residency conditions and fail to qualify for a category A or B pension, or receive less than the non-contributory rate. Age Addition is non-contributory and is payable to all recipients of state pensions aged 80 or above.
8. See Office for National Statistics, *Pension trends* (www.ons.gov.uk/ons/rel/pensions/pension-trends/chapter-2--population-change--2012-edition-/sum-pensiontrendshome.html).
9. See, for example, Elizabeth Jordan and Andrew Thomas, *Employer attitudes to collective defined contribution pension schemes*, Department for Work and Pensions Research Report No 623, 2009 ISBN 978-1-84712-692-4; the DWP is very much set against CDC systems, despite their clear advantages.
10. See Office for National Statistics, Annual Survey, December 2010. Fewer than 40% of men and women aged 22 to 29 contribute to a scheme offered by their employer. An estimated 8 million UK workers have no pension provision at all. It was these concerns (almost certainly misplaced) and the realisation that many millions will have to rely on the state pension – or around £5,000 a year –that led to the Pensions Act 2008 forcing employers to 'auto-enrol' their workers in pension schemes.
11. For the moment, very sensibly abandoned; see HM Treasury, *Early access to pensions*, April 2011, www.hm-treasury.gov.uk/d/consult_early_access_pension_savings_summary_responses.pdf.

CHAPTER 1

1. The figures are based on ONS Population projections and Life Expectancy estimates; the DWP's Centenarian Clerk works with Buckingham Palace to ensure centenarians receive a birthday card from Her Majesty the Queen on their 100th birthday. The analysis is published on the DWP website at research.dwp.gov.uk/asd/index.php?page=adhoc_analysis.
2. Before the reforms; see Fry and Smith, *Pensions and the public purse*, IFS Report Series No 36, 1990.
3. See www.gov.uk/calculate-state-pension
4. SSCBA 1992.
5. See Pensions Policy Institute, *The Pensions Primer*, 13 December 2011.

6. Pensions Policy Institute, *The Pensions Primer, Second Tier provision*, 12 May 2011; Department of Work and Pensions, *A detailed guide to state pensions*, NP46, August 2010.
7. HM Treasury, Budget 2011 (cdn.hm-treasury.gov.uk/2011budget_complete.pdf), para 1.130.
8. Form BR19 (available online at www.gov.uk/state-pension-statement) or, for the cash equivalent of the additional state pension (useful for calculating values for divorce purposes), Form BR20 (available online at www.direct.gov.uk/prod_consum_dg/.../dg_180317.pdf).
9. If you can bear to see just how complicated it is, have a look at *A detailed guide to . . . workplace reform for software developers*, The Pensions Regulator, 14 April 2011. Trying to write payroll and other employer software is going to be a major challenge for software providers, given the complexity and short timescales. You should be prepared for glitches in the early days.
10. See NEST website www.nestpensions.org.uk.
11. Based on an idea of behavioural economics set out in Richard H Thaler & Cass R Sunstein, *Nudge: Improving Decisions About Health, Wealth, and Happiness*, 2008, ISBN 978-0300122237.
12. The main three regulations are: (1) The Employers Duties (Implementation) Regulations 2010 (SI 2010/4) (Implementation Regulations), (2) The Occupational and Personal Pension Schemes (Auto-enrolment) Regulations 2010 (SI 2010/772) (Automatic Enrolment Regulations) and (3) The Employers' Duties (Registration and Compliance) Regulations 2010 (SI 2010/5) (Compliance Regulations).

CHAPTER 2

1. See, for example, defaqto, *Only 40% of people are saving for retirement – but they suggest what would make pensions more attractive*, Press release, 14 December 2010.
2. See, for example, Association of Consulting Actuaries, *Survey of smaller firms' pensions, final report of the ACA's small firms pension survey*, 4 January 2011.

CHAPTER 3

1. See, for example, the report by Alan Pickering (*A Simpler Way to Better Pensions*, DWP, July 2002), recommending the simplification of the then Pensions Act 1995 s67, which controlled the ability of pension funds to amend their rules. The DWP simplified it by removing the previous s67, which was around 300 words, and replacing it with the current version, which is 3,600 words.
2. Ellison, Rae & Salter, *Pensions on Divorce*, Lime Legal, 2010, ISBN 978-0-9552834-4-4
3. NAPF, Pension sharing charges, revised periodically, www.napf.co.uk/PolicyandResearch/DocumentLibrary/0180_Pension_sharing_charges_NAPF_guidance_0711.ashx.
4. NAPF, *Talking pensions: employer concerns and options for reform*, NAPF Research Report, NAPF, October 2009, 16pp.
5. The Pensions Regulator/Financial Services Authority, *Talking to your employees about pensions, a guide for employers*, 16pp, The Pensions Regulator, September 2009.

CHAPTER 4

1. See NAPF, *Talking pensions: employer concerns and options for reform*, 2009; The Pensions Regulator/Financial Services Authority, *Talking to employees about pensions, a guide for employers*, 2009.

CHAPTER 5

1. See, for example, 'The Annuities Market', 6 December 2006, Chapter 5, which clearly sets out what the Government regards as an improper use of tax-privileged pension savings. PBR Note 13, also published on 6 December 2006, announced that measures would be introduced to ensure that scheme pensions and annuities cannot be used as a means to pass on tax-relieved pension savings. HMRC have discussed these announcements with representatives of the pensions industry. See also Regulatory Impact Assessment 'Tax Relief for Pensions – 2006

Pre-Budget Report Reforms', 6 December 2006, and the full RIA 'Budget 2007: Regulatory Impact Assessment – Tax relief for pensions', 21 March 2007.

2. Finance Act 2007.

3. See, for example, www.hm-treasury.gov.uk/consult_early_access_pension_savings.htm.

CHAPTER 6

1. The importance of good scheme administration, Statement by The Pensions Regulator to scheme trustees and administrators, February 2011, www.thepensionsregulator.gov.uk/docs/ scheme-administration-statement-feb-2011.pdf.

2. The Pensions Regulator, *Guidance on transfer incentives*, July 2010; joint statement by the Pensions Regulator and the Financial Services Authority, *Enhanced transfer value exercises*, July 2010.

3. See, for example, Robin Ellison, *Pension Trustee's Handbook*, 7th edition, Thorogood, 2011. There is also guidance on the Pensions Regulator's website, as well as a training module (https://trusteetoolkit.thepensionsregulator.gov.uk/arena/index.cfm).

CHAPTER 7

1. *Conkright v Frommert* [2010] 049 PBLR United States: Supreme Court 2010 April 21 (US) Chief Justice Roberts: 'People make mistakes. Even administrators of ERISA plans. That should come as no surprise, given that the Employee Retirement Income Security Act of 1974 is "an enormously complex and detailed statute," *Mertens v Hewitt Associates*, 508 US 248, 262 (1993), and the plans that administrators must construe can be lengthy and complicated. (The one at issue here runs to 81 pages, with139 sections.) We held in *Firestone Tire & Rubber Co v Bruch*, 489 US 101 (1989) that an ERISA plan administrator with discretionary authority to interpret a plan is entitled to deference in exercising that discretion. The question here is whether a single honest mistake in plan interpretation justifies stripping the administrator of that deference for subsequent related interpretations of the plan. We hold that it does not.' Also *Jones v Verizon* (US). See also in the UK *Daventry District Council v Daventry & District Housing* [2010] 085 PBLR, [2010] EWHC 1935 (Ch), United Kingdom: England and Wales: High Court: Chancery Division, 2010 July 30 (parties are bound by the actions of their properly authorised solicitors; it is no part of any claim that they did not properly instruct them).

2. The Pensions Regulator, *Consultation response, Monitoring employer support: Covenant, contingent assets and other security*, November 2010, www.thepensionsregulator.gov.uk/ guidance/monitoring-employer-support.aspx.

3. Financial Services and Markets Act 2000.

4. For example, the retiring Chairman of the Pensions Regulator, David Norgrove, was reported on 6 December 2010 (*Financial Times*, 7 December 2010) to have expressed his concern that certain pension funds were gaming the Pension Protection Fund by investing in equities, which he regarded as risky and inappropriate, and not in bonds, which he regarded as safe and appropriate. If the investments paid off, full pensions could be paid; if they did not, the PPF would in due course underwrite the losses. In the same week, the PPF itself reported that its assets swung from minus £1.2bn to plus £400m the previous year largely because, according to its investment director, of its investment in equities and alternatives. Meanwhile, the former investment manager, government minister and Treasury adviser on pension investment policy Lord Myners, was reported to have said that increased pension scheme allocations to bonds are nonsense and that the bond market is an enormous bubble which will burst. (Norma Cohen, 'Watchdog plans clamp on pension bets', *Financial Times*, December 7 2010; Sebastian Cheek, PPF shoots into £400m surplus, *Professional Pensions*, 01 November 2010; Pension Protection Fund, Annual Report 2009/10, PPF November 2010, pp 16–17; Michael Bow, "Lord Myners warns bond market is 'enormous bubble which will burst"', *Professional Pensions*, 9 December 2010; Helen Winsor, 'Stop and think before you apply LDI', interview with Ian McKinlay, Chief Investment Officer of the Pension Protection Fund, Finance IQPC preliminary to a presentation by Mr McKinley at the Hotel Okura, Amsterdam, 25 January 2011).

5. See, for example, 'Eligibility' page of the PPF website; Pensions Act 2004 s126; Pension Protection Fund (Entry Rules) Regulations 2005 (SI 2005/0590). The levy can be waived. In

some cases (for example, where payment might drive the employer into insolvency) the PPF can waive either the whole levy or the risk-based levy (whilst leaving the scheme eligible for PPF protection); an application can be made (and repeated each year that it is claimed). Once the payment has been made, the waiver is not available, and the application can only be made after the invoice has been issued, so the window is very small and unfriendly (see Pension Protection Fund (Waiver of Pension Protection Levy and Consequential Amendments) Regulations 2007 (SI 2007/0771; PPF website, FAQs). A waiver application plus evidence should be sent to the PPF at eligibilityandwaivers@ppf.gsi.gov.uk.

6. Written Ministerial statement, Hansard, Lords, 14 September 2010 (Hansard, Lords, 5 Oct 2010: Column WS4); see also Law Commission, *Trustee Exemption Clauses*, Report 2006 (Law Com 301). Exemption clauses were blessed most recently by the courts in *Baker v J E Clark & Co (Transport) UK* [2011] 070 PBLR; [2006] EWCA Civ 464, United Kingdom: England and Wales: Court of Appeal: Civil Division, 2006 March 22.

7. See, for example, OPDU (Occupational Pensions Defence Union): www.opdu.co.uk.

CHAPTER 8

1. This is because of a decision in the European Court of Justice in 2011 (the *Test Achats* case – brought by the Belgian equivalent of Which?) which decided that there should be equal motor insurance premiums for men and women (and, by analogy, equal annuity rates as well).

2. See the Myners Report commissioned by the Treasury, *Institutional Investment in the UK: A Review*, March 2001, which concluded that training trustees in investments might only produce the kind of returns that investment managers were achieving, ie not very good.

3. There are organisations that manage proxy voting for pension funds; in the UK some of the more notable ones include RiskMetrics (a subsidiary of Morgan Stanley, an investment bank) (www.issgovernance.com/proxy/advisory), PIRC, which is particularly active on behalf of local government schemes (www.pirc.co.uk/services) and Manifest (www.manifest.co.uk).

4. See, for example, *United Nations, Principles for Responsible Investment*, which are somewhat selective (www.unpri.org), and Paul Palmer and others, *Socially responsible investment: a guide for pension schemes and charities*, Key Haven, 2005, ISBN 1–901614–24–7.

CHAPTER 9

1. Or not; there are cases where it makes sense to choose a jurisdiction where there is no double taxation agreement. See Finance Act 2011 s72.

2. See, for example, *Wielockx* (ECJ Case C-80/94), *Safir* (ECJ Case C-118/96) and *Danner* (ECJ Case C-136/00). Although the UK HMRC acknowledge the law, they make it rather difficult to make use of it.

3. Although see, for example, www.telegraph.co.uk/earth/3307052/Ice-melts-opening-up-Northwest-Passage.html; there is now a Northwest Passage.

4. See, for example, *Collective defined contribution schemes*, Deregulatory review of private pensions, Department of Work and Pensions, December 2009, 13 pp.

5. Cash balance plans come in many forms, but all try to share the risks (either investment or mortality or both) between the employer and employee. An example is a plan where an employer may promise whatever rate it chooses; it could use a fixed rate (eg 4% pa) or a variable rate (such as one linked to the growth in national average earnings). All 'credits' to the members' 'pot' are invested by the trustees in various different investments selected to support the promised return. The amount of the promised investment return might change from time to time (but in all probability, any change may apply only to new members). If actual investments achieved a lower rate of return, then the employer will have had to make further contributions to make up the promised 'pot'. If the actual return was higher than needed to support the promised kitty, the balance is held back to ensure that promised 'pots' can be supported in the future for all scheme members, without extra employer contributions. In a cash balance type of money purchase scheme, the investment risk before benefits is borne by the employer. Any shortfall on promised 'pots' are made up by the employer. In some large schemes, the scheme may also promise the terms on which the 'pot' is converted into a pension. In this situation, the employer is taking on the investment risk after the pension starts

and the risk that pensioners will live longer than the schemes advisers have assumed in setting these terms. The fact that the growth of the pot is 'promised' means that the pot based upon that return must be made available to provide benefits, irrespective of the value of the actual funds held by the scheme. Despite government assurances to the contrary, cash balance plans are hard to establish in the UK and are rare.

6. See also Chapter 6 for a fuller treatment.
7. 2003/41/EC on the activities and supervision of Institutions for Occupational Retirement Provision.